Victims as Offenders

Victims as Offenders

The Paradox of Women's Violence in Relationships

SUSAN L. MILLER

RUTGERS UNIVERSITY PRESS
New Brunswick, New Jersey, and London

Library of Congress Cataloging-in-Publication Data

Miller, Susan L.
    Victims as offenders : the paradox of women's violence in relationships / Susan L.
Miller.
        p.   cm.
    Includes bibliographical references and index.
    ISBN-13: 978-0-8135-3670-5 (hardcover : alk. paper)
    ISBN-13: 978-0-8135-3671-2 (pbk. : alk. paper)
    1. Family violence.   2. Victims of family violence.   3. Abused women.   4.
Female offenders.   I. Title.
    HV6626.M543 2005
    362.82'92—dc22   2005002573

A British Cataloging-in-Publication record for this book is available from the British
Library

Manufactured in the United States of America

For my son Connor, with love.

Contents

Preface

It would be foolish to claim that women do not use violence. Globally, women have been leaders or participants in political revolutions, protests against government, and acts of terrorism (Dasgupta 2002). In the most private of spheres, the home front, women commit acts of abuse against children and the elderly. They join gangs that perpetrate violence, are members of New Right hate groups that advocate violence, and engage in violence against their female partners in lesbian relationships. Indeed, women do participate in violence. However, the key question that guides the research conducted for this book is simply this: within intimate relationships in which women use violence, are they *batterers?* The question is profoundly important because of the rise in the numbers of arrests of women for domestic violence and the increased tendency of the criminal justice system to mandate arrested women to treatment programs often intended to address male batterers' behavior.

Accurately answering this question depends upon an understanding of the definition of battering and the contextual meanings of violence that occur within a relationship, as well as a thorough examination of the history of victimization. Some people confuse the issue, counting all uses of force the same and treating all users of violence similarly, which challenges much of the research that reveals that most domestic violence perpetrators are male while most victims are female. Although the bulk of women's violence entails self-defensive force, under some circumstances women do initiate violence or retaliate past hurts with violence. These facts are (mis)used to claim mutuality in abuse and to suggest that there are as many, if not more, "battered husbands" as there are "battered wives" in society. This contradicts the preponderance of research findings, namely that a more contextual examination of women's use of violence within relationships demonstrates that its use is related to their male partner's abuse. This division in the interpretation of women's use of violence stems from the nature of the methodology employed by researchers, a distinction that will be further explored in chapter 2.

The questions surrounding women's use of violence within intimate relationships have profound implications for criminal justice and treatment practices. Following the adoption of mandatory or pro-arrest laws that guide police in handling domestic violence situations, officers are responding "by the book": police make an arrest if the law is broken. It is easy to understand how this happens. Law enforcement is incident driven, not context driven, and arrests occur regardless of the history of abuse in the relationship or the meaning or motivation underlying the use of violence.

The arrest of women who may be battered introduces an ironic twist to the history of pro-arrest policies. Pro-arrest and mandatory arrest policies for domestic violence were designed and lauded as ways of responding uniformly to a problem that had suffered from years of police inaction and a trivialization of woman-battering. Although there is no reliable nationwide data on arrest rates, we do see that as a consequence of the implementation of more stringent arrest policies, more and more women are arrested on domestic violence charges despite many women's long histories of victimization and the possibility of compelling reasons why they resorted to using violence. There are some violent women who do fit the definition of a batterer, and in these cases and in other instances, women must accept responsibility for their actions. For instance, violence used as retribution for past abuses is not the same as violence used for self-defense measures.

Most women appear to use violence as a way to defend themselves or their children or to get back at their partners for past and ongoing violence. Women typically do not control, intimidate, or cause fear in their partner when they use violence, which is the opposite of the goals that most male abusers try to accomplish through their use of force against their female partners. To make matters worse, across the country female victims arrested for domestic violence are being sent routinely to batterer treatment programs intended for male abusers.

The situation raises a series of questions. Should the criminal justice system respond uniformly to a situation in which many gender differences in the use and meaning of violence exist? If arrested women are court-mandated to batterer treatment programs, should the curriculum be identical to that intended to address male batterers? What could be done so that battered women do not resort to using force? Surely, if the criminal justice system and other social institutions had not failed to address men's violence against women and hold them accountable in a meaningful way in the first place, women would have other recourses available apart from the use of violence. If such programs—batterer programs for women—exist, do they offer any positive outcomes for domestically violent women? Or, as I come back to my original key question that guides this research, does the outcome depend on whether or not these women are really batterers?

This book examines the complicated, vexing problem through the analysis of one state's practice. While I focus on one state's efforts to address women arrested for domestic violence, the findings are generalizable to the similar struggles that many states are experiencing throughout the nation.

I have been inextricably and deeply involved in the work of the battered women's movement that I describe. My initial concerns for the plight of battered women surfaced while I was in graduate school at the University of Maryland. I began volunteering as a hotline counselor at a battered women's shelter (and continued this work when I later moved to Illinois upon graduation). There, I saw things and learned things from the victims that opened up my eyes to the injustices of criminal justice system practices, as well as opened up my heart to them as individuals. At the same time, however, I was inspired by their stories of resiliency and empowerment, and how hard so many women worked to free themselves and their children from a life of emotional degradation and violence at the hands of their partners. Equally admirable was the commitment and tenacity of the female staff members who helped the women sort through their broken dreams and find the paths that were right for them to meet their goals. Their spirits were unbroken, and I witnessed firsthand the importance of providing tangible help and resources to disheartened women as they navigated through the convoluted machinery of the legal system while their belief in themselves and their abilities ebbed and flowed.

Since those early days, I have focused a good deal of my research efforts on exploring the criminal justice responses to the epidemic social problem of woman battering. In particular, I have been concerned with unintended consequences of policies that appear benign or beneficial but create deleterious side effects for victims the policies are ostensibly there to help. While I have been certainly affected by my work with victims, advocates, and activists, I also have been trained in the rigor of objective social science research principles. No one's research is ever truly value free, but I strive to consider and evaluate the domestic violence research fairly. I have also experienced the good fortune of working with committed, feminist (and sometimes non-feminist) women and men—law enforcement officers, probation officers, attorneys, and activists—who share my vision of justice for battered women, accountability for batterers, and hope for a world that is less violent and more egalitarian.

Thus, as both a volunteer in the battered women's movement's efforts to eradicate battering and as a researcher, I feel that my experiences have been critical in providing me with a wide repertoire of skills to use in evaluating domestic violence research. I hope that my efforts help others who work toward the goals of women's empowerment, gender justice, and the eradication of violence against women.

Acknowledgments

A book of this scope incurs a lot of gratitude, both personal and professional. The seeds of this project began to grow in 1994, when I was invited by Claire M. Renzetti to write a summary piece for a special issue of *Violence and Victims*. In the journal, Kevin Hamberger and Theresa Potente's article about the implications of treatment for women arrested for domestic violence—most of who acted defensively, not aggressively—aroused my interest. Although I was well versed both as an activist and as a scholar in the area of domestic violence, their topic was new to me—intriguing, a bit daunting, and perplexing. Since that time, I began my own examination into the phenomenon and have grown more aware of the complexities associated with the consequences of domestic violence arrest policies. This book reflects what I have learned.

Claire remains a true friend and colleague to this day. To all who know her through her editorship of the outstanding journal *Violence Against Women* and other work, she is a breath of fresh air, an inspiring scholar, and simply a wonderful person. I am proud to know her. Carol Post, of the Delaware Coalition of Domestic Violence, and Sue Osthoff, of the National Clearinghouse for the Defense of Battered Women in Philadelphia—hats off in admiration to both of you for all of your efforts to rid society of violence against women. Special thanks to Carol for her support and professionalism regarding various research endeavors.

I am fortunate to be a member of a terrific intellectual community, and grateful to the Department of Sociology and Criminal Justice and also the Women's Studies Program at the University of Delaware for providing an environment conducive to scholarly work and debate. Some of the research was funded by a University of Delaware General University Research grant. Nancy Quillen cheerfully provided crucial secretarial support. In addition, my editor, Kristi Long at Rutgers University Press, continuously encouraged me as I navigated the challenge of new motherhood while writing a book. Special thanks also to Raymond Michalowski, Meda Chesney-Lind, and Marilyn

Campbell for their assistance with the manuscript, and to Lyman Lyons for his superb copyediting skills.

Many thanks to my research team. For the police ride-along component, I thank Kaila Berkowitz, Cathy Conway, Shannon Dawson, Jaime Fisher, Danielle Joffe, Steve Keiser, John Kellenberger, Michelle Meloy, Pete Michaelides, Adam Siegelbaum, and Susan White for their hard work, long hours, and commitment to see the project through. I appreciate the state's Domestic Violence Coordinating Council for its help with arranging the police ride-alongs. Georgia Scott is transcriber extraordinaire—she managed to discern even the most inaudible conversations with her tenacity, fueled by her belief in this project. Very heartfelt thanks goes to Michelle L. Meloy, who was a doctoral student at the University of Delaware during the data collection phase of this project and is now an assistant professor at Rutgers University. She was instrumental in the data collection stages with the police ride-along study and the participant observation with the women's treatment groups. Her dedication, intellectual exchanges, friendship, and ability to stay awake on the long drives home are without bounds.

Very special thanks also to LeeAnn Iovanni, my dear friend for over twenty years, who provided encouragement, sage feedback, and tremendous support for my work on this book. This is a much better book for her insights.

Books are never written in isolation from people who touch our hearts. Thus, I also thank Lisa Bartran and family for making me take time-outs for long distance phone calls, sending corny jokes by e-mail, and taking annual vacations on Cape Cod; Nancy Getchell for coffee, companionship, adventures, and support; Ellen Lepine for her compassion and friendship; Dan Atkins, Ronet Bachman, and Frank Scarpitti for their friendship; and Patricia Tate Stewart for her wisdom and wit. And, last but never least, I would like to thank deeply my family. My parents imbued in me their sense of justice and always believed in me and surrounded our family with love. My sister Lisa was always a phone call away and ready to distract me with her optimistic spirit whenever I got bogged down, usually with stories involving Toni, Joey, or Samantha. Most of all, thanks to Connor, my bold, inquisitive toddler who was always willing to play and laugh and restore my energies.

Finally, I salute the activists, scholars, and practitioners in my state and elsewhere who contribute daily to the goals of stopping violence against women. Special thanks to the treatment group facilitator and the agency for their vision, openness, and support for research. Additional thanks and appreciation go to the many other respondents in my study who gave so freely of their time and knowledge. I am especially grateful to all of the women from the treatment groups for their courage and honesty, and their generosity in sharing their stories. So much of what I know about domestic violence comes from knowing them.

Victims as Offenders

Chapter 1   Defining the Dilemma

Beth cut her husband's throat so badly that he had to be
medivac-ed to the hospital; he almost died. He was
constantly abusing her throughout their six-year marriage
and at the time of the stabbing, she said he was beating the
crap out of her and she grabbed a knife—it was the first
thing that was near her . . . that's what she felt she had to
do to get out of the situation . . .

                              —PROBATION OFFICER #1

Jenny was sexually abused by her brothers, and violently
assaulted by her first husband continuously, and now, with
her second husband, more continuous assault. Basically,
what she did was after a particularly vicious assault, she
took his clothes out in the living room and set them on fire.
She was charged with arson. But the police records
document a number of times that she has been the victim of
battering . . .   —PROBATION OFFICER #3

THESE STATEMENTS ILLUSTRATE the varied situations experienced by many women who find themselves arrested on domestic violence charges by an incident-driven criminal justice system that responds uniformly to cases of domestic violence without examining the motivations and consequences of such acts.[1] In the two examples above, the authorities believed that the women broke the law, and these acts determined their subsequent arrests. By following the letter of the law, however, law enforcement officers often disregard the context in which victims of violence resort to using violence themselves. Often, what is most revealing are the antecedents to the incident that many battered victims share: they often act in self-defense, they may have long histories of victimization at the hands of their male partners, and they may use a weapon to equalize the force or threat used by their partners, who are bigger and stronger than they are. Hence, some of these arrests seem inappropriate, particularly when battered women act in self-defense or when women are falsely charged by their savvy (male) batterers who have learned how to manipulate the system.

So we see that there are victims of abuse who are arrested because they commit an illegal act, but this act occurs in the context of a long history of abuse (illustrated by Jenny in the second example above). This paradox gets to the crux of the matter: what is the appropriate criminal justice response to battered women who "assault" (as legally defined) their abuser, or do other illegal acts, and end up getting arrested, particularly when these acts of violence committed by victims are qualitatively different from acts of violence committed by batterers? The situation in which many battered women now find themselves is assuredly not the result that was envisioned when the cry for the criminalization of domestic violence was first heard.

In particular, these arrest policies and their consequences raise multiple questions: Just what should the police do in situations where victims of violence in turn commit a violent act? Are police doing too good a job of making arrests and enforcing the law? Do police miss important contextual clues by being incident-driven in their investigations, rather than being contextually based? Given the devastating impact an arrest can have on victims' lives as well as increasing their risk of further harm from retaliatory violence, how should we evaluate the success of domestic violence arrest policies? Are there actions that the police can take, such as determining the primary aggressor or uncovering the history of relationship abuse, that could have an effect on the course of action that police should follow? What if battered women *did* commit a technically "illegal" act—should they be treated the same as their (male) abusers? What do we want the prosecutor's offices to do? This book explores one state's experience grappling with the issues raised and faced by women who have been arrested for domestic violence offenses.

While this book is about women arrested for domestic violence and the appropriateness of sending them to batterer intervention programs, it is essential to place this phenomenon within the larger landscape of criminal justice ideology and practices that operate today. As part of a political climate that promoted increases in victim protections and diminished concern about offenders' rights, the 1980s ushered in an era of draconian crime-control ideology. The "war on drugs," introduced in the 1970s by former president Nixon, followed by the broader "war on crime" of subsequent administrations, attacked perceived loopholes in criminal justice policies, established more severe punishment practices, and expanded state efforts to surveil its citizens through the Clinton administration's addition of "100,000 more police" on the streets and a concomitant prison construction boom.

Prison populations have exploded, reflecting the consequences of specific policies such as "three strikes" laws, abolishment of parole, "truth in sentencing," mandatory and minimum sentences, and sentencing guidelines. These new policies virtually erase discretion, leaving judges to mete out routinized punishments that eliminate consideration of mitigating circumstances. The criminal justice system has been fortified, with increased surveillance of citizens by police, often under the guise of the "softer," more humane approach of community policing, a strategy that places officers in more direct daily contact with communities (Websdale 2001; S. Miller 1999). All of this growth comes at a huge economic cost, the burden of which is felt more acutely by poor people of color, particularly men (Mauer 1999). However, women are not too far behind (Danner 1998): Ten percent of the women in prison in 1979 were doing time for drug offenses; this grew to close to 40 percent by 1997, and more than two out of three of the inmates are women of color (Greenfeld and Snell 1999). Moreover, the female proportion of total arrests across all criminal offenses doubled from 10 percent in 1965 to 20 percent in 2000, with most of the increase attributed to minor property offenses, many of which are related to drug use (Steffensmeier and Schwartz 2004).

Men's and women's prison sentences reflect the smallest gap ever (Mauer, Potler, and Wolf 1999; Women's Prison Association 2003). Female offenders, who often benefited from chivalry extended to them by criminal justice authorities in the past, have found that rigid sentencing guidelines now override prior gender-based decision making. Women who commit particularly unfeminine crimes, such as using violence that is typically viewed as masculine, are punished even more severely for their deviations from perceived natural gender norms.

As part of the prison construction enterprise, building institutions to house female offenders has proliferated. Most women in state prisons have committed crimes of a petty nature—property or drug related rather than crimes against persons—and their prior records indicate more of the same. In state prisons, less than one-third of female inmates are violent offenders; some of those "violent" women faced situations that were precipitated by domestic violence (Women's Prison Association 2003).

Historically, patriarchal ideals about proper feminine behavior guided justice concerns, often resulting in more serious punishments for females who violated gender norms than males. This was particularly pronounced with states' efforts to control young women's sexuality; for instance, court records between

1900 and 1917 in Memphis, Tennessee, revealed that young women were harshly punished for any kind of sexual experience, forced or consensual, under "promiscuity" charges (Shelden 1981), a word and charge never associated with males (Belknap and Holsinger 2000).

The modern movement to criminalize pregnant drug-addicted mothers provides a contemporary example of the state's interest in controlling women, not crime (Boyd 2004). Thus, both historically and today, women experience "disparate justice due to the influence of sexuality and gender-based moral expectations about their behavior" (Anderson 2006, 3). However, research findings suggest that the majority of incarcerated women are motivated to commit crime for economic reasons, to support themselves or their families. While the growth in women's incarceration brings to mind a "field of dreams"—build it and they will come—there is also a greater willingness to incarcerate women rather than to create alternative sentencing strategies that could offer a more appropriate fit for their crimes. In any case, the incarceration rate of women has reached new heights (Mauer, Potler, and Wolf 1999).

Despite the closer parity reached in men's and women's sentences, we know that women who become involved with crime follow different trajectories than men, regardless whether women's paths lead ultimately to prostitution or substance abuse or gang affiliation. Women are far more likely to have histories of victimization from their childhoods; in fact, women in state prisons have histories of physical and sexual abuse at levels four to five times higher than male inmates (Women's Prison Association 2003). Beth Richie and others argue that this victimization puts women at greater "risk" for offending (see also Gaarder and Belknap 2004; Gilfus 1992). Criminal justice policies based on a norm of men's lives and needs fall far short with respect to women's concerns (Richie 2000). In addition, imprisonment of women exacts more profound costs on society in ways that damage families and communities, given women's central role in nurturing, caretaking, and maintaining parental and familial relationships (Women's Prison Association 2003).

Sentencing practices raise complicated questions about whether similar offenders who commit similar crimes should receive similar punishments—the equity versus special treatment argument. When sentencing for men and women becomes uniform (the equity argument), then extenuating circumstances that mitigate offender responsibility (the special treatment argument) become invisible. It takes no big leap to see the connection with battered women who use violence within relationships. If the context is invisible, then the practice of punishing similar crimes in a similar way flourishes unchecked.

Does the increase in the female prison population indicate that women have become more violent? While not indicative of a crime wave, women's arrest rates for violent crimes accounted for 17 percent of all arrests in 1995 and increased 61.6 percent in the previous decade (1985–95). If one were to follow media accounts, a profile of the angry, sullen female gangbanger emerges. Despite this kind of sensationalized coverage, the overwhelming statistical evidence suggests that women's offending patterns have not changed profoundly over time, and any increases reflect the consequences of increased drug offenses and concomitant changes in sentencing practices, as well as declines in the practice of chivalrous sentencing (Steffensmeier and Schwartz 2004). However, fueled by a backlash movement, arguments constructed by (mostly) men against women suggest that vengeful, weapon-bearing, violent women are commonplace. Many adherents to this perspective believe that men, as victims of women's violence, are overlooked and dismissed due to the political framing of crime where women are viewed exclusively as victims while men are viewed exclusively as offenders. This view is fueled by a profound abhorrence for and distrust of practices or policies perceived as feminist derived or endorsed. Nowhere is this hostility illustrated as perfectly as in the popular and quasi-scholarly discourse surrounding domestic violence and rape policies (S. Miller and Meloy 2006). Often, publications that appeal to a mass audience gloss over empirical findings to create sensationalized stories that reinforce victim blaming (in regard to female rape victims) or highlight male victims (in regard to domestic violence).

Despite national crime victimization survey findings that suggest otherwise, a vocal group argues for a redistribution of funds, resources, and sympathy away from female victims of male violence and toward male victims of female violence. The battered women's movement is targeted by challenges of validity. Part of this attack is predicated on the numbers that reflect that women are increasingly arrested on domestic violence charges. Arrest increases in general, however, do not happen in a vacuum but reflect a culmination of policy changes and criminal justice practices, in addition to actual behavior. This book explores this phenomenon.

The Crime of Battering: Politics, Policies, and Consequences

Anti-rape and anti-battering movements are firmly anchored in the second wave of feminism that emerged in the 1970s in the United States. Feminist efforts highlighted the personal inequalities and indignities endured by women in private relationships as being part of a larger continuum of structural inequalities that undergird society. Violence between partners, with women typically the recipients and men typically the abusers, was one area exposed. Keeping with the most-often used and accepted description of what makes the use of force "battering" is the understanding that battering shapes the dynamics of a relationship in which one partner, usually the male in a heterosexual relationship, uses coercive controlling tactics along with systematic threats and the use of violence to "exert power, induce fear, and control another" (Osthoff 2002, 1522). The battered women's movement was fueled by grassroots participants, who were joined by professionals (social workers, psychologists, and lawyers).

The movement's initial vision reflected both a sociopolitical analysis of women's subordinate status as played out within gendered relationships as well as a belief in social change. Over time, the movement has undergone great change, and the strong feminist and political principles and practices have been transformed into a more social service-oriented framework (S. Miller and Barberet 1994). This transformation is consistent with other analyses of state cooptation of splinter groups in which what is initially political work advocating broad social change gets reconfigured to providing therapeutic assistance to victims as well as other services.[2]

Because publicizing the social problem of battering by the battered women's movement entailed an exposure of cultural and structural gendered patterns of discrimination, it is not surprising that it generated a backlash. Shelters operated under enormous pressure to de-emphasize their feminist politics in order to secure funding. State and local government entities were uncomfortable with the movement's position that battering resulted from a patriarchal society (Dobash and Dobash 1992; Gordon 1988; Pleck 1987; see also Schechter 1982 for a wonderfully rich analysis of the early battered women's movement). Although many activists shifted their focus away from challenging structural factors that facilitate battering and toward victims' immediate needs, they still emphasized the need for change in criminal justice practices.

In fact, activism on behalf of battered women was instrumental in changing the traditional criminal justice response to domestic violence. Changes were not altruistically motivated, but reflected the surge in lawsuits launched against police departments by victims of Fourteenth Amendment equal protection violations as well as politicians' recognition that a "pro-victim" stance (and thus anti-offender) could garner votes. Most of the changes were directed toward police, who act as the gatekeepers to the criminal justice system through their decision making and action (or inaction) as first responders to domestic violence calls. Prior to the mid-1980s, police typically followed a pattern of non-enforcement when encountering "domestic disturbances," choosing to perform crisis intervention or use mediation techniques or simply to separate the combatants. Police reluctance to use formal law enforcement tools was challenged by research conducted by Sherman and Berk (1984a, 1984b), who suggested that arrest was a more effective police response to deter future domestic violence than was mediation or separation, based on their findings from a random experiment in Minneapolis. Many jurisdictions moved to enact mandatory and pro-arrest policies, to assert publicly that battering is a serious crime that will not be tolerated, to empower and protect victims, and to create uniformity with the hope of ensuring an end to selective enforcement based on race, class, or other extra-legal variables.

Although most states now provide police with the option to arrest in misdemeanor domestic violence cases that they have not witnessed, police officers may still rely on advising, mediating, separating the couple, or issuing a citation to the offender requiring him to appear in court to answer specific charges. Mandatory and pro-arrest statutes, which either limit or strongly guide police discretion, have become increasingly popular in current law enforcement efforts. These policies state that police officers *have to* (mandatory) or *should* (pro) arrest domestic violence perpetrators when probable cause for misdemeanor violence exists, even if the violence does not occur in the officer's presence and even if the victim does not desire prosecution (Iovanni and Miller 2001). By 2002 twenty-three states operated with mandatory arrest for some assault and battery domestic violence offenses; thirty-three states mandated arrest when police determine probable cause exists that restraining orders have been violated (Hirschel and Buzawa 2002, 1451). Today, all fifty states use at least one of these arrest types (mandatory and pro-arrest) (Buzawa and Buzawa 2003).[3]

The empirical research findings pertaining to the efficacy of arrest are at best equivocal. The widely publicized pioneering Minneapolis Domestic Violence Experiment (Sherman and Berk 1984a, 1984b) indicated that prevalence rates for subsequent offenses were reduced by about half with arrest. Although this result was welcomed by victim advocates, the study's results were intensely criticized for many methodological problems (Fagan 1989). Replication experiments in six cities followed, but only two provided any direct support for the specific deterrent effect of arrest (Berk et al. 1992; Pate and Hamilton 1992). In contrast, the majority of the replication experiments found that arrest was no more effective as a deterrent than any other intervention (Dunford 1992; Hirschel and Hutchinson 1992) or that arrest might actually increase the occurrences of future offending (Dunford 1992; Sherman et al. 1991).

In addition to the problem of contradictory research results, the focus on police practice and specific deterrence led some scholars to attack the naive assumption that arrest alone will deter the complex behavior of domestic violence (Bowman 1992; Zorza 1994). Although mandating arrest communicates the seriousness of battering, conveying that this behavior will not be socially or legally tolerated, opponents of arrest policies such as Buzawa and Buzawa (1993) note that relieving victims of their decision-making power by mandating arrest is ultimately patronizing to battered women. Often victims simply want the violence to stop in the given instance or fear the consequences that may accompany arrest, such as retaliation by their partner or loss of his income. Buzawa and Buzawa (1993) believe that true victim empowerment is achieved by giving victims control over the outcome of the police intervention and that a policy of victim preference is by far preferable to mandatory arrest. Moreover, arrest may be effective only for employed suspects who would incur legitimate losses if arrested (such as loss of job or reputation) (Sherman and Smith 1992; Zorza 1994). In addition, police often circumvent such policies due to the inconvenience of case processing, belief in stereotypes regarding battered women, and dissatisfaction with limits placed on their discretion (Ferraro 1989).

Other scholars have called attention to the unique problems of lower class and minority women in dealing with battering (Rasche 1995), as well as the fact that mandatory arrest policies can have unanticipated and negative consequences for these women (S. Miller 1989, 2000). Women from lower socioeconomic and minority groups may be more likely to call the police to solve problems in the private sphere because of their fewer resources, and this situation could result in disproportionately higher arrests of men in these groups (Hutchinson, Hirschel, and Pesackis, 1994). On the other hand, some women of color and poor women might be reluctant to call the police. According to Rasche (1995), African-American women may be hesitant to seek relief from a criminal justice system that they perceive as dealing more severely with nonwhite men, whereas Asian and Latino women may view expressing a preference for arrest as a betrayal of cultural norms that dictate privacy and deference to family authority. Poor women may also be deterred from calling the police if it means the loss of an employed spouse's income (Iovanni and Miller 2001, 309).

Despite the criticism that mandatory arrest fails to empower battered women to make the best choices in their own unique situations and that there is a potential for police bias toward the poor or people of color, arrest policies at a minimum represent a better criminal justice system response than decades of non-intervention (S. Miller 2000; Zorza and Woods 1994). As a consequence of these criminal justice policy changes (similar to police, many prosecutor offices created "no drop" policies so that victims cannot be intimidated by batterers to recant their stories), more arrests of domestic violence perpetrators have been made, and with this increase, more women have been arrested as well, either as the sole perpetrator or in dual arrests where both parties are arrested (S. Miller 2001; Hirschel and Buzawa 2002; Zorza and Woods 1994). Ironically, because the state is held accountable for women's safety through changes in law enforcement practices (Dasgupta 2002, 1364), many female victims of ongoing battering have ended up with less protection and fewer services, and have been labeled as an offender (Mills 1999). Furthermore, the consequences of mandatory arrest policies may be exacerbated for women of color in part because they are more likely to fight back (Wright 2000; Worcester 2002; Joseph 1997), more likely to minimize victimization due to their investment in perceiving themselves as capable of self-defense (Ammons 1995; Harrison and Esqueda 1999), or more reluctant to further involve the criminal justice system in the lives of men of color (Sens 1999).

Across the nation, as more stringent arrest policies have been adopted to target domestic violence offenders, the widening net has resulted in more and more women finding themselves arrested. A disproportionate number of battered women are now ensnared in the policies of arrest, despite research that shows that men who batter women account for 95 percent of domestic violence incidents (Dobash et al. 1992; Pagelow 1992). Nationwide statistics indicate that women who are prosecuted for domestic violence-related offenses represent about 5 to 10 percent of domestic violence prosecutions, although this number is growing (Hooper 1996). Following changes in arrest policies, the arrests of women for domestic violence crimes in California jumped from 5 percent of intimate violence arrests in 1987 to about 17 percent in 1999 (Blumner 1999); in Concord, New Hampshire, the same category increased from 23 percent in 1993 to 35 percent in 1999 (Blumner 1999). After mandatory arrest was implemented in a county in Minnesota, 13 percent of women arrested in the first year rose to 25 percent in the second year (Saunders 1995). Many jurisdictions are discovering that dual arrests have increased (Busch and Rosenberg 2004). For instance, Hirschel and Buzawa (2002, 1455) report that after the state of Washington implemented mandatory arrest in 1984, dual arrests increased to comprise one-third of all domestic violence arrests (see also Martin 1997; Zorza and Woods 1994). Thus, both research and anecdotal material from across the nation serves to raise concerns about a growing trend to arrest women as domestic violence offenders.

Does this mean that women are increasing their use of violence within relationships? On the one hand, part of this increase in arrests of women reflects the practice of an incident-based criminal justice system, where the concern is whether the law was indeed broken. When police determine that a domestic violence law was broken, under a pro-arrest mandate an arrest must be made. In this manner, people in violent situations are dichotomized into "victim" and "perpetrator" categories, with the context of the situation left unexamined. While many of these arrested women are victims of battering, it is easy to see how, by following a pro-arrest statute, a single act of a woman's violence eclipses her entire history of victimization. On the other hand, it is also possible that increases in the arrest of women on domestic violence charges could be attributed to police officers' desire to avoid accusations of gender bias. This logic introduces a gender-neutral approach to arrest that provides "equity" by holding perpetrators equally accountable for their actions, and demonstrates that the law is being applied fairly (Renzetti 1999).

Neither of these explanations, however, answers the question of whether more women are engaged in domestic violence or the increases in arrests reflect a change in criminal justice arrest policies rather than a real change in women's actual behavior. To compound the problem, women in general exhibit behaviors that easily facilitate police action: Even if they are victims of battering, women more readily admit their use of force vis-à-vis abusive men (Dobash et al. 1998); women have less to hide and fear from the criminal justice system and are less savvy about its operation (S. Miller 2001); and women are not socialized to use violence, so they vividly remember every incident (Kimmel 2002; Dasgupta 1999). These tendencies backfire for women when dealing with an incident-driven criminal justice system bent on arrest.

Among many direct service providers and scholars, the consensus is that battering must be explored and evaluated in context, by looking at the motivations, meanings, and consequences involved in violent acts. To better address the rigidity of police responses and to better prepare and train police officers, some jurisdictions recognize the problem of dual arrests or arrests of women who are really victims and have adopted protocols or statutes that encourage the identification of primary aggressors (S. Miller 2001; Hirschel and Buzawa 2002). Starting in 1985 in Washington, states began to add these kinds of protocols, with twenty-four states now having predominant/primary aggressor assessments (Hirschel and Buzawa 2002; N. Miller 1997). Statutes, such as in Iowa, Alaska, and South Carolina, instruct officers to consider the history of domestic violence of the parties involved (Hirschel and Buzawa 2002, 1460). Some declines in dual arrests have been attributed to passage of such laws and training in their enforcement (Haviland et al. 2001; Martin 1997; Zorza and Woods 1994).

The sparse literature on domestically violent women that currently exists indicates that women are less likely to use preemptive, aggressive force, but rather use violence in self-defense or to escape an imminent attack. The complexities of this debate will be discussed in far greater detail in the next chapter. However, when battered women are arrested, numerous deleterious consequences can accrue, such as losing their rights as victims (which could include transportation to a safe location, temporary refuge, and help from victim service workers), losing employment, incurring financial hardship, or losing custody of children. In addition, women could be more reluctant to report subsequent battering episodes to police, given the above consequences that occurred in tandem with their arrests (Hirschel and Buzawa 2002).

Not knowing what to do with the influx of women arrested on domestic violence charges, many jurisdictions have mandated them to batterer treatment programs designed to address male abusers' behavior. The surreal position of being a battered woman who is then formally processed as an offender exacerbates her feelings of confusion and powerlessness; being mandated to a batterer intervention program, especially one designed for male abusers, only increases this absurdity. Fortunately, recognition that the situation of women is different from that of men is increasing, albeit slowly, which could help in designing separate female offender programs with attention to victim status.

Batterer intervention programs are one component of the social, legal, and political measures developed to divert offenders, typically male, from incarceration while challenging them by using psycho-educational techniques. However, many practitioners and scholars involved in the battered women's movement express concern about the existence of these programs for arrested women. It is imperative to identify the *batterer* and send only that person to a treatment program. For women who have been convicted of a domestic violence offense but who are victims of abuse who used self-defense, the use of court-mandated programs seems wholly inappropriate. It is difficult to embrace programs that label victims as batterers and follow the goals of batterer treatment programs intended to confront male privilege and to treat male abusers (Dasgupta 2002; Pence and Paymar 1993). Moreover, a generic one-size-fits-all program fails to address men's and women's different needs.

Since the image of a violent woman attracts so much concern and attention, it is also important to discern how gender-based assumptions and expectations influence criminal justice actions, such as arrests. It is possible that women who do not conform to gendered notions of "pure" or "good" victims (i.e., nice, delicate, passive), but rather are more "masculine" (i.e., mouthy, aggressive toward police, drunk [Osthoff 2002]) are the ones who will continue to face arrest (Gilbert 2002, 1271 and 1287). When women use violence, they may evoke different reactions from authorities because their behavior contradicts gender role assumptions of submissiveness (Dasgupta 2002, 1379). Part of this perception is fueled by the legal system and the media's depiction of a battered woman as passive and helpless (Ferraro 2003), so when she does resort to violence, it is scary and surprising, despite studies showing that even the most timid victim of domestic violence can develop coping strategies for survival on an ongoing basis, such as ways to minimize injury (Campbell et al. 1998; Dutton 1992; Gondolf and Fisher 1988). Furthermore, evidence suggests that battered women who fight back are still not safe; they may face increased vulnerability to their partner's aggression (Bachman and Carmody 1994; Feld and Straus 1989; Gelles and Straus 1988).

Arguing that battered women who use self-defensive violence against their abusive partners or former partners do not belong in batterer treatment programs intended for male batterers revitalizes the equity versus special treatment conundrum. Prison reformers in the 1980s and 1990s demanded parity across men's and women's prisons; they sought equivalent care and services, based on the unique needs of each sex. I argue here for a consideration of parity in responding to domestic violence arrests of women. In general, the war on crime and the various "get tough" policies have led to unintended consequences for women (S. Miller 1998). For instance, women's prison programs remain inferior to men's, but women now have achieved equity in terms of being able to serve on chain gangs, attend boot camps, garner long mandatory sentences for nonviolent drug offenses, and face execution at the same rate as men—the worst of both worlds (Fischer-Giolando 2000) and what Meda Chesney-Lind (1998, 68) describes as "vengeful equity."

New police practices and criminal justice crackdowns have resulted in domestic violence victims being swept up with the tide of punitiveness, adrift from the structural and cultural context of battering. The contours of women's lives differ from men's, and this is particularly true in regard to battered women. Addressing inequities in past domestic violence arrest policies does not mean that justice can only be achieved if anyone who uses violence is arrested, regardless of the meaning or motivation of the act. Victims who use violence in self-defense are not the offenders that the law targets; sending victims to batterer treatment programs compounds the mistake. Yet many women continue to be arrested under pro-arrest laws and mandated to batterer treatment programs. It is time to fully examine the women involved in such miscarriages of justice, and my hope is that this book illuminates the multiple issues related to this policy by listening to the stories of the arrested women themselves.

Examining Women's Use of Violence

This book aims to weave together various data sources to create a more complete tapestry illustrating women's use of violence in relationships by untangling the snags that have plagued examinations of this topic. One way to explore these issues is to observe police behavior and attitudes while they respond to domestic calls for service. Another way is to examine the daily experiences and perceptions of criminal justice personnel (probation officers, police, prosecutors, public defenders) and social service providers (shelter workers, victim advocates, treatment providers, family court advocates). A final way to evaluate the use of violence by women is by revealing the perceptions of the arrested women themselves and allowing their descriptions of their own behavior to shape our understanding of their situations. I accomplish all three goals by gathering observational data from a systematic police ride-along study, by conducting in-depth interviews with criminal justice professionals and service providers, and by using participant-observation strategies to explore women's stories within their court-mandated batterer intervention groups.

Organization of Subsequent Chapters

The next chapter presents the empirical work relating to measurement of interpersonal violence by women and the findings associated with studies that examine women's use of force, arrested women, and women court-mandated to treatment. Chapter 3 provides background information and methodological material about the data collection and research settings. This chapter also introduces the treatment program philosophy and anchors the discussion of such programs to other efforts underway nationwide. Chapter 4 analyzes attitudes, perceptions, and experiences of police officers who were observed for three months while on patrol by my research team. Chapter 5 explores responses from criminal justice professionals and social service providers who work directly with women arrested on domestic violence charges. Chapter 6 takes the reader into a typical treatment group session for female offenders and discusses the themes that emerge during the program. The motivations and context of women's use of violence is explored in chapter 7 using data from three twelve-week female offender treatment groups. Finally, chapter 8 discusses the major findings of the study as a whole and their policy implications.

| Chapter 2 | The Controversy about Women's Use of Force |

UNDER CERTAIN CIRCUMSTANCES, women can be as aggressive as men (Bandura 1973; White and Kowalski 1994). There is a vast difference, however, between aggression and violence used in self-defense against an aggressor. The removal of the violent behavior from its context creates inaccuracies. Yes, some women hit. Some women use force in ongoing relationships or against former partners. There is no denying that women share some of the same base emotions with men: anger, jealousy, revenge. Women cannot be essentialized as the feminine, delicate counterpoint to men's masculine, aggressive self; this image belies reality and disempowers women by denying them access to use force legitimately under certain circumstances. However, the key questions surrounding women's use of force are contextual: What are a woman's motivations? What are the consequences of her violence? How do her understandings and use of violence differ from those of her (male) partner or former partner? And ultimately, what are the best ways to respond to her use of force, particularly if the meaning differs from men's use of force?

This chapter explores several bodies of literature along these lines. First, it examines the methodological, measurement, and conceptual issues that complicate the study of battering within interpersonal relationships. Second, it summarizes the literature on domestically violent women, drawing from studies that examine aggression, arrest, and treatment groups. In addition, the chapter considers issues unique to women with different race, class, and sexual orientation backgrounds.

The Gender Symmetry Argument

Once contextual factors are made clear, most of the empirical evidence to date demonstrates that gender symmetry in the use of interpersonal violence is a fallacy. While women do engage in using force, its use is very different from men's violence in terms of injury and motivation. There simply are not an equal number of battered wives and battered husbands. Yet this rancorous debate continues. A number of studies conducted by prominent scholars, endlessly rehashed and misinterpreted, continue to flame the fiery debate about mutual combat and are trotted out whenever one wants to suggest that women are equally or even more violent in relationships than are men. For instance, findings from two major reviews of the literature that look at seventy-nine and fifty-two studies respectively demonstrate that men and women are equally violent in relationships (Fiebert 1997; Archer 2000). These two studies received considerable media attention and challenged the focus of the battered women's movement on female victims of male violence, despite criticism about the conceptualization, operation, and interpretation of the studies' results (White et al. 2000).

Support for or against the mutual combat hypothesis is shaped by the type of methods used in the research as well as by the ideological positions of the researchers making the assertions; in fact, the debate gets downright acrimonious at times. The clearest way of assessing these different perspectives is to examine three types of research: the studies in the family violence perspective; the national crime victimization surveys; and the studies characterized as the feminist perspective.

FAMILY VIOLENCE PERSPECTIVE

Researchers in the family violence perspective tend to view abuse as incorporating a range of behaviors nested within a family constellation. Thus, family violence could include acts occurring between spouses, between parents and children, and between siblings. Given this wide range of possibilities, it is not surprising that many acts of violence are counted. The media sensationalizes evidence of mutual combat between husbands and wives without exploring who initiated the violence, if the violence was committed in self-defense, if injuries resulted from the violence, or if the nature of violent acts differed by gender (Osthoff 2002; Saunders 2002; S. Miller 2001).

The finding of mutual combat takes on a polemical cast in that researchers argue that the political focus should shift away from violence committed by men against women and that resources should be devoted to funding male victims and female violence prevention programs (Moffit and Caspi 1999;

Pearson 1997; Farrell 1999; Fiebert 1997, 1998). Anti-feminist men's groups ride on their coattails, arguing that there is strong evidence of husband battering by wives that gets ignored or trivialized when it comes to framing the issues or dedicating resources and funding support. They support shelters for battered men and reeducation of the criminal justice system so that prosecutors and judges become more cognizant of the violence wielded by women.

There is a powerful backlash force present in the debate that views the controversy surrounding female arrests as proof of gender bias against male victims that has been minimized or denied by the feminist advocacy movement (Burroughs 1999; Cook 1997; Pearson 1997; see also Messner 1998 and Savran 1998 for alternative views). Some men's rights groups claim that society is reluctant to believe that women are violent toward their male partners, and that "militant" and "victim" feminists drop their support for mandatory arrest laws when they sweep up women (Blumner 1999, 1; S. Miller 2001). This antifeminist stance is strongly supported by men's rights groups, the male members of which are typically joined by their second wives (Hart 1999; S. Miller 2001). As Michael Kimmel (2002, 1354) suggests, "It is an indication of the political intentions of those who argue for gender symmetry that they never question the levels of violence against women, only that the level of violence against men is equivalent. Their solution, however, is not more funding for domestic violence research and intervention but to decrease the amount of funding that women receive, although they never challenge the levels of violence against women." Men's backlash groups share uneasy alliances with conservative and right-wing women's organizations as well as with some feminist writers such as Katie Roiphe and Naomi Wolf who reject feminist emphases on victimization because these views reinforce traditional gender views of women as passive and fragile.

Exploring men's accounts of their use of violence in relationships reveals a great deal about these men's denial of responsibility, minimization of harm, and rationalization of their abusive behavior (Dobash and Dobash 1998; Hearn 1998; Ptacek 1990). Qualitative research that analyzes men's narrative descriptions of their violence finds that violence is used to punish partners who do not fulfill unspoken physical, sexual, or emotional needs (Anderson and Umberson 2001) or to graphically demonstrate that they are "men" in charge (Hearn 1998). Anderson and Umberson (2001) contend that relationship violence itself is a vehicle through which masculine identities are constructed. Using a sample of arrested men mandated to batterer treatment programs, they focus on listening to how differently the men discuss their own violence and that of their female partners and how these descriptions are linked to men's understandings of appropriate masculine and feminine behavior. For instance, men "depicted their violence as rational, effective, and explosive whereas women's violence was represented as hysterical, trivial, and ineffectual" (p. 363). To confirm their masculine status, the men constructed their own use of violence as more lethal and fear-generating, whereas women's violence displayed innate incompetence. The men refused to try to understand their partners' motivations and resisted any efforts to change the relationship. Moreover, Anderson and Umberson found that when the men did claim their partners were controlling, the men were unable to specify any examples of this behavior, "suggesting that these claims may be indicative of these men's fears about being controlled by a woman rather than the actual practice of their partners" (p. 368). Finally, Anderson and Umberson's research revealed various ways that men tried to deflect criticism: by claiming they were victims of gender policies within a criminal justice system that is biased toward women, and by chivalrously protecting their woman from arrest, despite their self-proclaimed innocence. The willingness of the men to erase all victimization or perpetration was telling; by constructing the idea that the justice system is biased against them, the men could excuse their own arrests and maintain the fiction of being rational, strong, and nonviolent.

Most of the family violence studies that claim evidence for gender symmetry rely on the Conflict Tactics Scale (CTS) empirical measure of domestic violence. In fact, fifty-five of the seventy-nine studies in Fiebert's review (1997) and seventy-six of the eighty-two in Archer's review (2000) relied on this measure. (Other studies in Fiebert's review offered no data or concentrated their study on dating violence patterns of young couples not married or cohabiting.) Hence, it is appropriate to examine the CTS-related measurement issues more fully here. The suggestion of "mutually violent couples" originates from the findings of three nationally representative surveys of households of married or cohabitating heterosexual couples that ask respondents about family violence in the context of conflict resolution techniques (Straus, Gelles, and Steinmetz 1980; Gelles and Straus 1988; Gelles 2000). These are important studies for the light they shine on what was going on "behind closed doors" (as one of their book titles suggest), despite the limitations of the data (discussed subsequently).

Murray Straus and his colleagues developed the Conflict Tactics Scale (CTS) and the revised version, the CTS2 (Straus et al. 1996) to explore family violence. Its opening paragraph, read to respondents, captures the socially palatable way of making individuals feel comfortable telling strangers about their private lives:

> No matter how well a couple gets along, there are times when they disagree, get annoyed with the other person, or just have spats of

fights because they're in a bad mood or tired or for some other reason.
They also use many different ways of trying to settle their differences.
I'm going to read some things that you and your (spouse/partner)
might do when you have an argument (Straus 1990, 33).

The CTS2 contains thirty-nine questions about violent and nonviolent
behaviors, each perpetrated and experienced, with finer distinctions made
about minor and serious violence than the original CTS and an effort to
include items that attempt to measure the consequences of violent events
(Iovanni 2006). Despite the measurement improvements associated with the
CTS2, the scale continues to be criticized for counting violent events without
providing information on the meaning and motivation of the event; i.e., it
does not distinguish aggressive or instigating violence from self-defensive or
retaliatory violence (DeKeseredy and Schwartz 1998).

Relying on quantitative survey responses that use large random national
or community samples is problematic on a number of levels. First, without
distinguishing between the contexts, the results provide the false impression
that intimate violence is committed by women at an equal or higher rate
than by men (Dobash et al. 1992; White et al. 2000). These results are
reported in work by Straus and his colleagues using the 1975 and 1985 National Family Survey as well as in findings reported in the National Youth
Survey data reports (Morse 1995); both surveys rely on the CTS to measure
domestic violence. For example, a man's "punch" may result in much greater
injury than a woman's, yet both are rated as "severe violence" using the CTS.
A specific illustration of this measurement difficulty is provided by Anderson
and Umberson (2001), whose research found that 61 percent of the sample in
which respondents reported "mutual" violence actually show something very
different:

> We started pushing each other. And the thing is that I threw her on
> the floor. I told her that I'm going to leave. She took my car keys, and
> I wanted my car keys so I went and grabbed her arm, pulled it, and
> took the car keys away from her. She—she comes back and tried to
> kick me in the back. So I just pushed her back and threw her on the
> floor again. (pp. 362–363)

Thus, without specifying contextual factors, merely counting violent acts
would lead one to a false assumption of gender symmetry.

Second, when respondents are asked to simply check a box to indicate if
they ever "hit or tried to hit," "shoved," "pushed," or "grabbed" their partner,
checking this designates that person as a perpetrator, regardless of the motivating

circumstances (such as self-defense) or whether it happened only once.[1] Thus, many researchers argue that this way of gathering data "erroneously portray[s] the gender similarities by exaggerating women's use of IPV [intimate partner violence]" (Melton and Belknap 2003, 335). Counting acts without attributing motivation is insufficient; it does not distinguish between how violence is used instrumentally, to control or achieve subordination, or used expressively with an absence of attempts to dominate or terrorize one's partner.

Third, self-report data suggest that a reliability issue is present in large national quantitative studies in that men underreport their use of violence (Campbell 1995; Dobash et al. 1998; Morse 1995) while women underreport their own victimization (Melton and Belknap 2003). When women are asked questions over the phone, as is the typical method employed with the national studies, women minimize or underreport their victimization experiences due to fear of reprisal, shame, or embarrassment, thinking the abuse is too minor to list, and not understanding that abuse is a crime (Melton and Belknap 2003). In addition, abusers might be present when the victim participates in the survey, which could affect the victim's disclosure, or victims might not trust interviewers who pose such personal questions (Smith 1994).

Fourth, as Kimmel (2002) suggests, it is important to examine what is excluded in the CTS measures, namely injury and sexual assault. While the measures of mild violence in the CTS find fewer gender differences in the use of violence, greater gender differences are found as violence (and injury) grow more serious. Women are six times more likely to need medical care for their injuries (Kaufman Kantor and Straus 1987) and more than ten times as many women report that their partners beat them up (Tjaden and Thoennes 1998). Four percent of murdered men are killed by their current or former intimate partners compared to about one-third of murdered women. (Bachman and Saltzman 1995). Yet the consequences of intimate violence are often not revealed in the CTS measures. In addition, battered women also face a wide array of health problems that are not directly related to physical injury (and thus not included in the CTS measures). These include clinical depression, sexually transmitted infection, gastrointestinal disorders, post-traumatic stress disorder, and frequent urinary tract and vaginal infections (White et al. 2000). White and her colleagues (2000) are especially critical of psychologists, such as Archer (2000), who endorse the "mutually" or equally violent position because it minimizes female victims' more serious injuries and "deflate[s] the momentum of efforts to change the structural conditions that support violence against women" (p. 693). In terms of sexual assault, the National Violence Against Women Survey reveals that 7.7 percent of female respondents were raped by their intimate partners (Tjaden and Thoennes 2000c), yet the category of "sexual coercion" is not included in the original CTS, the basis for a huge number of studies that examine gender symmetry.

Another excluded category identified by Kimmel (2002) is violence perpetrated by ex-partners and ex-spouses. The national crime victimization statistics that show that the intimate violence perpetrated against women by their former partners or spouses is eight times higher than rates for married women (Bachman and Saltzman 1995; see also Greenfeld et al. 1998). Some scholars feel that excluding former spouses and partners grossly underestimates the extent of interpersonal violence, perhaps by as much as one-third (Ferrante et al. 1996; Kimmel 2002). Failing to include the full extent of injuries, sexual assaults, and violence committed by former intimates casts serious doubt on the veracity of what the CTS measures.

Another way to challenge the gender symmetry perspective is to examine why female victims are disproportionately represented at battered women's shelters and hospital emergency rooms (Kimmel 2002). Advocates of the family conflict perspective believe that the absence of male victims demonstrates the humiliation or shame men would feel in admitting to police or hospital personnel that they had been beaten by their wives. However, existing data suggest otherwise: "Men who are assaulted by intimates are actually more likely to call the police, more likely to press charges, and less likely to drop them" (Ferrante et al. 1996, cited in Kimmel 2002, 1345). Calling the police to report women's violence may indicate a greater likelihood of men's vindictiveness than real victimization. "If men underestimate their own violence and overestimate their victimization while women overestimate their own violence and underestimate their victimization, this would have enormous consequences in a survey that asks only one partner to recall accurately how much they and their spouses used various conflict-resolution tactics" (Kimmel 2002, 1346).

Finally, the CTS fails to address the importance of fear and its role in understanding battering dynamics. Women may fear death or serious injury if their male partners, who are on average larger and stronger, are violent, whereas men may not experience fear until much more serious violence occurs, usually with weapons, and even when this occurs, men's fear is only temporary. As found in research by Hamberger and Guse (2002) and others (Barnett and LaViolette 1993; Barnett, Lee, and Thelan 1997; Hamberger and Lohr 1989; Jacobson et al. 1994), inducing fear is "the primary mechanism through which violent partners achieve control" (Hamberger and Guse 2002, 1301). It is a given that victims who fear injury or death will acquiesce to their partner's demands.

A directive from the American Association of the Advancement of Science (Lerch 1999) admonishes researchers who present findings in ways that are too easily misunderstood and misapplied and might engender incorrect policy assumptions:

> First, scientists must be sensitive to the implications of their work for the larger society and take steps to educate their non-scientist readers about the relationships of their work to the broader community. . . . [Members should] communicate the findings of controversial research in a way that anticipates its impact on policy, or more generally on the lives of people. (p. 3)

Given the interpretation problems inherent with the context-free nature of the CTS, it would behoove family violence researchers to rethink their "mutual combat" hypothesis.

NATIONAL VICTIMIZATION SURVEYS

National victimization surveys measure the extent of crime victimization using nationally representative samples. Two of the well-respected ones are the National Violence Against Women Survey (NVAW) and the National Crime Victimization Survey (NCVS). Compared to the family violence studies, these studies conducted or sponsored by U.S. federal agencies reveal dramatic differences in rates of intimate violence, lending strong support that the gender distribution is asymmetrical.

The NCVS, conducted by the U.S. Department of Justice's Bureau of Justice Statistics, is a nationally representative survey of forty-five thousand representative households comprising ninety thousand people. All members of the sample households age twelve and over are interviewed every six months for three years, and both in-person interviews (the first and fifth interviews) and telephone interviews are conducted (Iovanni 2006). The survey asks respondents about many types of criminal victimization, including violent intimate victimization. A revised version of the NCVS asks respondents directly about rape and violence in the context of intimate and other relationships rather than depending on respondents themselves revealing the context as in earlier studies (Bachman and Taylor 1994). As might be expected, improved question formats and wording resulted in higher estimates of domestic violence and sexual assault than in the earlier national crime surveys (Bachman and Saltzman 1995). The data showed that women reported six times as many incidents of violence as men did (Bachman and Saltzman 1995). While the results of the NCVS are certainly revealing with respect to female victimization, researchers are well aware that the context of criminal victimization could result in lower response rates for questions about intimate violence experiences, which respondents are reluctant to view as crimes (Iovanni 2006).

In an effort to address this reporting problem, The National Violence Against Women Survey (NVAW) was conducted in the context of personal safety. The survey relied on data from sixteen thousand households (eight thousand men and eight thousand women), and was sponsored by the National Institute of Justice and the Centers for Disease Control and Prevention (Tjaden and Thoennes 1998, 2000a, 2000b). The NVAW revealed that men used physical assault at three times the rate at which women used physical assault (Tjaden and Thoennes 2000b). Findings also included higher rates of domestic violence (IPV) for both rape and physical assault than the rates reported by the NCVS survey. Part of the reason is that the NVAW survey was framed within the context of personal safety and conflict resolution, thus sensitizing respondents to IPV questions; in addition, the NVAW uses a wider range of behaviors that meet the definition of rape in most states, and its questions and cues are also worded so that there is a higher probability of eliciting responses about intimate assault (Bachman 2000).

These national victimization studies fill in the gaps identified in the family violence studies because they include a wider range of assaults, such as sexual assaults and violence committed by former intimate partners. While they tend to find lower rates of battering than other studies, this is due to underreporting by respondents who may not perceive or report events as crimes, or due to the inclusion of household respondents over the age of twelve, which includes a younger age group less likely to have high rates of domestic assaults. Lower rates could also reflect respondents' fears of retaliation, since all family members are interviewed (DeKeseredy 2000; Gelles 2000).

With a more complete understanding of what studies measure and what they leave out, the persistence of gender asymmetry remains. We can acknowledge that women use violence without confusing the issue by a pretense that women's violence is as injurious or frequent as men's violence. As demonstrated by the national victimization surveys that correct for some of the measurement issues that plague the family violence studies, the notion of gender symmetry is simply not borne out by the data.

FEMINIST PERSPECTIVE

Feminist studies strongly dispute the conclusions reached by family violence scholars. Similar to the findings highlighted in national victimization surveys, feminist studies contend the contrary: interpersonal violence is a profoundly gendered phenomenon, and overwhelmingly women are targets of men's use of force. Rather than relying on national samples, these studies are most likely to be drawn from battered women's shelter samples, clinical samples, hospital samples, and police reports. Overall, the research findings indicate that men commit battering against their current or former female partners much more often than being victims of battering (Dobash et al. 1992; Johnson 1995; McLeod 1984; Saunders 1986). These findings of gender asymmetry are consistent with those reported by national crime survey data (i.e., victimization data that uses national probability sampling—see Dobash et al. 1992; Rennison and Welchans 2000; Tjaden and Thoennes 2000).

How can this wide discrepancy between the family violence perspective and the feminist perspective be explained? First, the methodological problems described earlier that are associated with the CTS/CTS2 are resolved by discerning the contextual factors related to the use of force within ongoing or former relationships. Qualitative instruments designed to elicit rich, detailed answers from respondents reveal a great deal about the different motives, meanings, and consequences that violence poses for men and women. Even the revised CTS2 does not effectively measure contextual factors, leading family violence researchers to mischaracterize and misrepresent the role of gender in violent relationships.

In contrast to the view expressed by the family violence perspective, feminist research reveals that when women do use force, their use is most likely in self-defense, in order to escape, or in an attempt to fight back (S. Miller 2001; S. Miller and Meloy 2005; Barnett, Lee, and Thelan 1997; Cascardi and Vivian 1995; Hamberger et al. 1997; Hamberger and Potente 1994; Saunders 1986, 1988; Browne 1987; Dasgupta 1999; Dobash and Dobash 1992; Hamberger 1997; Sommer 1994; Vivian and Langhinrichsen-Rohling 1996) or to escape an imminent attack on their children (Dasgupta 1999). A number of other studies revealed other motivations for women's use of force, such as retaliation, punishment for past hurt, expression of anger, stress, or frustration, or to gain emotional attention (Bachman and Carmody 1994; Dasgupta 1999; Faith 1993; Hamberger and Potente 1994; Hamberger et al. 1997). These reasons may not qualify as legitimate uses of violence in self-defense. However, the motivation for use of violence is gendered: men tend to use force to control and exercise power over their partners. Obviously, this goal results in women's higher levels of fear and intimidation. Women, on the other hand, tend to use force to express emotion, to escape violence, or to defend themselves or their children. Women are more likely to be injured and, in fact, hold a greater fear of physical injury (Morse 1995). The consequences for female victims are far more injurious and life threatening overall than for male victims (Tjaden and Thoennes 2000). Women are more likely to be killed (Fox and Zawitz 2000). Even when violence is used by women, it does not mean that women have control over their partners or inspire fear (Dasgupta 1999). As Worchester contends (2002, 1403): "It is crucial to keep asking who is afraid and who is not safe. . . . We know women can be effective at using emotional control, but whether it takes on the same level of threat to safety and whether the other person lives in constant fear may be a major difference between male and female use of emotional control." Dasgupta's research (1999, 2002) found that women were more motivated to achieve short-lived control over their immediate situation, while men's desire was to establish widespread authority for lengthy periods of time. Thus, women's violence rarely produces fear while men's violence often does (S. Miller 2001).

Michael Johnson's work distinguishes between four distinct patterns of domestic violence, patterns that address the degree of control that motivates the use of violence (Johnson 1995; Johnson 2000; Johnson and Ferraro 2000). *Common couple violence* encompasses relationships in which both partners use violence in a specific situation and the violence is of relatively low frequency, unconnected to control and unlikely to escalate or involve serious injury. The *intimate terrorism pattern* is one in which violence is one tactic used in a general pattern of control and is more frequent, less likely to be mutual, and more likely to escalate and result in serious injury (also called patriarchal terrorism in Johnson 1995). *Violent resistance* is used primarily by women and is not motivated by control. In relationships characterized as *mutual violent control*, both partners are violent and vying for control; this is considered to describe a very rare pattern. Research demonstrates that women rarely are the batterers in relationships (in Johnson's terminology, *intimate terrorists*) even if they—and many do—engage in hitting their partners (Dasgupta 2002; Hamberger and Guse 2002; Johnson and Ferraro 2000; Kimmel 2002; Stark and Flitcraft 1988).

Johnson's critique (1995) of the CTS-generated findings focuses on the distinction between two types of couple violence. Common couple violence is not controlling, but rather "consists of occasional outbursts of violence from either partner in response to everyday stimulus" (Johnson 1995, 285). Johnson notes that common couple violence is "less a product of patriarchy and more a product of a culture that tolerates violence" and "it rarely escalates into serious, sometimes even life-threatening, forms of violence" (p. 285). Johnson contrasts this with intimate or patriarchal terrorism, a form of terroristic control of women by male partners. He argues that this form of violence is a "product of patriarchal traditions of men's right to control 'their' women," and is more serious, occurs over a longer period of time, and is more likely to include economic subordination, threats, and isolation in addition to the systematic use of violence (p. 284). Johnson concludes that national probability- or community-based samples measure common couple violence, or expressive violence, while shelter, hospital, police, or clinical studies measure patriarchal terrorism violence. Moreover, he believes that these different kinds of samples measure almost non-overlapping phenomena (p. 286), which sheds light on the discrepancy between large-scale survey results, such as the Strauss and colleagues' National Family Violence Surveys, and the results from research conducted with people encountered by public agencies.

Thus, the preponderance of the evidence suggests that gender symmetry does not exist once researchers look beyond quantitative survey responses and tap into motivations and consequences of violence by gender. Male-perpetrated violence against women is more prevalent, serious, and consequently needs most of the available resources to combat it. Despite the empirical proof, however, the debate continues to rage. The unacknowledged result of this tenacious debate is a shift of focus away from social structural factors and toward pinpointing individual pathologies. Regardless of the source, it is clear that the trend toward the increased reluctance in arresting women for domestic violence offenses coincides with the seemingly unresolved question of gender symmetry. Findings from studies that examine the type of violence used by women who have been arrested for domestic violence, and often sent to batterer treatment programs, will be illuminating.

Women's Use of Force

No coherent literature on women's use of force is available to guide effective treatment and policies. Of what little there is, Lynn Dowd's work (2001) offers a summary of the state of the discipline's knowledge about partner violence perpetrated by females. Although feminist theories of domestic violence typically focus on heterosexual couples and exclude lesbians (Renzetti 1999), a number of studies have been conducted with lesbians, with findings that indicate that the prevalence of violence equals or exceeds that of heterosexual couples (Walner-Haugrud, Gratch, and Magruder 1997; Margolies and Leeder 1995; Renzetti 1992). However, making generalizations about lesbians' use of force is fraught with problems, given that the samples are typically small and collected from clinical settings or lesbian bars or events, and over-sample white and middle-class women. The studies also suffer from the use of unclear definitions of what constitutes abuse and methodological issues related to sampling: the samples are nonrandom due to the invisibility of lesbians as a whole and that lesbians have to explicitly identify themselves and disclose their sexual orientation to be included in a study (Perilla et al. 2003; see also Burke and Follingstad 1999; Turrell 2000; Giorgio 2002).

Despite feminist domestic violence theories' erasure of lesbian or same-gender[2] violence, it is critical to include this research in the discussion here because the roots and impact of same-gender violence is similar to heterosexual partner violence.[3] Domestic violence, whether heterosexual or homosexual, demonstrates unequal power held by partners. As Elliott (1996) contends, "The routine and intentional use of intimidation tactics in relationships is not a gender issue but a power one" (cited in Perilla et al. 2003, 20). Further, as "sexism creates an opportunity for heterosexual men to batter women, homophobia creates an opportunity for people in same-gender relationships to batter their partners" (Perilla et al. 2003, 20). Issues related to self-acknowledgment of being gay and the related disclosure risks with family, employment, and other social situations make it more difficult for victims to seek help. In addition, the source of power in same-gender relationships differs from that found in heterosexual relationships: "Whereas in heterosexual relationships gender is overwhelmingly the defining factor, power in same-gender couples may be a function of one or more variables interacting with one another, such as education, class, work status, ethnicity, earning potential, immigration status, and age" (Perilla et al. 2003, 20).

Looking at same-gender intimate violence assists in dismantling the "mutual battering" debate in that assessment and counseling tools deliberately look beyond gender to address other victim and perpetrator distinctions. As Nancy Worcester (2002) states, "Unlike those working on heterosexual domestic violence, people working on lesbian intimate violence have always had to look at how any behavior can be used as power and control, how any behavior can be used as a survival tactic, and the fact that victims may well identify as abusers" (p. 1401). Contextualizing intimate violence—whether heterosexual or same-gender—makes paramount the inclusion of a host of factors, both personal and societal, that help us understand the use, motivation, and consequence of violence.

More general research conducted on domestic violence makes clear that battered women are often survivors of childhood abuse and adult sexual victimization as well as the current abuse that led to their arrest. Using work by Walker (1984), Russell (1986), and Chu and Dill (1990), Dowd (2001) argues that women who experience sexual victimization in childhood have a much greater risk of re-victimization as an adult. Trauma is cumulative, and repeated exposure to victimization could increase levels of anxiety, depression, dissociation, and sexual problems. Moreover, Dowd (2001) explicates that there is a link between traumatized women and post-traumatic stress disorder, which manifests in "hyperviglilance and intense physiological reactivity when exposed to internal or external cues associated with traumatic events" (p. 85). This link does not excuse women's behavior, but helps to explain why women may use violence against an abusive partner when unprovoked in that immediate situation.

Dowd suggests that the link can exert a grave effect on women's ability to self-regulate their emotions, such as anger and aggression, which is exacerbated under circumstances that elicit memories of past abuse (p. 85):

> Van der Kolk (1996) notes that significant changes occur in stress hormone secretion, leading to a condition of chronic hyperarousal for some trauma survivors. This may result in a compensatory emotional shutdown, causing emotions to lose their function of alerting the woman to the need for adaptive action to manage internal or external events. She may then disregard the information, freeze, or overreact (Litz and Keane 1989).

Other researchers have looked at the links between various measures of trauma, anger, and distortion of reality based on studies with combat veterans, female survivors of incest, and substance abuse (Dowd 2001). Preliminary findings suggest that for many battered women, the use of force is indicative of coping or survival strategies; those women who have longstanding and extensive trauma histories may be more vulnerable to anger arousal. Less research has been conducted on how drugs or alcohol affects female aggression; in fact, most alcohol-related research in general has been conducted in laboratory settings with student samples. However, since there is evidence that childhood victimization may be related to subsequent substance abuse in women, this may be a fruitful avenue of inquiry given the strong relationship between battered women and prior victimizations (Najavits, Weiss, and Liese 1996; B. Miller, Downs, and Testa 1993).

Women Arrested for Domestic Violence

Who are the women most likely to commit intimate violence that warrants police attention? To date, only a small number of studies have addressed this issue. Overall, the findings of these studies suggest that unlike men, women tend not to have histories of arrests for domestic violence offenses (Busch and Rosenberg 2004; Martin 1997). Police scholars are well aware that police arrest decisions reflect a range of factors beyond the actual behavior of citizens and the parameters of law (Black 1980). Smith (1987) found that a history of previous calls to the police result in participants being twice as likely to be arrested. Citizen demeanor affects arrest decisions, with the likelihood increasing if one is disrespectful to police (Worden and Pollitz 1984), or if there is noticeable drug or alcohol use (Smith 1987), or if the victim's preference is for the perpetrator to be arrested (Buzawa and Buzawa 1993; Gottfredson and Gottfredson 1988). Women who deviate from traditional gender norms of femininity or passivity are also at greater risk of arrest for domestic violence (Visher 1983); for instance, young, black, rude women are more at risk of arrest than older, white, calm women who are deferential to police authority (Visher 1983).

In relation to the debate about dual arrests, the questions are: What determines arrest? Joint violence where both individuals are aggressors? Self-defensive action? Inadequate police training? Strict adherence to following mandatory arrest laws? A number of studies have begun to look at these questions. Martin's findings (1997) from a Connecticut study suggest that for the women arrested, the police were unaware of the women's arrest background. But she speculates that once a prior arrest record exists, police may be predisposed to arrest both the man and the woman since the violence was already flagged. Thus, arrest could happen even if one of the parties was not the primary perpetrator. It may also be the case that arrest samples reflect people who use more frequent and severe forms of violence so they are already well known to the police.

Martin's (1997) groundbreaking work on dual arrests deserves a little more attention. Three months after the state of Connecticut instituted mandatory arrest (with no primary aggressor protocol and no state policy about a defense against arrest for self-defensive action), she culled all family violence cases for six months, which resulted in a stratified sample of 448 cases in which 134 were dual arrests, or 30 percent. She matched these cases with court, police, and prosecutor files to gain a fuller understanding. In terms of prior victimization in a domestic violence incident, only 2 percent of the male suspects in dual arrests had been victimized previously, while 40 percent of the female suspects in dual arrests were. Unfortunately, this information was available after the fact; there was no way for police to obtain records at the time of arrest. Martin also found that white couples were more likely to be arrested in dual arrests, speculating that the police identify more with white male defendants and try to neutralize the effects of arrest by performing dual arrests. Most of the police knew that dual arrests result in *nolle prosequi* (no prosecution) in the courts, so perhaps they were not worried about arrest consequences. Moreover, Martin contends that "the arrest of white, unmarried and employed women may also be an attempt to punish some women for fighting back, for acting contrary to expected female norms" (p. 153).

Martin's findings highlight concerns about the appropriateness of dual arrests. If the female "offenders" were really battered women who rely on the police for help because the police are often their only resources, arresting a woman who acted in self-defense may reinforce her isolation, helplessness, and self-blame (Martin 1997). Dual arrests could deter women from calling the police to intervene in future incidents. In fact, Pagelow (1981) found that a lack of help from police resulted in the violent relationship lasting longer, while Brown (1984) found that the more helpful the police, the more it facilitated higher levels of self-worth in victims.

A series of studies conducted by Hamberger and his colleagues have addressed the motivations of women's use of force using samples of arrested women mandated to domestic violence counseling programs. With a sample of 51 women, Hamberger (1991a) found that 56 percent of the arrested women used violence in self-defense or retaliation. If the women indicated they used violence to control their partner, their narratives revealed that they did so in a preemptive manner in order to protect themselves from an imminent attack.

Hamberger, Lohr, and Bonge (1994) looked at the reasons given by 75 women and 219 men court-ordered for evaluations prior to beginning domestic violence counseling. They used the CTS to measure the level of violence in the relationships, but added this question: "What is the function, purpose, or payoff of your violence?" (p. 41). They found that women's reasons revolved around defensive action, escape from his restraint, and retaliation for prior physical violence or psychological battering when there was a history of such abuse. Men, on the other hand, used violence to assert dominance, to control women's verbal or physical behavior, to vent anger, or to demand attention. No men reported use of violence for reasons of self-defense, escape, or retaliation for past physical violence. These findings are consistent with other studies.

Saunders (1986) interviewed women in battered women's shelters and found that although 83 percent of them reported the use of at least minor violence sometime in the duration of their relationship, 78 percent used minor violence in self-defense and 71 percent used severe violence in self-defense.

Cascardi, Vivian, and Meyer (1991) interviewed thirty-six married couples (each partner seen separately) who experienced violence in their relationships and found that 58 percent of women who used violence did so in self-defense while only 5 percent of the men used self-defensive action; more than half the men used violence to control their partner. Barnett and Thelen (1992) report the same findings: male batterers used violence to control or punish their partners while the majority of women used violence in self-defense.

In Wisconsin, Hamberger and Potente (1994) found that most women arrested for domestic violence and court-mandated for treatment were battered women who used self-defensive or retaliatory violence against abusive males. The treatment intervention for the women focused on issues of victimization and oppression. From a sample of sixty-seven women, only three of the women were initiators or primary perpetrators. Several years later, Hamberger (1997) sought to further understand contextual factors that might contribute to women's violence. He found that 49 percent of the fifty-two women in his sample had been in a previous battering relationship, and over half had been exposed to violence between their parents as a child. About a third of the women revealed that they had a history of sexual abuse. In these women's experiences, males were clearly the initiators and primary users of violence in the relationships, but the women did report initiating violence some of the time. The women provided reasons such as: self-defense and protection; expression of tension or feelings; to get the other to shut up or stop nagging; to retaliate for a previous assault or to get a partner to talk. The context is missing for these women's stories of aggression, so it is unclear when some responses that seem controlling on their surface might be a function of self-preservation. As an interesting observation, in this Wisconsin study women "offenders" were placed in the same programs as women victims.

In another Wisconsin study, Hamberger and Guse (2002) explored the similarities and differences across three clinical samples: men and women court-ordered to a batterer intervention program, and women residing in a shelter. The most striking finding was the vast difference observed in the pattern of violence: men controlled the overall dynamics of the relationships, exhibiting more dominant behavior, while women tended to be reactive victims, not primary abusers or batterers who exerted fear and control over their partners. So, although women may become active participants when violence unfolds, they do not control their partners or the situation. Hamberger and Guse's findings are similar to other studies that show battered women are fearful but not passive (Holtzworth-Munroe, Smutzler, and Bates 1997) in that women respond with active resistance by fighting back or defending themselves (Johnson and Ferraro 2000; Saunders 1986).

Shamita Das Dasgupta (1999), a leading scholar on this issue, brilliantly articulates five gender differences in tactics and effects of violence in intimate relationships. With regard to the first tactic of battering, *intimidation*, men use multiple ways to cause fear, including glances, action, and gestures, with or without accompanying them by the threat or actual use of physical and sexual violence. Women, on the other hand, rarely cause fear in men "by sheer acts of looking, gesturing, or behaving in a particular way. This may be due to the fact that very few women can consistently back up nonphysical threatening conduct with the potential of severe physical violence" (p. 203).

Men can use *isolation*, the second tactic, to curtail women's contact with friends, family, and neighbors, and to prevent partners from working, going to school, or joining organizations. While a woman might wish to limit her partner's contact with people outside the relationship, she rarely can gain total control over his actions.

The third tactic, *economic control*, is easily exercised by men who often are the primary wage earners and financial decision makers; even women with incomes do not wield as much weight in financial autonomy or decision making, particularly when their incomes are meager or viewed as supplementary.

Men use their *personal power*, the fourth tactic, as a way to claim authority over all family or household decisions, and view this as their personal prerogative because they are male. Women tend to acquiesce more to men's authority and are less able to reproach his authoritarianism due to female socialization experiences that emphasize passivity.

Finally, in regards to the last tactic of *sexual abuse*, men are able to engage in marital rape and sexual assault as "weapons of terror," while women could "withhold sexual access and favors to manipulate their partners, [but] this denial hardly has the same impact as a violent sexual assault" (p. 203). These gender-differentiated tactics demonstrate the limited ability women have to control or intimidate their male partners without resorting to the use of force.

In Dasgupta's study (1999) of thirty-two women court-ordered to treatment programs in four cities, she found that the most consistent reasons women gave for their actions was to protect themselves. Yet, during her interviews with the women, she uncovered ten other reasons that women gave to explain their use of violence against their partners: to halt further abuse; to retaliate; to save their self-worth and stand up for themselves; to get some attention from indifferent partners; to gain a semblance of control over a situation that was about to erupt in violence; to force him to take responsibilities for household chores or childcare; to facilitate respect in a situation when a partner was paying attention to another woman; to exact revenge for his mistreatment of her; to retaliate when he had assaulted their children, family members, or pets; to stand up for themselves since they were taught not to be vulnerable (Dasgupta 1999, 206–208). Most of the reasons go beyond simple self-defense claims and instead suggest a constellation of expressive responses to the insidious, damaging consequences of male violence. Women want to end the immediate violent situation; batterers use violence to terrorize and control women in an on-going fashion. None of the women in Dasgupta's sample felt that their violent behavior inspired fear in their partners or controlled their partners' behaviors, a finding consistent with prior studies (Barnett, Lee, and Thelan 1997; Langhinrichsen-Rohling, Neidig, and

Thorn 1995; Morse 1995; Russell et al. 1989). If we go back to the original definition of battering that I provided in chapter 1, that it encompasses a systematic pattern of intimidation and control that creates fear and victim subjugation, then women's use of violence is qualitatively different the violence used by men.

In another interesting study, Melton and Belknap (2003) examine gender asymmetry in battering using both quantitative and qualitative data collected through pretrial services, police-completed forms, and prosecutor information in a sample of 2,670 misdemeanor domestic violence cases (p. 337). They found that 86 percent of the arrests involved male offenders, supporting research that shows that men are more likely to be perpetrators (R. P. Dobash et al. 1992; Johnson 1995; McLeod 1984; Saunders 1986). In addition, Melton and Belknap found that the men were more likely to have past domestic violence arrest records, while the women were more likely to be arrested in dual arrest cases than arrested as the sole offender. This finding lends support to self-defense explanations of women's use of force (Barnett, Lee, and Thelan 1997; Cascardi and Vivian 1995; Hamberger et al. 1997; Hamberger and Potente, 1994; Saunders 1986). Men were also more likely to make threats to victims and prevent their partner from calling 911.

Another finding from the same study revealed that the women were more likely to hit male victims with an object, strike with a vehicle, or bite. While this could be misinterpreted to suggest that women use just as serious forms of aggression as men, the authors believe that the finding lends support to the idea that men use their bodies to exact violence while women need objects to equalize force. "Thus, it may be that female defendants may be using other weapons, such as available household items, as a means of 'leveling the playing field' once abuse has been perpetrated against them" (p. 344). Indeed, women were more likely to cause scratches while men were more likely to cause bruises.

In particular, Melton and Belknap found that in the qualitative description of cases from the police narratives, gender differences were more emphatic in narratives than in the quantitative data. The qualitative data revealed that men used more detailed and hostile threats than women, and men were more likely to threaten their partners with violence if they cooperated with police or courts. If one were to only examine the quantitative data, this kind of intimidation would not be discovered. Moreover, the police narratives captured a string of abusive actions by men, while only documenting one or two acts by women. Female victims also reported greater fear, a finding consistent with past research (Barnett, Lee, and Thelan 1997; Cantos, Neidig, and O'Leary 1994; Morse 1995).

In sum, Melton and Belknap contend that "the differences between the quantitative police data and the qualitative data are important, whereas male and female actions may appear similar when simply checking boxes for hit, slapped, punched, and so forth, looking more closely, those actions may be qualitatively different for men and women" (p. 343). Thus, their findings aptly demonstrate the problems encountered by relying extensively on officially collected checklists that are solely quantitative. Qualitative data augments the checklist accounts of violence, finding significant gender differences in both the context and also the amount of violence. Their findings lend support to the feminist perspective on gender asymmetry in battering.

Using a sample of forty-five men and forty-five women arrested for domestic violence and mandated to a treatment program as a condition of probation in northern California, Busch and Rosenberg (2004) further examined gender similarities and differences in current and prior use of force, as well as substance use and injury levels. They used criminal justice records, which provided third-party views of the severity and degree of injury, as well as whether the violent acts were isolated incidents or part of a long pattern of abuse. While this jurisdiction is pro-arrest, it discourages but does permit dual arrests, and all offenders in the sample were arrested as primary perpetrators. As part of their sentence, the men and women were required to be on probation for three years, a sentence that included meeting weekly with their probation officers, doing community service, paying a fine, and attending a yearlong domestic violence intervention program. The participants were similar demographically across age, marital status, education and employment measures (although women earned less than men). Men were more likely to have a prior history of battering; more than half the men and about a third of the women had a domestic violence arrest history. Men used a greater number of severely violent tactics, but 90 percent of the sample overall used severe violence. Interestingly, there were no differences in levels of extreme to severe injury. Busch and Rosenberg account for this by the fact that women used a weapon or object, but men were able to use just their bodies alone to inflict serious injury.

When police arrived on the scene, 24 percent of the women, compared to 7 percent of the men, reported or showed evidence of abuse by their partner. Prior records also revealed gender differences: men were more likely to have committed at least one prior nonviolent crime and they were much younger than women when they did commit their first crime. However, men and women shared a range of problems in addition to battering (p. 54). Both men and women had experience with prior violent episodes outside of the home. Twenty percent of the men and 13 percent of the women had committed at least one violent crime; women's prior crimes were related to street fights, prostitution, and substance abuse. Many of the men and women appeared to be under the influence of an illegal substance when arrested (67 percent of women, 78 percent of men).

While the women were overall less likely than the men to have a history of domestic violence offenses, almost a third of the women had been arrested previously for a prior assault (p. 54). Similarly, in Martin's research (1997) on dual arrests, she found that primary perpetrators were more likely to have past domestic violence arrests than mutually aggressive parties (40 percent of men, 19 percent of women). Likewise, Busch and Rosenberg believe primary perpetrators might use more frequent and severe violence than mutually violent partners, which may attract police attention or precondition police to attribute responsibility as a primary perpetrator if a prior arrest exists. Since the women reported and displayed more signs of being abused by their partners, it may be that the women were acting in response to their partner's violence and thus were not necessarily "pure" perpetrators. Moreover, Busch and Rosenberg found that:

> Whereas men generally committed several acts of severe violence against their partners, women tended to use severe violence once, such as throwing a glass. In this study, men's violence was more consistent with the portrait of the male batterer who uses violence to dominate and terrorize his partner, whereas women generally fit the picture of a self-defending victim, someone who uses violence in the context of anger and conflict, or a combination of the two. Taken together, our findings are consistent with other research findings (e.g., Swan and Snow 2002) that although some domestically violent women are primary aggressors, most are victims who are defending themselves or partners in mutually combative relationships. (p. 55)

Other research reveals that there are significant differences in the context and quality of violence used by women and men. As Lyon (1999, 257) contends, looking at "who hit" only reveals one aspect of the incident, and in order to fully understand the complexity of the whole context, the "why and the how" need to be studied. Even Straus, the champion of the CTS (1993, 78), admits that men "typically hit or threaten to hit to force some specific behavior on pain of injury," while "a woman may typically slap a partner or pound on his chest as an expression of outrage or in frustration because of his having turned a deaf ear to repeated attempts to discuss some critical event" (see also Mullender 1996).

Using data collected from both partners from a sample of 199 military couples mandated for domestic violence treatment, Langhinrichensen-Rohling, Neidig, and Thorn (1995) found that although both husbands and wives used violence in 83 percent of the cases, the husband's violence was more severe, the husbands were less likely to be injured, and the husbands were far less likely to report any fear of their wives (see also Jacobson et al. 1994, 44).

In a study mentioned earlier in the chapter, Hamberger, Lohr, and Bonge (1994) examined the motivations for violence with 75 women and 219 men who were arrested and court-referred to domestic violence counseling programs. They asked respondents, "What was the function, purpose or payoff of your violence?" Women's answers revealed that they used violence as self-defense, as protection from or retaliation for prior physical violence and psychological battering, or to escape violence. In other words, when women used violence against their partners, it was almost always in response to the batterers' violence. Men, on the other hand, used violence as a means of control and domination over their female partners. It is important to note that sometimes, women may be the first to use violence as a tactical strategy to avoid getting hit (Bowker 1983; Feld and Straus 1989) or in response to perceived threats of physical or sexual violence (Browne 1987; Hamner and Saunders 1984).

One effort to address the situation typical of battered women who use violence was a national study of Canadian dating violence in which DeKeseredy et al. (1997) modified the CTS to include questions about the use of self-defense and protection, fighting back when the respondent is not the first to use violence by using preemptive violence before the partner actually attacked or threatened to attack. Their findings indicate most women use violence in self-defense or in fighting back; consistent with other studies discussed above, their data offer no support for the gender symmetry thesis (DeKeseredy et al. 1997).

Recent research also suggests that there may be racial or cultural differences in how women respond to their violent partners. For instance, African-American women may more often use violence (such as threats, slaps, hitting, and throwing objects at partner) against their intimate male partners in response to experiencing severe physical and sexual aggression (such as choking or attempted rape) and psychological abuse (West and Rose 2000). In a study comparing white and black women, black women were more likely to fight back when physically assaulted (Moss et al. 1997; see also Clark et al. 1994). Black women may be more likely to fight back due to a "long history of physical abuse and oppression, both within their homes and in the larger society, [so] they had to be prepared to defend themselves" (West and Rose 2000, 488). However, black women often minimize their victimization due to their investment in perceiving themselves as capable of self-defense (Ammons 1995; Harrison and Esqueda 1999). It may also be possible that people who live in disadvantaged neighborhoods and experience the stress of poverty and racism may use violence as a survival strategy in self-protective measures. This may also indicate that African-American women have an overall greater risk of victimization due to more limited options and resources inherent in their marginalized socioeconomic status. Overall, the studies that examine racial differences are similar to the earlier studies reported in that they demonstrate that women's use of violence is typically reactive or protective, while men's use of violence is consistent with power-control patterns of abuse.

The evidence of racial differences notwithstanding, some commentators remain unpersuaded and maintain a gender-neutral stance, arguing that all violence and assault, regardless of the context in which the violence occurs, constitutes criminal behavior independent of an assailant's gender. They further argue that policies that fail to hold women accountable for violence they perpetrate should not be endorsed (Lyon 1999, citing Straus 1993). However, as Lyon asserts, the danger that men face occurs when women "resort to violence when they are left (or believe they are left) with no alternative ways of escaping from the damage that male violence does to them." Clearly, this is not the same danger faced by women.

The research literature reviewed here leaves little ambiguity with respect to the following factors. First, women's use of violence is most often related to their partners' violence. Women resort to violence mostly for self-defensive reasons, in order to escape an attack against themselves or their children, or in response to men's previous abuse. Second, measurement choices confound the issue, with family violence researchers measuring "common couple" violence which is not gendered and unconnected to power and control dynamics. When context is taken into account, violence is significantly gendered, with men more likely to use violence as one tactic in a general pattern of control that causes greater fear and injury for women. Third, women are much more likely to be injured in violent relationships. And finally, the contours of violence vary by differences across race, social class, and sexual orientation.

Discussion

In a fascinating study of political magazines and men's magazines, Berns (2001) reveals that discussions of woman battering contained within are reframed to be portrayed as "human violence." Gender is removed from the framing and discussion of the problem, which obfuscates the role of gender and power in battering (p. 265). This erasure makes it easy to ignore the structural factors that foster battering. Concomitantly, after "de-gendering" violence, the magazines' themes focus instead on women's culpability, resulting in blame that is gendered. For instance, Berns (2001) contends that the ways that blame is gendered include: "(1) highlighting women who are abusers, (2) holding female victims responsible for their role in their own victimization, (3) critiquing the social tolerance for women's violence but not for men's violence, and (4) blaming battered-women advocates" (p. 269). This strategy is reminiscent of that used by advocates of the family violence perspective to argue that men and women are equally violent.

It is clear from the studies and methodologies reviewed in this chapter that statistics can be manipulated in order to serve different agendas. Perhaps the most accurate approach to discerning whether or not the gender-symmetry argument holds water is to accept the nonpartisan findings of the national victimization surveys. They provide a middle-of-the road approach to resolving the debate, not being fully without context as is the family violence perspective, or directly attributing battering to patriarchal systems of power and control, as endorsed by the feminist perspective. The findings reported from the national victimization surveys provide strong support for the position that the gender distribution of violence is asymmetrical, with men responsible for a much greater share of domestic violence offenses.

What this literature review also underscores is the importance of conducting research that triangulates the data collection so that multiple perspectives can be evaluated. The studies reviewed in the latter part of this chapter that focused on women who have been arrested on domestic violence charges are important in telling the story. But the studies are limited by their coverage of select parts of the full process. By analyzing results from a police ride-along study, in-depth interviews with criminal justice professionals and social service providers who work directly with arrested women, and observing the female offender's program developed to treat arrested women, the present study will be better able to address questions about women's violence and appropriate policy responses to the soaring numbers of arrests and the development of treatment programs nationwide. The following chapter introduces the research project and pays particular attention to the research site and methods of data collection and the philosophy of the female offender's treatment program.

Chapter 3

The Research Project

Female Offenders and the Criminal Justice System

THE MATERIAL PRESENTED in this book reflects the culmination of a three-year research project. Through my various professional connections and friendships within the domestic violence community in a mid-Atlantic state, people would tell me about their concern that they were seeing more and more women arrested on domestic violence charges. They wondered what it meant: Was there something triggering an increase in women's use of force? Was there a change in criminal justice policies that affected police arrest strategies? Or some other explanation? I was puzzled, too, despite the anecdotal nature of such informal inquiries. I began to search the scholarly literature, finding that this phenomenon was occurring all across the country. It clearly warranted a closer investigation.

The state in which the research was conducted is small, with a total population in 1999 of 760,691. It has only three counties (County A is the largest county with 491,407 inhabitants; County B, 143,007; County C, 126,277). The state's police departments do not follow state-wide mandatory arrest policies, but rather operate with pro-arrest emphases that reflect considerable variation across state, county, city, and local police departments. In 1984 the state code gave police the authority to arrest without a warrant for misdemeanor offenses committed outside the officer's presence. In 1988 the state's police chief council adopted a model law enforcement policy for domestic violence, and individual departments were then free to adopt all or part of the protocol. The protocol allows police to retain discretion in misdemeanor cases, as long as the decision *not* to arrest is fully documented. The protocol does not address the determination of primary aggressor.

The state's efforts to document domestic violence incidents came on the heels of several well-publicized domestic fatalities in which it was generally believed that if the police had responded more quickly and seriously, some homicides or suicides might have been prevented. (For instance, in the southern part of the state, a police officer had responded to a domestic dispute the night before but did not make an arrest. The next day, the husband killed his wife and another relative, and then himself.) Police faced scrutiny by advocates and the press to improve their responses and to follow the laws exactly or be subjected to disciplinary action or lawsuits. The rise in the number of domestic violence arrests of women may be a result of this increased pressure to rectify past police inaction.

Components of the Study

In order to most fully explore the arrests of women on domestic violence charges and what happened to these women following arrest, I needed to hear from the arrested women, as well as explore the perceptions and experiences of people directly involved with this phenomenon, namely, the police and the female offender treatment providers. Thus, there were several stages of data collection for the project. The gathering of information was triangulated (Denzin and Lincoln 1994; Denzin 1997), using in-depth interviews, ride-along studies, and participant observation in the field. For those less familiar with the methodological term of triangulation, this means that data are collected and analyzed from three sources to better ensure reliability and validity of the findings.[1]

The *ride-along study* entailed a member of the research team accompanying police officers on their daily shifts in their neighborhoods, and observing and recording their actions and comments. Ten advanced undergraduate students and one graduate student were trained to conduct the ride-alongs, a process that is further described in greater detail in chapter 4. In order to maximize the possibility that the police would be dispatched to respond to a domestic violence call for help, ride-along shifts were selected to over-represent evening and weekend shifts. During each ride-along, researchers queried police officers about their perceptions and experiences with women and domestic violence. The ride-along component covered the entire state.

County A is what I refer to as the northern part of the state, and it is the largest and most populated county. It was over-sampled because it experienced much larger domestic violence caseloads and had more criminal justice professionals and resources devoted to responding to domestic violence. I refer to the other two counties, County B and County C, as the southern part of the state.

In-depth interviews were conducted with thirty-seven criminal justice professionals and social service providers. All of the major players in the state that had direct experience with this issue and worked with domestic arrests were interviewed. While some of these professionals were likely interview candidates because of their particular position, such as the police detective in charge of the domestic violence task force within the state police, others were identified during the interview process and later contacted (a sampling technique known as "snowball"). Thus, the sample is both deliberate and snowball. The respondents included: two directors of battered women shelters, four case workers in shelters, seven victim service workers who are affiliated with police departments (city, county, and state—four are social workers and three are police officers), three treatment providers (who run counseling groups for arrested women), five probation officers, five prosecutors and social workers, five public defenders (lawyers and social workers) and six family court advocates.

The interviews with the thirty-seven respondents lasted between one hour and three hours. When conducting the interviews, I followed Lofland and Lofland's interview preparation guidelines (1995, 78–88): I initially explained who I was and gave a broad outline of the project; I adopted the language of the respondents and tried to be sensitive to what made sense to them; I structured the questions around general clusters and topics, beginning with less-sensitive material in order to build trust and rapport; and I developed probes that took into account both what the respondents mentioned and what they did not mention. Although for consistency I followed an overall checklist with each interview, I also followed a flexible format and stayed open to pursuing other issues of merit. Respondents were free to interrupt, clarify my questions or their responses, and challenge my questions (e.g., on the grounds of style or content). They were also free to turn off the tape recorder at any point or ask me to erase any of their comments. Re-interviews occurred when new issues were raised and clarification was sought. The analysis of these interviews appears in chapter 5.

Participant observations were also conducted. After the previous six months of conducting interviews with criminal justice professionals and social service providers throughout the state, it was clear that the arrested women themselves had to be heard in order to place the perceptions and experiences of criminal justice professionals and social service providers, as well as the police data gained from the ride-along study, into perspective. These participant observations entailed myself and a graduate student attending the twelve-week female offender's treatment programs. These groups were observed weekly for three months each in two of the state's three counties. Although we sought admittance to treatment programs in all three counties, permission was obtained in only two. The two counties incorporate both urban and rural dwellers. One treatment program serves the two counties, and it is offered under the auspices of a private treatment agency, with a total of three groups operating each week.

All three groups follow the same philosophy and format, and are led by the same facilitator; they are offered at different times (day and evenings) and locations in order to increase accessibility for women who work, have childcare responsibilities, or must travel some distance to attend the programs. In the six months of observation, only one woman was not court-mandated to the program as a condition of her probation. Therefore, with one exception, the women were on probation and their completion of the female offender's program met a condition of probation. In addition, participation in the female offender's program was often a condition of the court's first offender's program, which was monitored by the probation department.[2]

Treatment groups were observed for six months, from February 2000 through August 2000. The female offender's program mandates a twelve-week commitment from participants.[3] It allows for open enrollment whereby women can start treatment any week rather than wait until a new group forms. This design provided the opportunity to observe a larger number of women than might otherwise be possible. Ninety-five women participated in these programs during the months of observation. On a weekly basis, the size of a group varied between five and eleven women. The open enrollment strategy also meant that women who were in various stages of the treatment process were able to raise different issues and offer different insight in the weekly discussions, with many of the longer-term participants offering emotional and practical support to the newcomers.

Of the participants, fifty-eight were white, twenty-nine were African-American, two were Latina, and six did not provide racial information. All of the women except one had at least one child. Many had drug or alcohol problems (often they were simultaneously ordered to treatment programs for drugs or alcohol). It was not uncommon that a participant's male partner (current or ex-) was ordered simultaneously to a batterer's treatment program for men; the treatment programs for men were conducted by the same organization using different facilitators.

The Female Offender's Program Philosophy

The female offender's program that we observed follows a feminist philosophy that seeks to empower women through raising issues and conducting group discussions to encourage self-realization. The curriculum includes group discussions, video viewing, worksheets to read, homework assignments, and, at times, role-playing. The female facilitator, Mary,[4] holds the women accountable for their behavior, pointing out that they made choices to respond or act in a way that facilitated their arrests. However, she does not focus on labeling women as "victims" or "offenders"; rather, she focuses on accountability, options, and choices, leaving the personal designation (of victim or offender) up to each participant. Understanding and transforming old behavioral "scripts" or patterns are program goals.

As both part of her standard introduction for new group members (which occurs nearly every week) and sprinkled throughout each session, Mary walks a thin line between victim and offender designations. She recognizes that the women are mandated to the group because they broke a law, but she sees the group as an avenue to create greater awareness of both self and also of the larger fabric of the women's daily lives. Thus, without excusing the use of force or ignoring the law broken, Mary contextualizes both the women's use of violence as well as the institutional responses by the criminal justice system (and others) to their actions. For these women, this therapeutic style seems effective, for it empowers the group members while remaining cognizant of the pushes and pulls the women feel toward their partners, family members, and other important people in their social networks, and the criminal justice system. Using similar words to those quoted below, Mary states the following in the group sessions:

> This group provides information about domestic violence. What it is, how to recognize it, how to not put yourself at risk so you find yourself in a similar situation that brought you here. I don't label you. Some people see themselves as victims. Some people see themselves as an offender. You know who you are. I don't put a label on you. I give information from an abuser's viewpoint and from the victim's viewpoint so that we have sort of a real-life situation.

> We [the counseling agency] want the fighting stopped. That's why we have this class. You have the power; the only person you can control is yourself. You can't control your partner. You can't control your brother, your sister, your friend. You can't control the other person. You can't control your partner's drinking. You *can* control your own behavior. You make choices. If you're in an unhealthy relationship,

then you need to get out because you can't fix it, you can only fix yourself. Who are you? Are you the person who has been doing the abusing? Or are you a victim who has fought back? Or are you a woman who is violent to everyone? You tend to fall into one of those categories.

As captured in the quotes above, Mary operated the three treatment groups in this particular female offender's program with an emphasis on accountability for one's behavior. Mary, who is a social worker, maintained that the women were not "bad" women, but rather that they were women who made some bad choices. If Mary believed that any woman was truly a "pure victim," and not a female offender, she exercised the option of switching the client to the victim's support group. This option was not always followed, however, because in some instances a male partner (abuser) would not "allow" a woman to attend a victim's support group, but would tolerate her participation only in a female offender's group.

Although the state follows a uniform treatment protocol designed by a representative statewide committee of therapists and social workers who conduct these groups, program philosophy can be radically different from one program to another program. The philosophy used in the three treatment groups observed ostensibly follows the feminist treatment model created by the Domestic Abuse Project (1998) in Minneapolis, Minnesota, which holds the belief that most arrested women are not the primary perpetrators of violence in their relationships. In addition, Mary had run the victim's group for over eight years prior to running the "offender's group," thus giving her a very solid understanding of the issues that battered women face. It is crucial to note that such a perspective would vary according to the facilitator's background and the program's philosophy.

Each time we attended a group session with a new member present, Mary introduced us, explained the research project, and obtained release forms (via university Human Subjects Review Board protocol). We reinforced the confidentiality protection in addition to Mary's discussion. Mary vouched for us, and she and her organization wholeheartedly endorsed the project. The women, in turn, clearly trusted Mary's judgment and seemed eager to accept our presence. We received unanimous support from the members in every group.

Although the process used to obtain members' permission might sound coercive (for instance, maybe the women did not feel as though they could decline because they were not in the group voluntarily and because we and the facilitator were present when permission was sought), it was explained that the women had options to pursue if they did not want to be part of the research.

In addition, and perhaps what was most effective in achieving "buy in," we explained personally to the women that we felt it was crucial to hear from the women themselves about their experiences and not just rely on official records or police reports to speak for them. When the women heard this, they were excited to participate, exclaiming that no one else had asked them to tell their stories. Their enthusiasm and eagerness were consistent with the feelings expressed to us when the facilitator was absent, so we believe that her presence did more to vouch for our sincerity, and not to coerce their cooperation. At times, we were active participants in the sessions, such as asking the women follow-up questions. They talked to us on an informal basis before and after groups, telling stories about their children, how their school or jobs were going, and teasing us about our long car ride home after the group session ended.

Group sessions were tape-recorded and later transcribed. Transcripts were coded using grounded-theory methods, and patterns of data were identified as they emerged. Following grounded-theory methods, themes were utilized only if they were discussed at length by at least three respondents (Lofland and Lofland 1995). The data were examined using coding techniques described by Strauss (1987). Each transcript was read exhaustively and analyzed into emergent conceptual categories. Once no new conceptual categories were unearthed, theme identification was believed to have been achieved (Krueger 1994).

Philosophies of Other Female Offender's Programs Nationwide

In the 1990s, as more and more women were arrested for domestic violence, there was no standard institutional response in place to handle these offenders. Moreover, there is no literature on any outcome studies on domestically violent women who have completed treatment. Typically, violent men were diverted from jail to batterer intervention programs that would provide treatment under the auspices of the jurisdiction's probation department.

The creation of a separate female offender's program caused a good deal of unease. Many advocates struggled with the message that a women's treatment program would deliver, fearing it would suggest that women who use violence in their relationships were no different than male batterers. At the same time, however, criminal justice professionals and some social service providers and activists acknowledged that women's violence sometimes fell outside the legal parameters of self-defense law. A handful of programs were created around the country to address the treatment needs of female offenders. While some of these programs were guided by the recognition that women's use of force stemmed from their male partners' ongoing abuse and created programs that steered clear of labeling women as offenders, other jurisdictions sent women to treatment programs intended for men; some programs simply included women in their male batterer populations.

The Duluth model, originally intended for male batterers, has been the blueprint for most treatment groups (Pence and Paymar 1993), in combination with anger management and assertiveness techniques and an acknowledgment that women occupy positions of both victim and offender. While some goals may overlap with men's treatment programs, most treatment providers believe that a recognition that women's violence is shaped by a history of abuse is central.

In Kenosha, Wisconsin, following a struggle over the appropriate response to women's violence, a treatment program was created, the Kenosha Domestic Abuse Intervention Program. To ensure that "domestically violent women," as they were called, were not seen or treated as synonymous with male batterers, the program's format and philosophy focused on women's empowerment and was developed in direct collaboration with the battered women's shelter (Hamberger and Potente 1994). Its philosophical orientation stated that "women commit acts of violence in response to having been victimized, either in the current relationship or a previous one" (p. 130), a position based on data analyzed from the program's clients. While the program staff believed that women should take responsibility for their behavior and strive for nonviolent and safe responses, they were insistent that the use of the word "responsibility" did not imply blame:

> As noted previously, most domestically violent women are caught up in a system of control, terror, and violence brought about by their male partners. One might argue that these women never would have chosen violence in any other situation. Nevertheless, their use of violence, although understandable, has brought them more untoward negative consequences: often, more battering from their partners plus arrest and adjudication, along with the attendant feelings of humiliation, futility, and loss of energy to continue the struggle. (p. 131)

Both the Kenosha program (which is no longer operating due to legal changes in arrest policies) and a Denver program modify a curriculum intended for male batterers in order to address gender differences, focusing on women's past victimizations and behavioral accountability (Dowd 2001).

A different Duluth program, the Domestic Abuse Intervention Project, worked to create a program specifically for women who use force. It refers to arrested women's treatment groups as "groups for women who use violence," and not "abusers' groups" (Dasgupta 1999). Perhaps the most comprehensive outline of the issues that must be considered in an intervention program for women has been done by Dasgupta (1999):

1. Since the majority of women have been and are being battered, it is important to address the issue of battering and power and control.
2. Since the justice system tends to focus on incidents of violence, it is likely that women's behavior will be viewed in segments rather than in their contextual entirety. Therefore, it is important to train appropriate personnel to understand women's use of violence holistically and contextually.
3. Frequently, alcohol or drug abuse plays a significant role in violence of any kind. The issue of substance abuse needs to be addressed in women's intervention programs.
4. Exploring behavioral alternatives to violence in any given situation must be included in any intervention program.
5. Issues related to race, class, ethnicity, nationality, and residency status in the United States must be incorporated in the curriculum. (p. 218)

A final example is found in Lynn Dowd's work (2001), which describes a twenty-week anger management program located at the University of Massachusetts Medical Center. The program was formed for both court-mandated and self-referred women who have exhibited assaultive behaviors towards partners, family, friends, strangers, and police officers. Similar to the treatment group described in the present study, the Massachusetts program emphasizes a psycho-educational support group approach that meets weekly. While Dowd does not analyze the process and outcome of the treatment groups, she details the structure of the program, its goals and curriculum. The culture of the group is described as including "supportiveness, hope for change, expectation of commitment to non-violent behavior and accountability, overcoming social isolation, and ensuring one's own safety, and openness about aggressive behavior" (p. 92).

The program begins with thirty to forty-five minutes of check-in time, which follows a pattern similar to the present study's female offender's program in that women can discuss their challenges, stresses, and successes of the previous week and how they handled anger if it arose. Again, similar to the female offender's program, the Massachusetts program uses the remainder of the session to cover a topic using various lectures, video, role-playing, or other techniques. In particular, the program identifies several skill-building topics to cover, and the concepts are reinforced throughout the program. These include emotional education, basic skills in self-awareness and conflict management, conditions that undermine emotional and behavioral stability, relationship issues, communication skills, thinking errors, and stress management and relaxation techniques.

Overall, beyond the studies just discussed, there is a dearth of articles published about programs developed for women arrested on domestic violence charges. The features that the existing programs share include an emphasis on women's prior victimization experiences, ways to avoid violence, safety issues, anger management techniques, and other daily stressors (such as children and substance abuse). However, these programs have not been evaluated to determine their effectiveness.

Feminist Research Design

Feminist researchers explore "what knowledge is, what makes it possible, and how to get it" (Harding 1991, 308), challenging "gender-neutral" theories and practice when these deny the gendered nature of crime and victimization. In general, feminist research has been characterized by four major themes: topic selection, methodology, interruption of power and control hierarchies, and acknowledgement of researcher subjectivity (Gelsthorpe 1990; Flavin 2001).

With regard to topic selection, the argument is that the topic should be relevant to women, with the hope that the research will have some kind of political and practical significance (Gelsthorpe 1990, 90). Another feminist researcher, Maureen Cain (1990), argues that this does not mean that feminist research has to be solely on, by, and for women; rather, it seeks to explore relationships. Within criminology and criminal justice areas especially, it would be difficult to exclude men and masculinity from research on the system. Because my study examines gendered patterns of violent behavior (aggressive or defensive) in relationships and the criminal justice system's response to women's use of violence, my questions and topic clearly reflect a feminist approach. Whether the findings will have practical or political significance for women raises another recurring theme. Research findings should speak to audiences beyond academia. I believe that my analysis will be useful to people outside the world of scholarship, including police, court, and treatment personnel as well as interested citizens who know little about arrest policies for domestic violence or women's use of intimate violence. Since violence against women is so widespread, issues such as these have the potential to touch all of us.

The second theme involves selecting and using methods. Typically, feminist research uses qualitative methods; however, not all feminist research is qualitative and not all qualitative research uses a feminist orientation (Flavin 2004). For their part, quantitative methods have been criticized for being narrowly objective and for often reflecting only male experiences, thereby excluding in-depth coverage of the experiences of women. Social status, gender differences, and their implications are often masked in quantitative studies. By contrast, feminist research encourages techniques such as conducting interviews and constructing ethnographies and life histories. These are more of a two-way process, so that respondents are not objectified and interviews do not lose "personal meaning" (Gelsthorpe 1990, 91). As I have stressed, I followed a two-way, interactive style in my interviews and participant-observation components, and trained my research team to do the same when conducting the police ride-alongs. Our questions were phrased so as to convey to respondents that we were not experts and that we did not believe there was one objective "truth" to uncover. Rather, there could be multiple truths, and part of the research process was to uncover and untangle them by recognizing that respondents have expert, intimate knowledge of the events, issues, and situations of their own lives and work.

The third theme explores ways to interrupt conventional relations of power and control between the observer and the observed. Feminist researchers tend to adopt a more interactive method so as not to produce hierarchical relationships between interviewer and interviewee. By using an interactive style of communication, I became more than a body holding a tape recorder who asked scripted questions from printed pages. I remained engaged in the conversation, probing issues raised by the respondents and actively challenging both them and myself to push beyond simple surface responses. As this was taking place, I indicated my intense engagement with the issues and with the respondents by introducing relevant information from prior knowledge, research, or my own experiences.

Because of my own middle-class, white, educated, female status, I was cognizant of the nexus of issues involving gender, race, social class, education, and sexual orientation. I did not consider respondents as outside their contexts, but rather saw them as belonging to many affiliations beyond being a criminal justice professional or an arrested woman. Moreover, I asked them what other questions I should ask, thereby creating an interactive exchange with them. I also sought their interpretation of data collected from other components of the study.

The fourth, and last, theme concerns the acknowledgement of research subjectivity—that "feminist research is characterized by a concern to record the subjective experiences of doing research" (Gelsthorpe 1990, 93). As Stanley and Wise point out (1983):

> Whether we like it or not, researchers remain human beings complete with all the usual assembly of feelings, failings, and moods. And all of these things influence how we feel and understand what is going on. Our consciousness is always the medium through which the research occurs; there is no method or technique of doing research other than through the medium of the researcher. (p. 157)

No research is ever value free. My analysis, like that of any other investigator, is conducted through my own eyes and interpretations. As Flavin (2001) contends, in any kind of research endeavor, subjectivity is unavoidable, but it could also serve as a strength: learning from respondents can help researchers better understand and appreciate the respondents' experiences. Moreover, as Dubois (1983) asserts, "A rejection of the notion of 'objectivity' does not mean a rejection of a concern for being accurate."

In sum, I explored the question, Are the women who are arrested for domestic violence really batterers? I sought the words, knowledge, and experiences of people who directly grapple with this question, both within criminal justice and service provider systems as well as with the arrested women themselves. I did not let one point of view create the "truth," but I listened and watched for how the people I talked to made sense of their world. All research should seek to uncover the standpoint of those researched. To paraphrase Loraine Gelsthorpe (1990): Is this feminist research, or just good research? Many of these themes and analyses related to feminist research methods have been integrated into mainstream criminological research, contributing significantly to a greater understanding of criminal justice policy-making in both the academic and the public arenas.

The next chapter focuses on the police ride-along study to explore police officers' perceptions and actions regarding women's use of violence, pro-arrest policies, and other related topics.

Chapter 4

On the Beat

The Police Ride-Along Study

As the initial responders to a domestic violence call for help and as the "street level" interpreters of the law, police play an integral part in implementing domestic violence policy. Day in and day out, police are exposed to people's problems and have to interpret people's behavior, officially responding to it within the parameters of the law. While law enforcement strives to be nonselective and evenhanded, officers' personal attitudes, beliefs, and priorities shape their actions. Given their exposure to the complexities of citizens' private lives, police officers also make wonderful informants about social problems such as domestic violence.

This chapter describes the police ride-along component of the research project and analyzes the content of the conversations conducted with police officers and the situations observed. Ride-along studies entail a systematic effort to record police-citizen encounters by sending a trained observer to "partner" with a police officer during her or his shift. Observers are not randomly placed, but observe during a chosen time and day in order to increase the opportunity to observe the desired events. Since the goal was to observe domestic disputes, the focus was on the police shifts during which observers would potentially see the most action. Based on prior research findings, domestic skirmishes and violent eruptions were more likely to occur on Thursday, Friday, and Saturday evenings and during the shifts from 4 p.m. to midnight and 6 p.m. to 2 a.m.

The research team included eleven observers: ten advanced undergraduate students and one graduate student, seven females and four males. All students were trained in participant-observation skills and taught to recognize various issues related to domestic violence so they would be able to discuss these issues with police.[1] While some themes emerged independently from the observation process (an inductive approach), others reflected prior theoretical understandings of the phenomenon under study (an a priori approach). "A priori themes come from the characteristics of the phenomenon being studied; from already agreed on professional definitions found in literature reviews; from local, commonsense constructs; and from researcher's values, theoretical orientations, and personal experiences" (Ryan and Bernard 2003, 88; see also Strauss and Corbin 1990). In particular, the study was designed to reveal how the police feel about responding to domestic violence compared to other calls, what officers' perceptions were about whether women play a more active role in domestic violence than in the past, and whether women's violence and arrests have changed over time. In addition, observers were trained to ask questions about the dynamics of dual arrests and how police are able to distinguish between aggressive behavior and self-defensive behavior.

Observers carried a small notebook with them to document what occurred during their shift. They transcribed field notes from the notebooks into longer, more descriptive typed versions within twenty-four hours of the shift's completion. I reviewed their field notes and maintained an ongoing dialogue with members of the research team to resolve any points of confusion. The fieldwork team met weekly to talk about situations that were unclear and to troubleshoot any problems. Each notebook had a checklist of questions for the students to address sometime during the shift. Generally, once the topic of domestic violence was raised, most of the questions on the list were spontaneously addressed by the officers in the course of their discussions.

In order to best cover the demographic and geographic variation across the state, we solicited the help of the state's three major police departments: the state troopers, the county police in the largest county in the state (County A), and the city police of the largest city in the state (located in County A). Within the state police department, we conducted ride-alongs with three troops so that all three counties in the state would be represented. The largest county, in the northern part of the state, and the largest city located within that county were over-sampled because of the larger volume of calls and the higher population density. (The county handles three times the caseload of the other counties and has the largest number of criminal justice professionals and social service providers dealing with women arrested on domestic violence charges.)

For 1998, domestic violence incident reports revealed the following numbers of incidents counted by police: County A: 9,711; County B: 3,067; County C: 3,252. A total of ninety ride-alongs were conducted in summer and early fall of 1999. Most of these occurred during the evening shifts on Thursday, Friday, and Saturday nights to maximize opportunities for witnessing domestic calls. The ride-along study put the fieldwork team in contact with slightly over one hundred police officers.

Limitations of the Ride-Along Study

Although we had received approval to conduct the ride-along study from high-ranking officials, including the state's criminal justice coordinating council, it became apparent that there was a discernible pattern to whom the student researchers were assigned within the city police department. First, more than 80 percent of the ride-alongs were conducted with officers who had been on the force for three years or less. Officers with less seniority have little control over whether they were to take a ride-along with them on their shifts.

Second, the squad cars with ride-alongs on board were typically sent as the backup responders to the domestic calls. It was the city police's policy to send two cars in response to a domestic call; the first responders to the scene were generally responsible for making the arrests and completing the paperwork. While this might have been a benign pattern—or even one that was genuinely orchestrated so that the students would not be pulled off the streets to watch an officer fill out hours worth of paperwork—the result was that students could not observe many of the actual arrests or ask the basic questions one would want to know about the situation and the decisions of the officer who was most involved in the domestic call.

Finally, a number of ride-alongs were assigned to officers working overtime on a special summer grant that responded primarily to nuisance calls, such as disturbing the peace, noise violations, and so forth, and often responded to these calls on foot. These three administrative decisions made by the sergeant on duty that night happened too frequently to believe they occurred merely by chance. Moreover, at roll call, officers groaned audibly when they were assigned a ride-along for the night, although they often apologized to the students in private later and told them not to take it personally.

On the surface, this systematic assignment of ride-alongs to the youngest, least experienced officers might lead one to question the representativeness of the officers' comments. Also, a red flag might be raised that newer members of the force might be less critical of aspects of the criminal justice system and less willing to let down their guard and tell it like it is for fear of jeopardizing their positions. However, contrary to these expectations, these officers were consistent in their answers to questions, and volunteered uncensored responses, often making sexist, homophobic, and racist comments without apology.[2] It was the more veteran officers who exhibited the most consistent professional manner in their conversations with citizens and in their descriptions of their district's problems and residents. For example, the comments of this white male officer with more than ten years' experiences typified many things veteran officers said: "The most important thing is to treat people with respect. It works better than using force to solve problems." This belief contrasts sharply with sentiments that were common from the officers having less than three years' experience: "These people are animals. [The officer is describing a poor, dilapidated housing project with all African-American residents.] They think foreplay is beating your partner with a baseball bat. One hour they're fighting, and the next they're making love."

Despite these potential limitations, it became clear over the course of the summer that the younger city police officers' philosophies were not anomalies but were consistent across departments in the entire state. Since the full research project includes several components, the ride-along study is a valuable part of the triangulated data collection, and the police data can be scrutinized for reliability and validity once the other components (in-depth interviews and participant observation in treatment groups) are included in the analysis.

Characterization of Domestic Violence Calls

Out of the ninety ride-alongs conducted during June through September of 1999, 63 incidents of domestic violence were observed by the research team; these 63 domestic incidents were part of a total of over 400 calls for police service or police-initiated encounters during the ride-along study. A caveat is important here: not all of these domestic incidents involved partners and former partners because the state has an expansive definition of what constitutes domestic violence. Multiple types of family disturbances are collapsed with intimate violence into a general domestic violence category. For example, based on statistics gathered from police departments by the state's statistical center, the percentage of female domestic violence suspects comprised 32 percent of all domestic arrests in 1998. However, an initial inquiry revealed that the 32 percent reflects the way "domestic violence" is defined: the statute includes people who are related to one another by blood, marriage, and cohabitation, plus non-cohabiting couples and third-party disputes that involve one of the intimate partners. Thus, under this classification scheme, a sister fighting with her brother would be classified as a domestic incident in the same way a woman arrested for assaulting her partner in self-defense or otherwise would be counted. Once these cases are separated from intimate partner or ex-partner violence, the smaller percentages obtained are more consistent with national estimates. One other note: different departments will be distinguished when the officer's point is germane to that specific department; if an officer's comments reflect other officers' experiences across the state, I will not use specific department identifiers.

Almost all of the county and state officers across the state mentioned that there are too many petty domestic calls ("bullshit calls") that involve people other than partners or former partners. They resent this because they see a lot of these calls as "stupid kids' stuff" that pulls them off the street for hours doing paperwork. Many feel this also results in some officers not taking "real" domestic calls seriously. Also, officers feel that there is too much widening of the term "domestic": "Everything is a domestic. If we get one hundred domestic calls a night, eighty-five do not have to be classified as domestic." Officers see this as an example where their discretion has been taken away. City police officers, too, echoed the state and county officers' frustration with the all-encompassing list of what constitutes a domestic call, believing that the term was now too vague and included tension between anybody—siblings, parents and children, boyfriends and girlfriends who had been together for a week or less.

The analytical focus here is specifically targeted to the fifty domestic calls that involved altercations between intimate partners and former partners, which excludes the thirteen additional domestic calls involving siblings, parents, children, grandparents, and non-romantic roommates. Of the fifty domestic calls involving partners or former partners, seventeen occurred with the county police, eleven with the state police, and twenty-two with the city police. Of the ten arrests, only two were of women, one was a dual arrest, and the remaining seven involved male suspects who had either violated Protection From Abuse orders or used aggressive force against females. Eight of the ten arrests involved white citizens, one was African-American, and one involved a man of unknown race. In addition to the arrests, nine warrants were issued (or victims were instructed to bring police reports with them to the courts to file warrants). Only one of the nine warrants was issued for a woman (for a current girlfriend who was verbally harassing an ex-girlfriend). The remaining eight warrants targeted men who had been physically violent toward women or engaged in Protection From Abuse violations or "terroristic" threatening. There were two domestic calls in which it was unclear what happened or what the outcome was. Finally, twenty-nine domestic calls resulted in no arrest or warrant. Of the twenty-nine incidents, six involved women's use of violence, but that count is misleading because in only one of these incidents did a woman use aggressive force instead of defensive force. With two of the domestic calls, the gender of the victim and suspect were unclear because no one was found at the locations upon police arrival. Twelve incidents involved male suspects while nine involved both a man and a woman; these twenty-one incidents were mostly verbal in nature. (See the Appendix for summaries of the domestic calls by county, city, and state.)

Previous Research on Police Domestic Violence Policies

Previous research on police responses to domestic violence reveals two general themes (S. Miller 1999). First, police hated answering such calls for a variety of reasons, among them cynicism as to the efficacy of arrest, a belief that domestic calls are not part of "real" policing, and perhaps unfounded worries about their personal safety (Buzawa and Buzawa 1993; S. Miller 1999). Police officers responded to domestic violence calls by supporting the offender's position, challenging women's credibility, blaming women for their own victimization, and trivializing women's fears (Karmen 1982; Stanko 1985; Gil 1986). Police training manuals reinforced officers' reluctance to arrest by stressing the use of family crisis intervention or separation tactics rather than making an arrest (International Association of Chiefs of Police 1967; Parnas 1967). These policies sent the message that it was a waste of police time to initiate criminal justice proceedings when reconciliation might occur and make the matter moot (Field and Field 1973; Lerman 1986).

The second general theme relating to police response to domestic violence is that police typically did not arrest batterers. This was true even of those officers who worked in jurisdictions that had mandatory or pro-arrest policies. When police had the discretion to make arrests in domestic assault incidents, they largely chose not to. For example, three studies indicated that police arrest rates in domestic violence incidents were 10 percent, 7 percent, and 3 percent (see Buel 1988). In Milwaukee, although 82 percent of battered women wanted their abusers arrested, police took only 14 percent of the offenders into custody (Bowker 1983). In Ohio, officers arrested only in 14 percent of the cases, even though in 38 percent of them victims had been injured or killed (Bell 1986). Additionally, until new legislation was enacted between 1977 and 1991, in virtually all states, "domestic violence has . . . been characterized as simple assault, a misdemeanor, unless accompanied by aggravating circumstances such as use of a weapon, intent to commit murder or to inflict grievous bodily harm, or a sexual assault . . . police officers were legally unable to make warrantless arrests unless the violence continued in their presence or a previously existing warrant had been issued" (Buzawa and Buzawa 1990, 34). The new legislation has resulted in increased domestic violence arrests, although negative police attitudes toward responding to domestic violence calls have not really changed much (Buzawa and Buzawa 2003).

Domestic Violence Policy in the Research State

For this particular state, since 1984 the police have the power to arrest without a warrant for misdemeanor domestic violence offenses committed outside the officer's presence. If police exercise discretion not to arrest in misdemeanor cases, they must fully document their decision. There are no state statutes that mandate primary aggressor identification for domestic violence calls. The state troopers have the most clearly articulated policy:

> Although arrest should occur in misdemeanor incidents where proba-
> ble cause exists, the discretion not to arrest in either type of misde-
> meanor incident remains with the officer. When an arrest is not made,
> the decision must be fully documented in the incident report and the
> potential for continuing violence must be addressed.

State police policy also instructs that "dual arrests are not favored" and that officers "are required to determine the predominant aggressor and to explore a potential self-defense claim." County and city police departments do not have similarly articulated guidelines, thus making for fractured and inconsistent arrest policies across jurisdictions. In fact, there was some confusion about the policies of arrest for state, county, and city police departments among the officers, as evidenced by the number of times they referenced "mandatory arrest" or "pro-arrest" policies (defined in chapter 1) without delineating the distinctions in their discussions with the student observers.

Generally, officers believed that the state had a very strict and aggressive policy about domestic violence—a change in what police used to do ten or so years ago when they would just separate the parties. Now, arrest conveys the message that domestic violence is taken very seriously. Officers from all departments used the terms "mandatory arrest" and "pro-arrest" interchangeably. They explained that an arrest had to be made if any element of a crime existed. Officers could make warrantless arrests if both parties were there and there were signs that a crime has been committed. Both department policy and the law mandated that the aggressor must be arrested if there were obvious signs of abuse. The county police followed the policy of locating the primary aggressor and making an arrest. The officer can arrest the suspect if he or she is still on the scene or if he or she returns during the incident. If he or she is not there, the victim needs to sign the warrant.

Essentially, most officers stated that if there is any apparent physical injury, someone should be arrested.

Across all police departments in the state, the standard policy is to send two cars out to handle domestic calls so that victim and officer safety can be assured and so that combatants can be separated. Officers believe in separation so that they can get full stories from each person for investigative purposes. As one officer says, "If it smells like a domestic, it is a domestic," so if there is any sign of an argument, it has to be reported. State law also allows for the additional charge of endangering the welfare of a child if any children witness abuse. Some officers commented that the decision to file such a charge was a difficult one because of the concern about where the children would go if both parties were arrested. Another option exercised, mentioned by some officers, was to have the victim sign a "refuse to prosecute" form if she refused to cooperate. The officers made sure that this happened so that "she wouldn't get spiteful six months from now and dig up that shit and screw the guy on it."

The state troopers often mentioned that the pro-arrest policy's goal was to prevent homicides, not necessarily prevent domestic violence. While a few county officers mentioned the need to arrest to prevent a later murder, it was a very prevalent theme for the troopers. Many mentioned that the state trooper policy is one of zero tolerance. Part of officers' perceptions about domestic violence policy stems from their training and beliefs. Most of the officers were emphatic that the reason for their caution stemmed from a case that occurred in the southern part of the state in which officers were called repeatedly to a house where the husband was violent, but made no arrests. Finally, the husband killed his wife, her mother, and himself, and the department was sued because of their inaction at earlier points in the case. There seemed to be a party line: "We can get sued, so it's better to cover our asses and arrest someone," as one state trooper summarized.

Both state troopers and county police believed they needed to arrest an offender and not leave the decision up to the victim, because if the offender later returned home and seriously harmed the victim, the officer who initially responded would be held liable for the victim's injuries. "You have to make arrest because if something happened later to the victim and it was revealed that you didn't do anything, you would probably lose your job" (county officer). Most officers used the term "mandatory arrest" and stated this was the policy to follow, even if there were no injuries. Basically, the officers said the policy is to arrest if there was a physical altercation, but there was more room to maneuver if the dispute was verbal only.

Many officers attributed any increases of women's arrests to hyper-vigilance that grew out of fear of lawsuits ("cover your ass"), rather than any real increase in women's use of violence: "The last thing I want is for a domestic to bite me in the ass."; "I write paper on everything I can because I don't want shit getting me later on in life." A number of officers said that this concern was reinforced by the O. J. Simpson case in which police were blamed for failing to do more to address domestic violence and prevent the murder of Nicole Brown Simpson. "The media would eat the department alive—again—if that happened," as one trooper explained.

Overwhelmingly, most of the officers from the city police department described their domestic policy the same way: if there is any sign of injury, an arrest must be made. Most officers said that statement verbatim, as if they had it memorized to use when responding to questioners. One officer summarized: "If I see an injury, my hands are tied. I'm gonna have to lock somebody up. If there is not an injury, and we usually pray there isn't, then it's my discretion. I can just write verbal altercation on my sheet. It's really my choice if there is no injury, but, boy, you better cover your ass and write up those reports well." A number of officers mentioned that if the welfare of any children was endangered, arrests would occur.

Officers who had been on the force between five and fifteen years were nostalgic about the "good old days" when arrests were not encouraged: "When I first came out here, a domestic took five minutes. We would just tell one or the other to leave for the night, and that would be the end of it. Now, with all the bullshit laws and papers, we can lose a fucking officer for four or five hours." As another put it, "Before all the high profile cases, police could just adjust the call, respond to the call, go in and settle down the situation and leave. Now we have to report everything and cover our asses."

Covering one's ass was mentioned repeatedly. "I will make an arrest on a domestic. Liability, man. You can't take a chance with that shit. It could be dangerous. Someone could die. Plus, my sarge would have my ass if I did not make an arrest or at least get a warrant on the guy to cover my ass." Or, as another officer stated, "Arrest is best because it covers everybody's butts." To illustrate the point further, a number of officers told the research team members stories such as this: "One of my buddies had arrested a male in a domestic last year. He was lucky that he did, because the next day the guy made bail, went home, and killed his wife. If the cop hadn't arrested the guy, the city would have come under a lot of shit. We need to cover our asses out here. Domestics are very sticky situations."

While the more veteran officers talked wistfully about how handling domestics were far more simple in the past, the officers with the least amount of experience focused on how much time domestic calls took officers off the street. They felt badly that their fellow officers were stuck with all the calls, and they hated all the hours of paperwork they would need to complete: "Basically, once there is an arrest, it ties me up for the whole shift while the rest of my platoon is getting their asses handed to them and I'm stuck doing fucking paperwork." This antipathy towards the time and paperwork of domestic calls is not surprising, given that these activities are in opposition to fast-paced crime fighting that police think of as the hallmark of policing and masculinity.

It was rare for officers from any of the police departments to speculate beyond the facts of an immediate situation. One officer explained, "Police are just so busy. We don't have time to put in the social work aspect of calls." This seemed particularly true for the city police who said that the county and state officers had a lighter load and might be more farsighted in their approach. Overall, the officers responded to the crisis at hand: "I don't look at it that deeply. They teach us to just look at the surface. What do you see here and how and who. I can't go into that other life stuff with them. We are just a Band-Aid."

There were only a handful of officers who took a broader outlook on domestic violence, seeing it as a social problem and expressing concern about arrest policies and what they saw as their failure to work. Most of these officers felt that an arrest was a quick fix that did nothing to ameliorate the conditions under which violence thrived. While some officers thought it would be futile to address underlying conditions because of the abject poverty they saw, other officers suggested strategies to supplement arrest. For instance, several officers thought that social services should provide financial assistance for families so that women were not so concerned about how an arrest might affect their "bread and butter." Other officers believed that having mandatory long-term counseling was a good idea. Others mentioned that filing bogus Protection From Abuse reports might be more effectively deterred by fines than by arrest.

A number of officers across all departments expressed misgivings about a pro-arrest policy. For instance, a few officers felt arrest makes things worse because the guy loses pay from work or even his job, and has even less money than he did to begin with, which was probably one of the trigger points that was stressing him out. Many officers mentioned that battered women just want men to stop abusing them, but the women do not want the men arrested because of childcare and financial issues. This causes the women to turn on the police after they begin arrest proceedings. This theme was particularly underscored in the ride-alongs with the city police department. As one officer said: "Women welcome us at first, but after the arrest, we go, in her eyes, from her hero to her enemy." There was a lot of concern that she would turn against the police and attack them for their actions. Many officers shared stories about women who "changed their minds" and came after cops with "a frying pan or whatever she could grab to hit us, crying and begging for us not to arrest him."

Many state troopers were aware that the "refuse to prosecute" tactic is used by county police, and they did not see it as a viable option for state troopers: "The state police are expected to do more work than that." They saw themselves as having a higher level of professionalism: "Troopers are hands down the best; we are the best trained and we handle everything."; "Unlike other departments, we take great pride on the thoroughness of our work. We don't do a half-ass job." They assess who is at fault by examining physical harm done, investigating and questioning witnesses, and identifying primary aggressors.

Two county officers talked about circumventing domestic arrest by writing up an incident as disturbing the peace, and separating parties for the night. They viewed this option as an acceptable loophole. A few of the city police mentioned similar strategies, ones that reflected their unwillingness to arrest on what they deemed as a petty "bullshit" offense or to arrest when officers were nearing the end of their shift and did not want to pursue an action that might take them an additional three or more hours to complete. During the ride-alongs, two city officers on different domestic calls, both with less than one-and-a-half years of experience on the force, wrote up a domestic call as a disturbing the peace call, even though one of the combatants had a restraining order filed.

Similarly, veteran city police officers justified these sleights of hand as ways they could use their discretion, based on many years of experience. They said things such as: "I only make mandatory arrest if there are children involved or if they are married or in a secure relationship, not for situations like the one-week wonder relationship" (eleven years on force); "They encourage us to make arrests, but if you do or not, it's up to each officer. A lot of times they won't because they don't want to fill out the paperwork. I mean, you have the higher-ups coming up with the philosophy, but it's up to the officers to implement" (ten years on force).

PAPERWORK

Almost all officers mentioned the excessive paperwork required to document domestic calls. While some officers felt that documentation was necessary, it was common to hear paperwork referred to as "cover your ass." As one officer stated, "We don't have a pro-arrest policy; we have a pro-paper policy." Everything was documented so that an officer would not get into trouble later if it was revealed he or she did nothing at a domestic violence call. Many officers believed that the pro-arrest policy, as well as the extensive paperwork it entailed, was related to liability issues.

County police felt the paperwork took about three or four hours to complete. Only one officer mentioned that felony paperwork was worse than a domestic call. Excessive paperwork was a common complaint: "It sucks because it's very time consuming, with paperwork and computer programs and warrants that need to be signed by a judge—takes four or five hours, just stupid." A number of officers expressed concern that since paperwork took so long to complete, it kept them off the streets and unable to help their fellow officers on the shift; some felt like shirkers, especially if they did not like dealing with domestic calls to begin with. Also, if domestic calls were seen as "bullshit" ones, such as petty fights between siblings, officers felt paperwork was even more excessive and unnecessary.

State troopers felt paperwork could take up the majority of a shift. Like other officers, they believed that paperwork is "cover your ass" policy and excessive. Paperwork is even required for verbal altercations, including taking the histories of both parties involved and use of an incident checklist. Most state troopers understand the need for paperwork for domestic disputes involving partners or ex-partners, but loathe the work entailed for other victim/offender combinations. This relates to another oft-voiced complaint: "It's ridiculous how everything is now considered a domestic. That makes a lot more work for us." While some troopers shrugged this off (e.g., "It's a long grueling process that nobody likes but we have to do it."), others were very frustrated and annoyed. "If one answers two or more domestics, no way you'll go home on time; you're looking at overtime." They feel that domestic violence paperwork is more excessive than any other report. As one trooper said, "When you think about it, it's crazy. I can handle a homicide and do the paperwork (which is on one form) in a matter of minutes." Moreover, with domestic calls, troopers have to complete all of the paperwork and turn in the forms to the supervising sergeant before they can exit shift and go home.

Part of the antipathy toward paperwork can be understood in a larger context. Many officers see their job as one of "crime fighting," and doing pen-and-paper work does not reinforce their macho image. For example, in her work with New York street cops, Jennifer Hunt (1984) found that their assessments of office cops were not flattering, and that these assessments were described with gender-based language. The street cops saw the office cops as

> . . . engaged in "feminine labor" such as public relations and secretarial work. These "pencil-pushing bureaucrats" were not involved in the "masculine" physical labor which characterized "real police work" on the street. (p. 287)

Another downside to paperwork, according to several officers, is that they will spend less time on the scene talking to the victim because they just want to get out and get the paperwork done:

> All the paperwork required in domestics may actually hurt victims. Let's say you get called to a domestic. You know this means two hours plus of paperwork. So what do you do? You can cut on the time you are at the scene and the amount of time you spend investigating and listening to the victim. It's like you don't really care what she has to say about what happened to her because you just wanted to get out of there and get the damn paperwork done.

This insightful comment raises the possibility that the paperwork required by pro-arrest policies may hinder effective investigation and victim assistance.

DUAL ARRESTS

One of the concerns about the consequences of mandatory or pro-arrest policies is that police will arrest both parties involved in a domestic dispute, which might reflect overzealous enforcement of the law and an inability or unwillingness to take the time and care needed to identify the primary aggressor and victim or distinguish between battering and self-defensive behavior. Although more than a few of the arrested women discussed in chapter 7 were part of dual arrests, at the time of the data collection the state did not track the numbers of dual arrests of intimate partners or former partners that occurred annually.

The county police department frowns on dual arrests and trains its officers to believe there is almost always an aggressor. This tenet was enough to deter many officers from making dual arrests. Other county officers reinforced department policy with the understanding that the court system does not encourage dual arrest. Officers are trained to look for signs of physical injury, so in order to make a dual arrest, both parties would need marks that did not indicate defensive use of violence. If the man is claiming self-defense, officers say he better have received some serious injuries to show for it, reflecting officers' opinions that women rarely harm men very severely. Witnesses are important, too, in order to add more to the standard "he said, she said" story. County officers stated that injuries made by self-defense are easy to determine, and separating a couple is the best way to get the full story and thoroughly examine injuries.

An interesting theme arose with a number of county and state officers who believed that dual arrests were appropriate if the woman fought back after some time had elapsed from when she was hurt (this possibility was never raised in the ride-alongs with the city police). For instance: "If he came home and pushed her down, and then he went upstairs, and next she grabbed a knife and went after him and cut him, then they would both be arrested." At one domestic call during a ride-along, even though the husband was violent, the officer felt that the woman was also the aggressor because she had many chances to get away from him and instead kept following him around the house. Another officer's example:

> Let's say your husband has been beating on you and you do what you
> can to get out of the house. You kick, slap, whatever. You run over to
> the neighbor and call the cops. I come talk to you and I can tell by what
> you're telling me and what I see that you did everything you could to
> get out so you aren't getting arrested. But if he was slapping you around
> and then *later* you started thinking about it and got pissed so decided to
> hit him with a frying pan—now you are getting arrested too.

Officers never mentioned that context, motivation, or history of abuse were important factors to use when trying to assess a situation and determine primary aggressor status. When asked about what to do if the primary aggressor could not be identified, one officer stated that he did not really care about the background: "Listen, I don't go there to figure out what happened. I don't care what happened. My job is to decide whether or not a criminal act occurred and if so, what criminal act and who committed it."

State troopers framed the dual arrest quandary slightly differently. Unless there are compelling circumstances, a dual arrest indicates that the trooper is being lazy or judgmental or not doing his or her job. They believed that well-trained officers know how to determine who is in the wrong. Troopers do echo county officers' thoughts in that they feel a dual arrest is appropriate if there is a "break in the action" or if "the woman or man has a chance to get out of the house, then it is not an acceptable excuse if violence is used in a relationship, or, if the victim decides twenty minutes later to hit back—that doesn't work either." The troopers took pride in their (perceived) greater professionalism and training, and believed the county police arrest everyone they can in domestic violence calls and make no distinction between primary aggressors and victims.

Sometimes troopers acknowledged that it is difficult to tell whom to arrest:

> If you get there and the one partner had to fight back, so the other
> ended up with a scratch on their face, yeah, violence occurred on
> both ends, but that is where mandatory arrests fail, for there is no
> need to punish someone acting in self-defense. It's a fine line that is
> hard to distinguish who is at fault. But for the majority of calls, unless

the wife has been sweet-talked by her husband, it is obvious the man
is the aggressor.

Some state troopers wished there was some alternative to arrest, such as in
situations in which "you don't want to arrest the woman but you have to because she committed the crime. You know she is just trying to defend herself
and she has been beaten for years, but you still got to arrest her." A few troopers suggested that the dual arrest policy does not really look at the totality of
circumstances, a view expressed by troopers on the force for more than four
years. Other troopers expressed concern that dual arrests can make a woman
think she is to blame for his abuse. Nonetheless, troopers felt when they did
make dual arrests, their actions were appropriate.

Very few city police officers admitted that they made dual arrests. First,
they believed that it was frowned upon by "the brass, the D.A., and the
courts." A number of officers shared stories along these lines: "I did a dual once
and after the trial, the judge asked me what the hell was I thinking doing that.
You try to cover your ass, but then I had the judge yelling at me!" Similar to
the state troopers, the city police felt that a dual arrest would indicate a lack
of professionalism: "The brass would think it means we didn't do our job because every domestic instance should have an aggressor and a victim. If you
don't find that out, you fucked up." Second, they didn't believe that most
women could be the aggressor: "Unless the guy got the shit kicked out of him,
and most of the time the woman didn't do shit, she was just getting beat up on,
so no arrest of her would be made." Finally, the majority of the city officers explained that if they thought a woman was protecting herself, an arrest was inappropriate. Several officers even explained that they try to make only one
arrest when there are children present because they do not want to have to
take the children to family services. Overall, city officers believed that dual arrests were very rare. This rarity may also reflect the limited number of years of
experience that many of the city officers had.

Police Perceptions of Women's Use of Violence

Overwhelmingly, the officers from all departments stated that they did not believe there was an increase in women's use of violence. At the same time, however, many officers believed that women were starting to "stand up for
themselves" and fight back. While officers acknowledged that self-defensive
measures were not synonymous with battering, they did not feel protective measures included situations in which a woman makes an aggressive move beyond
self-defense, such as a woman attacking a man minutes after he has hit her, after

he has already left the room and calmed down. They viewed self-defense as an immediate, spontaneous response to violence.

Although officers declared that women were less likely to use preemptive or aggressive violence, they still projected a profile of a violent woman they deemed blameworthy. Typically, a violent woman was described as a drunk or a drug addict, and was "nasty." "The worst person to deal with in the world is a drunk, pissed off chick. You don't want to fuck with her; they have nails that are like claws that will chop you up." Alcohol and drugs were highlighted as the trigger for women's violence, especially since many officers believed "alcohol makes women mean." Alcohol, combined with youth, makes women bolder and more willing to fight back and less likely to walk away. In general, however, officers believed that alcohol fostered a greater use of violence in women against anyone, not just male partners: "Women messed up on drugs or alcohol get into fights with other women, children, men, neighbors, you name it. Women are nasty when they have been drinking or drugging."

Many officers admitted that they had never arrested a woman as a primary aggressor. However, all officers revealed strong opinions about women's use of violence despite their lack of experience with arrest. They believed that women "pushed men's buttons and she can be just as much at fault." But while women do fight back and "pull stupid shit to get revenge," officers did not believe that the women's use of violence had increased. Some officers attributed the increase in the arrests of women to the pro-arrest policies that encourage arrests, and felt that women get caught up in the push to arrest: "Women now know there's gonna be an arrest made, so they call the police to help make the guy stop beating on her. But her fighting back now gets attention too." As previously mentioned, some women were arrested because of a new law that stated an arrest must be made if violence was committed in front of a child.

Quite a number of officers believed that "women's lib" has encouraged women to stick up for themselves more, and with this new independence comes a greater visibility for women when they do more than "just sit there and take it." So, while officers believe that women's use of violence has not increased, arrests for women's assertiveness have increased. Moreover, some officers applaud women's initiative "because they are not putting up with guys' shit anymore. Instead of taking it, like the past hundred years, women are giving it back. Which I think is good. I am sick of going to a scene and seeing a battered defenseless woman. And I'm sick of going back to the same scene another day and seeing the same battered defenseless woman."

A number of officers suggested that women are beginning to realize there is a better way of life out there, but they seem stuck in their circumstances because of poverty or misguided love, so they feel they have no choice but to fight back. Younger women in particular are asserting that they are just as good, just as tough, and just as independent as men. This "women's lib" theme was more pronounced in the ride-alongs with the city police. Most of the city officers believed that women may be using more violence because they are sticking up for themselves, getting more frustrated with their situations, and getting tired of taking it. These explanations were offered with a sense of understanding, if not even tacit approval.

Officers from all departments deplored the repetitive nature of domestic calls and hated to return to the same house over and over, which might help to explain their empathy for women who fight back. Officers believed that women's tactics differ from men: women tend to slap, pull hair, push, whereas men use their closed fists. Women often pick up a handy object in an attempt to equalize the force between them and male combatants, which often means a kitchen object such as a knife, pan, glass, or dish. "The weapons women use are usually strange, and you can tell that they grabbed them in the heat of the moment trying to save themselves. Men usually just use their fists." Not a single officer said that they encountered a battered man in the way that they describe battered women: bloody, bruised, and with broken limbs. As one officer succinctly stated, "Women don't beat up men. They use force, but it is never a situation where a woman is coming home drunk and giving her husband a few lashes; it's more like self-defense." Another officer said that "most of the time the man is the abuser and he doesn't have a scratch on him since he has his woman completely under control." Several officers noted that one common way that women fight back is to cut up the guy's clothes and throw them out of the house.

Many officers contended that women get violent at the point when the police arrive, whereas men will stop fighting in the presence of an officer. A common refrain was that women become violent when they realize that their breadwinner is getting arrested, even though they wanted the violence to stop. Only one officer mentioned that he had seen women violent in lesbian relationships, in a couple of calls.

The state troopers, even more so than the county police, took pride in saying that they had never arrested a woman who used violence in self-defense. This pride no doubt reflects their sense that if they did their investigation thoroughly and correctly, they would not have missed the determination of the primary aggressor. Even with the new paperwork requirement that entailed taking the histories of both parties involved in the domestic violence situation, and the troopers' boasts that they never arrested women who used self-defensive violence, most were loathe to look beyond the immediate incident to gain a more complete understanding of women's lives. The superficiality of

their understanding is in accord with their reluctance to engage in more victim assistance, an action viewed as akin to social work rather than crime fighting. It was very rare for troopers to describe contextual factors related to use of
violence; officers were more focused on whether or not violence was used by
women, and not why it was used.

Troopers were also the only officers who raised the possibility that women's
violence towards men represented a way of reacting to abuse when other options of escape were blocked. The connection to alcohol was seen as very
strong; as one officer put it, "If it weren't for alcohol, I wouldn't have a job."
City officers also talked a lot about how drugs and alcohol can make women
"tough" or "mean and nasty."

Time and time again, officers mentioned that it boils down to "cover your
ass" and that concerns about liability down the road guide police in writing
more thorough reports that detail the use of force by all parties, whereas before
their focus was on the aggressor's actions and not the reactions to these actions. However, their understandings of gender differences were reflected in
typical charges filed: "Women will get charged with offensive touching, while
men usually get charged with third degree assault, mostly due to the worse injuries that men inflict."[3] State troopers in particular noticed that men seem
more willing to report violence committed by women. Several officers speculated that the man's greater willingness to report may be a way of regaining a
sense of power over the woman, especially if she had a restraining order
against him. A few city officers mentioned that sometimes the man calls the
police himself to report violence, thinking that the woman will get arrested
when the police arrive. But the police stated that it is easy to see through the
man's manipulative techniques.

Protection From Abuse Orders

Civil orders of protection, or restraining orders, are a national strategy developed in response to the reluctance of the criminal justice system to handle effectively the criminal nature of domestic violence (Klein 1996). These civil
court remedies permit victims to circumvent the criminal process, yet still obtain some relief or have an additional tool at their disposal. Initially, restraining orders were difficult to obtain. Prior to the 1970s, women had to begin
divorce proceedings to be eligible (Chaudhuri and Daly 1992).

Today, restraining orders (also called civil orders of protection in some
states) are more accessible and can actually provide various types of relief.
They not only establish limits to abusers' access to victims but may also include
financial arrangements and restrictions on child custody. They may limit access

to residence, place of employment, children, and children's schools. Restraining orders also serve as an alternative form of victim protection if the level of evidence does not meet the standard of a criminal proceeding or if the victim would be a weak prosecutor witness due to drug or alcohol abuse (Finn and Colson 1990). Because violation of a restraining order is a criminal offense that can result in arrest, these orders expand police power and increase officers' ability to monitor repeat offenders (Finn and Colson 1990). The effectiveness of restraining orders ultimately rests on law enforcement's response, and it can be enhanced with serious prosecutorial and judicial actions and meaningful punishment for violators (Gelb 1994, cited in Iovanni and S. Miller 2001, 313).

In this state, restraining orders are called Protection From Abuse (PFA) orders. During the ride-alongs, officers had a great deal to say about PFAs. On their surface, PFAs represent potentially wonderful resources for victims. PFAs can develop a paper trail that documents trouble, which will be very helpful later in court in proving violence occurred. At the same time, however, officers stressed that they were "only" a piece of paper, one that could give victims a false sense of security: "If someone wants to kill you, a PFA won't stop him." Officers were torn about their assessments of PFAs. They hated them because PFAs were so often abused by victims seeking revenge, yet they also appreciated them because PFAs extend their arrest powers.

Officers were candid about the advantages they attributed to PFAs. Several mentioned that PFAs were helpful in that they ordered that the offender's weapons be taken away. Police also were "thrilled," as one officer described it, that PFA enforcement extended an officer's power to arrest. Violations were clear cut, giving officers more to work with and making it easier to make an arrest. The officers repeatedly mentioned that PFAs give them more power, "more ammunition."

The complaints that officers raised in regard to PFAs far outweighed these benefits, however. First, officers felt that PFAs were too easy to obtain. There was no proof required, just a victim's statement to the court: "No one—police or judge—will question a woman who is claiming to be victimized because of the mistakes made in the past, such as not arresting or not serving restraining orders that then led to murder." Second, officers were disgusted with the frequency in which they saw victims using PFAs as "payback" or revenge: "Ninety percent of our calls are for bullshit like bogus PFA violations. People trying to use us to get back at one another. If you were to call the police for something real and it takes awhile for us to get there, it's because of bullshit cases like that."

Officers were adamant about how often PFAs were abused and used incorrectly. For instance, the most common scenario described by officers was one in which the woman ends up forgiving the offender and giving him another chance, and invites him back to her house. Then when things start getting sour again, she calls the cops and says he is at her house in violation of the PFA, and then he gets arrested. Another common scenario described by many officers was when the woman tricks the man, sometimes using children, to get him in trouble, a situation that seems especially prevalent when the couple is undergoing a divorce or child custody decisions. Officers observed that PFAs are becoming more like "he said, she said" battles, because they see that men are now cross-filing for PFAs against the women.

Officers felt that many victims in the past were not aware of PFAs, but now "women are getting smarter to the system and know how to abuse them." Officers were loath to arrest on bogus PFA calls: "I hate those; it's almost like you feel bad arresting the guy, even though he did the original abuse." They were dismayed about the waste of time and resources taken up by chasing bogus PFAs. They believed that the large number of bogus PFA calls may inadvertently hurt "real" PFA violations because officers would approach a violation call with suspicion. Only two officers commented that violence could increase after a PFA is secured if the aggressor wants to regain power in the relationship. Despite the considerable amount of discussion by officers about PFAs, during the three month ride-along study, only three suspects were arrested on PFA violations and one warrant was issued based on a PFA violation.

In the poorest section of the city, comprised mostly of African-American and some Latino neighborhoods, the city police officers believed that most of these residents did not take out PFAs. In fact, officers felt that this particular section of the city rarely requested police assistance for domestic disputes. As one officer explained:

> These people handle it themselves. They rarely call the police. It's apparent shit is going on there, but they don't want to involve us. Too many drugs and stuff. They have their own code out here and they just don't like cops. Especially white cops. I hear them calling me "cracker" and they tell me to get outta here.

Regardless of the officer's race, they shared the sentiment that the very worst part of the city was underrepresented in domestic calls.

Race and Class

During the ride-alongs, the student observers were exposed to the officers' personal philosophies, not only about domestic violence but also about the world the police patrol. On the surface, the officers seemed to frame their explanations about violence using racial themes. Many used derogatory statements and expressions in describing residents, neighborhoods, and behaviors. When one digs a little deeper, however, their descriptions seemed more about the social class positions of residents rather than purely race. For instance, when an officer from the less populated, rural counties talked about residents as "dirtbags, scum buckets" who were unable to "control their violence because they are trashy and don't know any better," the officer was generally describing poor white neighborhoods, often trailer parks. Almost identical language was used by the city police officers to describe poor inner-city black residents who resided in public housing projects. The words used could be interchangeable, except for the racial identifiers. In fact, many officers across the state were surprised when domestic calls came in from nice, middle-class neighborhoods; these were the same officers who admitted that if they saw a BMW or Mercedes in a really bad neighborhood, they would stop and ask the driver and occupants a few questions to determine why they were there.

In the more white, rural part of the state, a few officers believed that poor women are more independent, so they fight back more than women in suburban areas. Only a few county and state officers stated that black women fought back more than white women, and these officers patrolled primarily African-American neighborhoods. Many city police, who were more exposed to African-American citizens and neighborhoods, believed that black women fought back more than white women, and suggested it may be because black women were poorer and had less to lose and were "raised in violence." The officers who patrolled poor white neighborhoods, especially more rural trailer parks, believed that "poor white trash" fought back more. Thus, their comments seem to say more about a woman's precarious economic position than her race.

Officers from the county and state tended to dismiss women's violence as a part of their overall crummy lifestyle:

> They just don't care. You see a lot of that in this line of work. The places we are called to, kids running around in the streets and no parents are around. They just don't care about anything. So when they get mad or upset about something, they lash out violently. Hell, they see it all around them. That's how disputes are handled in these poor areas.

Thus, these officers believed violence to be part of a "poverty lifestyle."

City officers offered extensive commentary on the ways they thought lifestyle affected the use of violence:

> They were raised differently. They were conditioned to be violent. Look at this place. What kind of chance do you think these kids

have? Look around. This place is a shit hole. The only sources of income here are welfare and drugs. These kids run around unsupervised. God knows where their parents are or what they are up to. They grow up hearing "fuck you" and "fuck this." They learn to be violent. They are conditioned to be violent. That's how they learn to handle all their disputes. Animals. The men grow up to beat their women and the women grow up to think they have to take it.

A few officers speculated about larger social factors and attributed high levels of violence in general to the media's portrayal of violence on TV, violent TV shows, and feelings of economic desperation.

Student observers' field notes cited multiple times when officers treated poor white or black citizens with outright hostility and suspicion, noticing a difference between the officers' attitudes towards them and more "upstanding" citizens. Other field note write-ups indicated that some officers would share their private racist or classist (or sexist or homophobic) thoughts with the student observers in private, but said that they would not let their discriminatory beliefs affect their treatment of citizens, and in fact talked to citizens respectfully. This example, what an officer told the student in private after a traffic stop of an African-American man, is illustrative: "I didn't believe that asshole from the start. If it had been an upstanding guy like you from the start I would have cut him a break, but he was a dirty man." Although this particular officer felt this way, he still maintained a professional detachment and respectful demeanor with the citizen as he questioned him and issued a traffic ticket.

All officers across the state believed that domestic violence is more prevalent in poorer neighborhoods, even though the incidents are less likely to be brought to police attention by victims. Neighbors often called in with domestic complaints because of the noise. The police believed that domestic violence occurred more in "bad" neighborhoods since so many residents are without jobs and stay close to home: "One thing you have to deal with here is trash. There is plenty of it in this place. People here don't want to work so they just sit on their ass all day and collect the check." Officers stated that middle-class or richer people did not like to get the police involved because they had more to lose, such as a good job or reputation, or because they feared the embarrassment of having a police squad car parked in front of their houses.

Officers in the two less-populated counties believed that domestic violence involving "poor white trash, you know, trailer people and hillbillies" was reported more by neighbors because of the close proximity of trailers and modular homes. City officers patrolling all-black neighborhoods said that domestic violence involving "dirty people, dirtbags, and scum" come to officers' attention more because neighbors are stacked on top of each other in housing projects or subsidized housing where no privacy exists.

Officers admitted they like to ride around nice neighborhoods during their shifts or answer security alarm calls there because "those people deserve patrol because they pay their taxes and our salaries." The visual contrast between the "nice" neighborhoods and the "slums" were often a source of conversation by the officers. Responding to a domestic call in a poor neighborhood presented physical discomfort because of the summer heat; as one officer stated, "Heat causes bad tempers. If everyone had air conditioning, the domestic violence rate would drop by 50 percent. I went to one domestic call last week and it was so hot in the house I felt like saying, 'Lady, it's so freakin' hot in here, I'm about to hit you too.'"

Officers who had served on the force for over ten years took a more thoughtful approach to race. One white male officer, with fifteen years on the city police force, captured their tone with this reflection:

> You got parents out there working or doing whatever, and ain't nobody watching the damn kids, and they are just running wild. I grew up in Wilmington, and I was never racist. I'm not sure if I am that way anymore. I think being a cop in this town can make you that way. You are just exposed to so much shit. And there's a lot of futility there when we know we don't make a difference.

Another veteran officer with over ten years of experience on the city force added, "There are a lot of decent, hard-working people in the city, but they are unfortunately stuck in a bad place."

These reflections by veteran officers conflict with the musings of less-experienced officers. Here are two quotes from city officers, each with two years of experience on the force: "These people feel they are the victims of society. I wish I was a victim because then I could sleep all day, not get a job, collect welfare, and commit crimes. Law is a nuisance to these people"; "This place used to be nice until all the black people moved in." The officers with less than three years of experience tended to mimic a black dialect and roll their eyes in a mocking way when dealing with black citizens. This derision was not shared by veteran officers, but it should be kept in mind that the data is limited because the ride-alongs were conducted with far fewer veteran officers than with officers relatively new to the profession. Perhaps the difference is that the younger officers do not have the career longevity to draw upon that might offer them enough positive experiences to challenge their stereotypes, nor do they share a tendency to think of the larger picture the way some veteran officers do.

Discussion

Mandatory and pro-arrest policies for domestic violence emphasize uniformity and decrease officer discretion and flexibility. While a welcome change from earlier police inaction, arrest policies have the potential for creating disastrous consequences, such as arresting victims who fight back or increasing dual arrests of both victims and offenders. The ride-along component of this study permits an examination of officers' perceptions and attitudes related to domestic violence policy as well as reveals their behavior toward citizens when enforcing the law.

Most police officers held strong opinions about the extent to which women used violence in intimate relationships, believing that most women are not primary aggressors but rather use force under three conditions. First, self-defense, which is seen as justified by the officers; they say they do not arrest women under this circumstance. Second, officers feel that women fight back because they feel more "free" to do so because of advances in "women's lib" that enable women to not just "take it" but strike out against their abuser out of frustration and anger. Officers even expressed tacit approval of such action, perhaps underscoring their frustration with responding to the same dwellings over and over to handle domestic complaints. Again, this description of women's violence illustrates the use of defensive behavior rather than preemptive, aggressive violence, according to officers' interpretations. Finally, officers acknowledge that they encounter women who are drunk or strung out on drugs, and their actions are often violent, crazy, and nonsensical. They feel some women are more violent when under the influence of drugs or alcohol.

Officers' strong opinions about women's use of violence support the fact that most officers admit they have never arrested a woman as a primary aggressor under the state's pro-arrest policy. In fact, when analyzing the arrest data from the ninety ride-alongs conducted, out of the ten arrests made, seven involved male offenders, while only two involved female offenders and one involved a dual arrest of both a man and a woman. The motivations of the two arrested females entailed revenge or retaliation for past violence the women endured from a male partner or former partner. The dual arrest involved a boyfriend and girlfriend who were both drug addicts and very high at the time, and verbal sparring escalated into mutual pushing and shoving. Not surprisingly, the arrests of the seven male offenders entailed three PFA violations and four instances of aggressive force used against females. Of the nine arrest warrants issued, only one was for a woman; this case involved a man's new girlfriend making threats to his former girlfriend. The other eight arrest warrants issued where men were the suspects reflected a variety of physical violence and "terroristic" threats that the men made against their current or former female partners.

Across the state, officers contended that dual arrests were rare, and in fact only one occurred during the ride-along study. Officers framed dual arrests as rare because they believed that their skill and professionalism enabled them to conduct sound investigations and to determine who the primary aggressor was without having to resort to making a dual arrest. The only time that officers said dual arrests were acceptable outcomes was when both parties were injured very severely.

For any domestic violence call, including one involving a dual arrest, officers felt that the paperwork required was excessive. Officers regretted the time it took them off the streets and the burden it placed upon the other officers on the shift to respond to the volume of calls with a shortage of officers. One officer mentioned that the downside to spending so much time completing paperwork was that police spend less time on the actual crime scene or with victim assistance. Although only one officer provided this insight, it is easy to see the impact this could have on conducting thorough investigations to determine the context of domestic violence incidents (such as the motivation for the violence and the identification of the primary aggressor) or to allay victims' concerns about safety and to provide information and referral resources to victims.

Officers were also very consistent with their explanations for gender differences in the use of violence. Almost all believed that men used violence to control their women and the situation, whereas women used violence as a way of getting back at men for cheating or treating them badly or battering them. When women did use weapons, officers saw this as an indication that women were trying to match men's greater strength, and not as indicative that women were meaner or more weapon-prone. Still, a mythology of the "violent woman" persisted, with many officers re-telling a story of folklore proportions about a female offender who put a guy in the hospital.

In all police-citizen encounters, police wield a lot of power. According to domestic violence policy in this state, police possess limited discretion over their responses to a domestic violence incident. Yet, the ride-along study revealed multiple times when discretion was exercised. Police seemed to thrive in flexing power and autonomy. Throughout the ride-alongs, officers commented on how much they loved being police, despite their frustration with paperwork and the necessity of "covering their asses" on every call. As one officer exclaimed to a student observer, "Where else could you get a job as fun as this? I can fuck with anyone I want; it's really cool!" The impression left by many officers is that they enjoy being police because "you get to call the shots," or, as another officer phrased it, "patrol is great because there is always something to do and always people to fuck with." While most officers put their personal feelings aside and treated citizens with courtesy and respect, they lowered their guard when talking with the student observers and spoke at length about their frustrations with domestic violence in general and with people they characterized as "problems."

Moreover, officers tended to categorize people as either "losers" or "hard workers," and often this characterization determined whether officers felt they deserved "a break" or a punitive action. These prejudices were exacerbated when officers felt the people were "dirt bags" or "trash," which appeared to be connected to low economic status of poor whites in the rural parts of the state and poor African-Americans (and sometimes Latinos) in the more urban settings.

Officers were very vocal in their dislike of responding to domestic violence calls, particularly with their frustrations with making repeat calls to the same address, and they also voiced their displeasure with the women who "took the abuse." Although the officers did not blame the women explicitly for their victimization, they did criticize the women's refusal to do anything, their inability to leave a bad relationship, their willingness to let the children see the domestic strife, and so forth. The officers did not show much sympathy for the men, but they did focus on why the battered woman didn't leave the relationship rather than why the batterer felt he was entitled to hit her. In a study of police officers' attitudes in a different state that, at the time, had a warrantless arrest statue for misdemeanor assault, Saunders (1995) found that officers who arrested women in domestic violence calls were less likely to feel comfortable talking with victims and more likely to harbor traditional stereotypes, believing that domestic violence was justified in the case of infidelity and that victims of domestic battery remained with their violent partners for psychological rather than practical reasons. The officers in the present study seemed to share similar beliefs about women's traditional roles; they did not understand the difficulties women face when leaving abusive relationships, even if the ride-along results did not reveal a large number of female arrests.

One final observation from the ride-along data suggests that police are rigidly trained and guided by a criminal justice system that is simplistic in its approach to battering: did the event occur or not, and if so, follow the law or department policy and make an arrest. This incident-driven philosophy that is devoid of contextual understandings and explanations of violence was illustrated by a number of officers' quotes, such as: "I don't look at it that deeply.

They teach us to just look at the surface. What do you see here and how and who. I can't go into that other life stuff with them. We are just a Band-Aid"; "I don't go there to figure out what happened. I don't care what happened. My job is to decide whether or not a criminal act occurred and if so, what criminal act and who committed it."

Despite the limited number of times that officers during the ride-along phase of the study arrested women who used violence in intimate settings, the state has experienced an overall increase in the number of women arrested and mandated to treatment programs intended to address males who batter females. Thus, the additional components of the larger research project extends the inquiry in two ways: First, by exploring the perceptions and knowledge of criminal justice professionals and social service providers in the state who directly work with women arrested for domestic violence; and second, by observing batterer treatment groups for arrested female offenders. The next chapter turns to an examination of information gleaned from in-depth interviews with criminal justice professionals and social service providers to understand their experiences with women arrested on domestic violence charges.

Chapter 5   After Arrest

Criminal Justice Professionals and Social Service Providers

This CHAPTER FOCUSES on the perceptions and experiences of criminal justice professionals and social service providers who play a direct role in addressing the issue of women arrested for domestic violence.[1] Thirty-seven structured, in-depth interviews were conducted, during which respondents answered a number of set questions as well as took the opportunity to raise additional issues they deemed relevant. Each interview began by asking respondents if they felt that women's violence against their partners was increasing, and if so, would this change account for the increase in the number of women arrested.

Without exception, none of the respondents (e.g., treatment providers, counselors, shelter directors and workers, prosecutors, police officers,[2] defense attorneys, public defenders, probation officers) believed that women's aggressive violence was increasing and thus justifying increased arrests. Rather, they indicated there were other reasons that could explain why more women were being arrested, such as their use of violence in self-defense. Most respondents were aware of the 1984 shift in police response and the emphasis on a pro-arrest policy, stimulated by fear of civil lawsuits. Both probation officers and shelter workers asserted that all of their clients had histories of victimization, but the police are now directed to make arrests. So rather than ignoring women's behavior as they had in the past, the police focus on the violence itself and not the context in which it occurs. As one probation officer said, "The guy might hammer her three times and maybe even get charged and convicted; and she hammers him once in response and gets charged during the fourth incident."

In fact, often if a woman was on probation for relationship violence, the probation department also had her male partner on the caseload. Victim services personnel said that they often received calls from women who were arrested— women they knew from earlier episodes in which the women were victims. A social worker in the prosecutor's office also talked about these women:

> A lot of our female "victims" have had a long victimization history. I think that a lot of our female victims just reach a point, even if it is just verbal abuse, where they can't take it anymore and then they lash out; and it's true, they are getting a criminal charge and that criminal charge can be sustained. But there is usually a history that goes with that as to why they're here.

As a prosecutor stated:

> I think in a lot of these situations . . . they're both verbally abusive . . . and they both get in each other's face and I think sometimes she gets arrested. But I still think that he's the dominant figure . . . he controls everything . . . He's still the man and he's still the head of the household and that's probably where half the problems come in—when you challenge that authority figure that he is, or you want to go against him or do something he doesn't want you to do.

Interestingly, what these statements show is that members of the prosecutor's office (prosecutors and social workers), whose job it is to prosecute the women as offenders, view them as and call them "victims," not "offenders."

Overwhelmingly, the respondents dismissed the idea of mutual combat or equivalent danger, and instead talked about the reasons why women used violence.

> . . . most of the time it is to tell him to "stay away" and then as he approaches, sometimes he gets stabbed. (treatment provider)

> Women typically say that "he was assaulting me and I was trying to get away from him." The women are more likely to admit what they did, like they'll say, "Yeah, I stabbed him!, but this is why." The men a lot of times will not even admit that they struck her unless you say, "Well then, how did she end up with a broken nose?" Even then, the men still sometimes don't admit it, even when you have the facts right there. (probation officer, domestic violence unit)

What also was consistent across respondents was that they believed that the police are being overly cautious: "If they see any mark, any scratch at all, police will charge, regardless if it was due to fighting back or inflicted because of being the initial aggressor. I think police are far more free or willing to charge both parties these days than they used to be" (shelter worker). The respondents stated repeatedly that women's motives differed from men's motives; in particular, that women's use of violence was not part of the power-control dynamic associated with battering. According to probation officers, women often seemed "at the end of their rope." The probation officers raised the issue of self-medication: women take drugs and alcohol in order to cope or because they do not feel strong enough to leave. Police officers echoed this belief; as one male police detective said, "Women use substances as a momentary escape because of the hell that she may be in."

The arrested women were often charged with misdemeanors (except those using knives or guns) and typically caused little damage to the men. As one victim services worker claimed:

> Most of the time, they are arrested for offensive touching—occasionally, assault, but more typically it's for a scratch or something . . . we don't have a man who's beaten to a pulp or anyone with a black eye or bruises all over the body and broken bones.

Overwhelmingly, the respondents believed that the women did not have the same kind of power that men possess in relationships. The men were not in fear of their lives (unless she had a weapon, but even so, men's fear would be temporary; men rarely live in fear as many battered women do) and if the men wanted to defend themselves, they could easily do so. The women also did not control the men's autonomy: give them a curfew or tell them who they can call on the phone, who they can socialize with, what clothing they can wear, whether they can visit with family members.

Even so, a few respondents (typically, the police members of domestic violence units and members of victim services units that were closely affiliated with police departments) stated that if women did commit a crime, "they should be arrested the same as a man. We shouldn't differentiate just because she's a female" (victim services worker). If there were inconsistencies, they believed the prosecutors should resolve them. What distinguished the two scenarios (of arrested men and arrested women) was that "you don't see the same kind of power and control structure with women; it's probably a situation where she just lost it" (head of domestic violence unit, state police).

Thus, not a single respondent believed that women were getting more violent. Rather, they believed that the increase in females arrested for domestic violence reflected changes in police policy in that police were trained to make an arrest on any domestic violence call rather than use their discretion to handle the situation in alternative ways. The respondents strongly asserted that women and men have different motivations for using violence, with women being frustrated or defending themselves. A number of respondents believed that women should be punished for criminal acts as long as context was taken into account and aggressive violence was differentiated from self-defensive action.

Manipulating the System

Another significant theme that emerged from the interviews relates to the ways in which the criminal justice system could be manipulated by offenders who are familiar with its process. Respondents indicated that more men today seem willing to call the police to report violence committed against them by their female partners or ex-partners. While this could indicate an increase in the numbers of women using violence against their male partners, national data as well as the data from the research state indicates that the increase in arrests may be more accurately attributed to men's greater awareness of how to use the criminal justice system to their advantage. In fact, national survey results from the 1973–82 National Crime Survey reveal that men are not shy about calling the police: men assaulted by their wives call police more often than women assaulted by their husbands (Schwartz 1987). Kimmel (2002) suggests women are more likely to forgive their abusers and "normalize it with statements that he really does love her" (p. 1345).

The respondents in this sample were adamantly clear about the ways that men manipulated the women or the criminal justice system. The respondents either directly observed these deceptive behaviors or heard about them from victims. These behaviors included men intimidating women to waive their right to trial by claiming that the woman would lose her children if she lost at trial and went to jail; men self-inflicting wounds so that police would view the woman as assaultive and dangerous; men being the first ones to call 911 in order to pro-actively define the situation; and men capitalizing on the outward calm they display once police arrive—his serenity highlights the hysterical female. As one detective explained: "He's calm because he was all pissed off before we got there and he beat the crap out of her. So now, of course he's calm, and of course she is hysterical because she just got beaten up! But we did not realize that years ago" (detective, head of domestic violence unit).

According to one supervisor from a family court-based advocacy program, the program averaged three or four calls a month from women whom the advocates considered being victims, but whose partners called 911. This supervisor noticed that more women who have a history of victimization were fighting back, and the battered women told the advocates that they were sick of the violence.

> What we're seeing is dual arrests where they're both being arrested. And we have victims who will say to us "he's threatening to have me arrested" because maybe he's done it before, or he's called the police . . . I actually have one who said that he took a knife and made little marks because she had been arrested for scratching him, but this was after he had initiated it so what he did was took a knife and made little scratches and said "Go ahead, call the police, because you're just gonna get arrested because they'll think that these are scratches!" (supervisor, domestic violence project, family court)

All of the treatment providers said that one of the most common statements they heard in batterer treatment groups for men was "get to the phone first." Relatedly, a male batterer may use the pending case against the woman as another mechanism of control. For example, a woman might not be aware that when a case is dismissed without prejudice, it is rarely reopened, but a batterer may tell her that he can get the prosecutor to reopen the case at any time; this way, he holds it over her head indefinitely.

> The men aren't dumb about how the process works, and unfortunately, they are going to use that to their advantage whenever possible. They will threaten the women with it—if they are still in the relationship, they will use it against her: "I'm going to call 911; I'm gonna call your probation officer; so you better do what I say" or "If you don't do what I say, say good-bye to your kids." (director of treatment facility)

> We've had guys wound themselves, cut themselves, and say "She did it!" and know that she is going to get in trouble, and often these are guys who have been perpetrators for some time. And they've learned to do that through their experience with the system. (shelter worker)

The shelter directors and workers believed that as the pro-arrest legislation aged, men who have been through the system more than once knew how it worked and they manipulated it. In one instance, a woman called a shelter in hysterics; her husband had beaten and choked her, but the bruises would not appear for a few hours. Her husband heard her call the police and he calmed down and lay in bed, pretending to sleep. The police did not make an arrest in this case. The lack of protection from the police angered and confused women, who felt they had no redress since they were novices in negotiating the system.

Respondents also believed that the police did not take the time to thoroughly investigate incidents, but rather granted greater credibility to the citizen who made the 911 call. But when officers did question ambiguous or puzzling situations, a clearer story emerged. One police officer from a county domestic violence unit described several incidents where they questioned the initial stories they received when dispatched because officers knew the men from previous domestic violence incidents as the offenders, and this time the men called and identified themselves as the victims: "We sneaked up on one of them, looked through his windows and saw him punch himself in the face, probably thinking, 'I got the injury now, so the police will lock *her* up—hey, it's a little payback.'"

Overall, the interview data reveal that respondents seemed troubled by incidents of men's manipulation of domestic violence laws. The respondents shared several beliefs: Men have become savvy and know the ins and outs of the criminal justice system; men manipulate women with threats, particularly over children and custody issues; and men self-inflict wounds. These findings demonstrate the need for police to thoroughly investigate the context of the situation, not just rely on "he said she said" commentary from the combatants or automatically accord greater credibility to the authoritative voice of men, a practice common in male violence against women (Taslitz 1999).

Concerns about the Criminal Justice System

Social service providers and criminal justice professionals raised many concerns about police behavior, case processing, and legal decision making. The main police issues revolved around dual arrests, displaced frustration with bureaucratic paperwork, over-enforcement of pro-arrest laws, and victim-offender ambiguity. Respondents in all three counties believed that changes in police policy, such as movement towards mandatory or pro-arrest policies, have resulted in dual arrests. Many of the respondents raised this issue—seeing it as troublesome—even before being asked about it. Overall, respondents felt that they were seeing an increase in the numbers of dual arrests, which was discouraging because it meant that the police were not thoroughly investigating the context of the incident in order to determine the primary aggressor. Respondents felt that police took the easy way out by arresting both parties, which left charging decisions up to the prosecutor's office.

One of the common explanations that respondents gave was that police felt over-burdened with excessive paperwork requirements, causing them to be less attuned to the intricacies of domestic violence situations.

They are getting flooded with paperwork, to the extent that they are getting desensitized to the proper way to deal with intimate partners. They are having to deal with minor offenses, such as where it is a brother-sister fighting over a remote control. And they are having to do that long form because that is what is required for a domestic. And one of those minors is going to be identified as the perpetrator and that is going to be recorded as an offender in a domestic. But it is not intimate domestic violence . . . (victim services worker)

Part of the problem was that the police were required to document every domestic violence call, which covered a range of victim-offender combinations. So when they were writing up a domestic violence call that involved intimate partners, they were frustrated in general from the excessive paperwork and just wanted to complete it and not spend time analyzing the incident. As one respondent explained,

It used to be that when police responded to a domestic they calmed the people down and they would try to get one to leave and they would write that up as a disturbance, like you were rescuing a kitten from a tree. So that was not adequate; that was clearly not adequate. But they have gone from that to this extreme—it takes eight hours if there is an arrest made . . . So what we've got is these police officers who come aboard wanting to do the right thing, but they are frustrated. (director of shelter)

Overwhelmingly, the respondents believed the police may be over-enforcing, or at least not taking the time to make the wisest decisions. As one of the directors of a treatment facility says, the police "are following the letter of the law, which is that if someone has an injury, if there are allegations made against the other party, then that party must be arrested . . . So it is almost as though they are doing too good a job." Police officers' fear of liability was also apparent: "They don't want to be the officer coming back the next day hearing that they have gone out for a domestic and then didn't arrest someone and then there is a major incident; the police are concerned about this and they will tell you that." As the head of a county domestic violence police unit said, "Victims do not wake up police departments; lawsuits do." He explained: "Police attitudes haven't necessarily changed; what changes a lot are the lawsuits." He believed it reflected a training issue: "They do not *have* to get it, they just *have* to do it. They can go home and complain all they want, but if they fail to act, now, that's a big deal."

Several respondents also suggested that the police were weary of being seen as "the problem" in providing adequate responses to domestic violence.

Respondents believed this resentment emerged in hostile ways: "If men are going to be held accountable, so will women and despite the fact that the dynamics are very different, police are going to make that arrest" (treatment provider). In fact, a treatment provider in the northern county said that it has become a common refrain to hear a police officer tell the couple: "According to police policy, I have to arrest both of you." The head of the county domestic violence police unit framed the issue in terms of providing protection for the victim:

> If they are both injured and we have reason to believe that both broke the law, they may both be arrested, and at least they'll get that time off, that cooling off period . . . It is not always that clear cut, but we're gonna make sure we take some action to protect them that night.

Several respondents mentioned that police have indicated to a female victim that they regretted making the arrest since she did not fit the stereotypical image of a violent, out-of-control woman, saying things like, "We're sorry, you don't look like somebody who is a batterer, but I have no choice but to arrest you" (treatment provider). Remorse from the police sometimes consoled a victim and made her more compliant. A city victim services worker believed that some officers have empathy for the women, yet they still have to arrest them because of the policy requirement. Yet many victims ended up feeling as this victim did, telling her counselor: "I just can't BELIEVE that I'm being arrested! Even though there's a knife wound, but I'm the victim! I called the police five times because there were black eyes, broken shoulders, and here I'm getting hauled off when I was just trying to keep him off of me!"

One respondent speculated that police action might be altruistically motivated so that the victim would get some help: "The police really want to see anyone arrested who is in any way violent, even if they *know* it is the victim and they are fully aware that the victim is also violent; they want her involved in the system so she can have some options and a record of the abuse." (Although only one professional respondent mentioned this, several women enrolled in female offender treatment groups raised this as something positive.) When the prosecutor's office inherited a dual arrest made by police, the prosecutors focused on the criminal or victimization histories of the parties. Prosecutors provided a typical scenario they encountered: a woman scratched her boyfriend or husband (which constitutes the misdemeanor charge of offensive touching), and they have a long history of domestic violence between them; she finally says "enough is enough" and reacts with some form of violence rather than call the police as she may have done in the past.

We see cross-charging quite a bit, where the police can't determine who the aggressor is: you know, he says that she scratched him and she says well, he hit me first and that's why I scratched him. And the police may cross-charge because they can't make a determination, which is real difficult for our office because then we have to mesh out who was the aggressor. And to tell you the truth, we can't always tell. A lot of time with cross-charges, we'll *nolle prosse* both of them because if we can't go into court and sustain a charge, figure out who the aggressor was, who the first person was who did it, then we really can't go forth on the charges. But we do see a lot of the scratching and a lot of slapping in the face [by women] and those are all true charges that can be brought against a person and we really have to look at whether we are going to pursue them or not. (social worker, prosecutor's office)[3]

Another problem identified by the prosecutors was that when both parties were arrested, often the man had the ability to make bail, but the woman could not. The perpetrator would not necessarily bail her out, thinking that this was a way to teach her a lesson. She might remain in jail four or five days until arraignment.

The issues raised by respondents concerning the court experience included women's unfamiliarity with the court process, their limited knowledge of their options, and their perception of themselves as powerlessness in the negotiation process. Women's legal problems were compounded once they arrived at court. Many respondents advised women who acted in self-defense to hold out for a trial. However, the process was not that simple: most women were not accustomed to being charged as an offender and they were mystified about the criminal justice process. Women were eager to get the case over with and return home; thus, they accepted a guilty plea without full appraisal of the consequences of having a record. These consequences could include being barred from certain employment opportunities, denial or loss of public housing, denial or loss of welfare benefits, immigration status problems, and problems related to custody hearings—all things which disproportionately harm women since they tend to be the primary caregivers (*Double-Time* 1998). In addition, respondents expressed concern that arrested battered women could be court-ordered to attend a treatment group designed for abusive men.

Women found the court process to be intimidating and stigmatizing:

Women have an awful lot of pressure put on them when they get to the courts to just plead guilty. But the women don't seem to understand that there are reasons why they might not be guilty, even though they did scratch his face. I have even had clients whose partners were on top of them and they were pushing his face away and they broke his glasses and got scratches on his face and the next day the woman gets arrested . . . (family court advocate)

Public defenders and prosecutors acted less as adversaries than as a friendly courtroom work group, ensuring the efficiency of case processing.

The public defenders are so accustomed to working with the attorney generals in negotiating the plea bargaining that they will really encourage the victim to go ahead and plea—it's just easier. It's faster and the victim will be taking a big chance in going into court and then if found guilty and then how about having a record . . .

Women were encouraged to plead guilty as first offenders, which placed them under probation supervision and mandated their attendance at a twelve-week treatment program.

I think a lot of people get screwed in that way, since they are really encouraged to plea guilty then they have it on their record or they get this first-offenders program through family court so that it won't end up on their record in the long run except for being arrested. It won't show up as a conviction so it won't affect their employment or if they were going to be found guilty then that's a good deal too, because then they are not going to have a conviction so that could affect them later. The whole thing is a big mess—who needs a record? And they don't know what is going to happen so they don't know if they should take the pleas . . . (director of shelter)

The social service providers and criminal justice professionals (with the exception of the public defenders and prosecutors) seemed to feel that both public defenders and prosecutors took advantage of the women's confusion and manipulated them into decisions that benefited their own positions by increasing their conviction rates or benefited the system's need to dispose of cases quickly.

It's very dehumanizing. The women already feel stigmatized by having been arrested, they don't understand the process . . . and I'm not gonna tell you it's all that different for men. The process often takes place in a waiting room, you are told what can happen if you chose to plead not guilty and are found guilty, and then they are told what they can do if they plead guilty . . . so a lot of women are buying into it because it seems like the simplest thing to do . . . they're afraid of going to jail . . . (treatment provider)

Respondents also felt that the attorneys strong-armed the women into accepting a guilty plea in exchange for what was presented as an ideal opportunity: "The women hear about this wonderful offender's program where you go to treatment and you are on probation for a year and then your charges will be expunged off your record, so they agree to the program, but they just don't have a clear understanding of what they are agreeing to" (victim services worker).

Shelter workers, victim services personnel, and treatment providers believed that the women would be better off going to court with self-defense justifications: "At least three-fourths of the time if they had taken it on to trial, they could have gotten out of the charge and been found not guilty" (shelter director). However, social service providers and other domestic violence advocates typically were not involved in the case at the arraignment stage since the women were not yet identified as victims. Consequently, the women did not receive any alternative information or encouragement to plead innocent. The arrested women were also very concerned about the time and money the process took; the program for first offenders offered an attractive option just at the point when the women were most vulnerable.

A treatment provider in the northern county believed there was a problem with the way options were presented and that women gravitated towards life preservers thrown at them: "You're told that you have a choice of going to jail or staying with your family, and maybe that language is what makes the difference." Women easily capitulated once they were threatened by having a criminal record and perhaps having their kids taken away from them. ". . . And for all practical purposes, you deem the women powerless and they believe themselves to be powerless. So consequently, if there's the remote chance that they are going to be convicted and they could lose their kids, they'll plead."[4]

There was tremendous pressure on the prosecutor's office to resolve cases with guilty pleas because there would be a guarantee:

> If a case goes into a court hearing, it's fifty-fifty that the judge could find them guilty or not guilty. If there is more than one charge, they could find them guilty of one, you know, split-the-baby where you find them guilty of one and not the other. But with a guilty plea, the person is definitely saying that he or she did *something*—not always that charge, but at least it is a guarantee. With a guilty plea, you don't have the appeal issue, because in family court there is actually a two-fold appeal. If you go in front of a commissioner, that charge can be appealed to a judge and then appealed to superior court. So it's like three times that it could be appealed. (social worker, prosecutor's office)

Since cases handled in family court can be appealed to superior court for a jury trial, the prosecutor's office acknowledged that this could result in a long, frustrating process and that the process itself wore people down. In reality, very few cases are appealed to superior court or end up actually going to trial. One social worker, who had been in her position for nine years, thought only three or four cases took this route.

In sum, the interview data also revealed that the respondents were very cognizant of the layers of confusion that surrounded the handling of women arrested for domestic violence. Police were under pressure to make arrests, yet respondents felt that the police did not spend the time necessary to distinguish between victim and offender behavior, which often resulted in a dual arrest. This victim-offender ambiguity was resolved to some extent by the prosecutor's office, but other issues emerged. In particular, women felt abandoned by their attorneys and threatened by the potential consequences if they did not accept a plea bargain, and their confusion was exacerbated by their lack of familiarity with the court process.

Common Themes

Comparing the themes that emerged during the police ride-along component of the study with the in-depth interviews conducted with criminal justice professionals and social service providers reveals a good deal of consensus, despite the fact that logistically, the police are introduced to citizens involved in domestic violence at a much earlier point in the process than public defenders, prosecutors, victim services workers, or social workers. Without exception, all the police officers from the ride-alongs and all the criminal justice professionals and social service providers expressed that women's violence was not on the increase, but rather that other factors accounted for the increase in women's arrests for domestic violence. Both groups offered similar explanations about the rise in arrests: the change in the state laws and corresponding police department policies that removed officer discretion to favor pro-arrest strategies.

The sample of criminal justice professionals and social service providers, however, offered additional insight about this. They claimed that the legal changes resulted in assessments of the violent encounters without context, since police were just focused on answering the question, "who hit," and clearing the call with an arrest. Very few police officers during the ride-along observations, however, acknowledged their failure to examine the contextual factors involved; a few officers were even adamant about how that examination was beyond the scope of their obligations. Excessive paperwork, a theme raised by both groups, exacerbated the problem because less time was available to conduct a more thorough investigation because officers were bogged down with filling out forms.

Respondents from both groups also agreed on the reasons underlying women's use of force. Most did not see women as primary aggressors, and no one felt that women were able to achieve the kind of power and control over their male partners that are typically in place in relationships where the male batters the female. The reasons for women's violence included her need to escape from the abuser, her frustration about her victimization, or her need for self-defense. Drugs and alcohol were also suggested as common antecedents to women's use of violence. What is most telling is how many respondents from both groups mentioned that they do not encounter male "victims" who are "bloody, bruised, and broken" the way they find female victims. Law enforcement officers mentioned that there were times that they felt badly about making an arrest of women, similar to the police ride-alongs, but they were equally quick to state that the law was intended to be gender neutral, and they would not practice selective enforcement if there was visible signs of injury on the man.

The most striking differences between the two groups involved beliefs about men's manipulation of domestic violence laws, dual arrests, and more generalized legal issues. During the ride-along phase, officers suggested that dual arrests were rare and, more than anything else, dual arrests indicated that police were not conducting a thorough enough investigation. If they were competent officers, their law enforcement skills would enable them to ferret out the primary aggressor in the situation and avoid arresting the victim. This understanding contrasted sharply with the data analyzed from the criminal justice and social service professionals, who believed that dual arrests have increased. These professionals placed the blame squarely on the officers' shoulders for over-enforcing the law and failing to look more closely at the context of the situation for fear of liability. The professionals in general also expressed greater concern about the consequences of arrest for women (inability to meet bail, greater willingness to plead guilty even if they acted in self-defense just to get home to the children or avoid jail time, diminished self-esteem, and so forth).

Many of the professionals believed that male batterers are finding more ways to manipulate the system in their favor through intimidation of their wives or girlfriends (e.g., using threats that they would lose custody of their children if they were arrested for fighting back), being the first to call 911 and define the situation to the police (claiming they were the victims), and even going as far as to self-mutilate to set up the woman as the violent person in their relationship. Only two officers in the ride-along study mentioned batterers' greater cognizance of how the system could be manipulated. This difference may reflect that the professionals hear stories from victims, whom they might have more frequent and sustained contact with, which could also include more information on the longevity of the relationships and the nature of those dynamics. In contrast, police officers experience a one-time contact with the parties involved, and do not have the time or interest in pursuing victim narratives about their relationship history.

Unlike the police from the ride-along study, the criminal justice and social service professionals talked at length about how the court process alienates victims and implicitly encourages them to accept a guilty plea just to ensure efficient case flow in order to satisfy the court's organizational needs. They expressed concern over the overall fairness of the process that begins with the false identification of the victim as the offender, continues the miscarriage of justice with the absence of both legal and advocacy resources available to the victim who is now officially designated as the offender, and finally facilitates the acknowledgement of guilt in order to halt the adjudicatory process and send the "offender" to a court-mandated treatment program originally intended for addressing male violence committed against women. However, this was one of the few aspects in which the two groups diverged. Overall, the consistency in perceptions, understandings, and experiences between the two groups was high. The respondents from both groups agreed on many things, yet their astute understandings of women's violence, of the role of legal and policy changes, of the backlash emanating from male batterers, and of the anomic criminal justice process did not result in any tangible challenges to the continued arresting and processing of female victims as offenders—certainly not enough to derail the next stage in the process, when women are mandated to female offender treatment groups that are modeled after batterer intervention programs intended for male batterers.

Drawing on the understandings gleaned from interviews with criminal justice professionals and social service providers, it is easy to follow the path of a woman arrested for domestic violence and see why she might plead guilty regardless of justifiable reasons for her use of violence. Rewarded for her willingness to plead guilty, she is presented with the opportunity for treatment by attending the female offender's program in lieu of jail. The next chapter explores the inner workings of the female offender's program and discusses the themes that emerge in the group sessions.

Chapter 6

A Day in the Life

Inside a Female Offender's Treatment Group

This chapter accomplishes two goals. First, it documents the process of a female offender's treatment group, and second, it describes the ongoing themes that characterize the sessions within an analytical framework. Each session consists of a ninety-minute block of time, and I have reconstructed a typical group meeting by using a compilation of several groups' transcripts. Redundancy is filtered out and readers have a more complete picture of the kinds of conversational exchanges that happen during the treatment sessions. The synthesis of several group sessions is the best representation of the kinds of issues that are raised and discussed by the women in the groups and the group facilitator. My aim here is simply to present a typical treatment session for women mandated to domestic violence offender programs and then to explore and analyze the issues that emerge from the pattern of the session.

Each of the three treatment groups met once a week for twelve weeks. In Location A (County B), there was a daytime group and a nighttime group. The groups commandeered a temporary home in a social service building in which there was a clerical office and several multipurpose rooms where community groups such as Alcoholics Anonymous met. In Location B (County C), there was one nighttime group. This group met in an old house that had been renovated for meeting space for the counseling agency. A family lived in the apartment upstairs, making the background noise loud at times. The room where the group actually met was what was formerly known as the parlor. Old wallpaper and furniture, banging radiators, and comfy chairs dominated this room. There was no sense of a sterile office environment (except, perhaps, for office supplies stored in the large bathrooms). Mary (a pseudonym), the facilitator, carried all of her paperwork, books, videos, handouts, brochures, and the cash box with her. In neither location were there signs announcing that the female offender's group met at that site.

The women trickled in from the parking lot, as close to the start time as possible. Some weeks, the women seemed genuinely glad to re-acquaint themselves with the other members; other weeks, the women approached the group room staring straight ahead, and moved glumly to their chairs. Part of this difference reflected how long the members had been together and how comfortable they felt with one another, while the other possibility was that the women felt frustrated or annoyed about being there. Women often had to negotiate hassles related to childcare, transportation, and other inconveniences prior to arrival at the group session. Most of the glumness dissipated as the meeting got underway.

Group Meeting Structure

The structure of the meeting followed a clear pattern each week. Group members knew to place their chairs in a circle prior to the start time. Each meeting ran an hour and a half. The first five to twenty-five minutes of the meeting consisted of "check in." As Mary told the group:

> I have found that the group check-in is probably the most important part of this program. You could rent a video or you could get a book and read. Or get an audiotape and listen to it. You could go down to the local library and get all the same information that I put out to you. But it's check-in time when you get to talk about what's going on for you individually that makes a difference for this program, and I've seen the groups done with it and without it.

Three tasks were accomplished during this time. First, Mary conducted record keeping, such as taking attendance and relaying information pertaining to a member's absences, money paid or owed, and so forth. Next, Mary introduced and welcomed any new members to the group; the new member would tell the group why she was there (what was she charged with—the "Reader's Digest version") and Mary—with other group members chiming in—would go over the group rules (e.g., no name calling; no drugs or alcohol; punctuality; excused absence policy). For the new members, their "Reader's Digest version" of the incident leading to their arrest was either short and sweet (if they were embarrassed to be there or shy), or vitriolic (if they were incensed that they were arrested and mandated to group treatment). The women could not minimize their actions since Mary held their case file (which included the charges as well as the probation officers' descriptions of the incident). Finally, Mary would go around the circle and ask a few check-in questions of each group member: "How was your week? Any issues with anger or violence? If so, how did you handle it?"

Obviously, the "check-in" time length varied, depending on how big the group was and how much had occurred in the members' lives in the past week. If any member was at her final session, Mary would tell her that she would need to do an evaluation and she would be asked to talk about her experiences in the group at the end of the session. Mary exercised the option of terminating a participant from the program if she was re-arrested or if she failed to adhere to the group's rules. Mary could also extend a member's length of participation, usually by six weeks, if she felt the member had not absorbed the curriculum. Mary worked in tandem with each member's probation officer, and could recommend extending the program or could present accolades to the probation officer about the member's progress. Members were also welcome to call Mary during the time between meetings for additional information or other assistance.

When Mary walked into the room, many of the women's faces relaxed (because they knew the session would start) and others clamored for her attention so they could receive answers or kudos regarding events that happened during the past week. Rarely was there a woman who exuded outright hostility. Mary established a folksy rapport with the women; she lived in the same town or a nearby town as many of the women in two of the groups and attended graduate school near the other group's location. She was not clinical in her approach or with her language, and was apt to provide a lot of examples from her own life experiences of her family, herself, or her friends. The women could relate to Mary and felt comfortable talking with her. Yet at the same time, Mary did not pretend that she had walked a mile in their shoes: she was clear about being in a long-term, happy, non-abusive marriage. Her insights came from years of working in a shelter and running support groups for victims of domestic violence, as well as other experiences in her social worker occupation. I believe her honesty and sharing of some personal stories went a long way in establishing trust with the women in the groups. Mary was able to laugh at herself and this freedom was contagious as the weeks went on.

Mary would make eye contact with each woman as they walked through the door or as she assembled her paperwork. She took notes during the group meetings, and ensured that everybody introduced themselves so that the women would learn each other's names.

Reconstruction of a Typical Group Meeting

"Hello Everybody! As always, my name is Mary and you can reach me at this number. Don't just call the main office because I won't get the message until much later," says Mary in her initial greeting. "Because I'm the world's worst with names, as we go around the room if you could be nice enough to say your first name and just to tell about how your week has been as far as anger and domestic violence or any other situation that may have arisen that you're feeling some stress about or might need the support of the group." Mary explains to the new women in the group that this is the pattern they follow with every meeting.

MARY: On the first night you are here, you get a chance to say what you were arrested for, what you ended up with, and basically your version of the incident. Let's start over on this side of the room.

TERESA: My name is Teresa. I had a pretty good week.

MARY: So, what does a pretty good week for you right now mean, Teresa? Because a pretty good week eleven weeks ago was probably very different.

TERESA: We haven't been fighting a lot or arguing so we're doing OK. If he says something, I guess I just try and learn how to deal with it a little better. You know, like using the time out thing and stuff like that. That's really been helpful to me because trying to argue with somebody who's hardheaded, you're not going to get anywhere.

MARY: Probably we wouldn't want to call anybody hardheaded. We have a couple of rules here, and one of them is that you can't use any derogatory terms.

TERESA: Well, let me see. How would you put it then?

MARY: Just for Vicki's [new member] sake, what are the rules?

(At this point, most of the women chime in, reeling off the rules of the group.).

MEMBER: Don't put yourself down or call yourself any type of bad names.

MEMBER: Don't let anyone drop you off or pick you up.

MARY: They can drop you off or pick you up. But, they can't come into the building with you. They can't wait out in the parking lot for you.

MEMBER: No drinking, no drugs.

MARY: If I suspect that you've been using these types of substances, you will not be allowed to attend the meeting.

MEMBER: Confidentiality.

MARY: What goes on in the group stays in the group. Who you meet at this group stays in the group. If you see anybody out in public, unless she told you in here that it's OK to speak to her, you cannot speak to her out in public. Why? Because how would she explain how you know each other?

(Mary goes on to explain that if she sees a group member in the community—and she runs into a lot of them at the local Wal-Mart—she will not acknowledge them unless they speak to her first. She explains, "I'm not being stuck up. It's the policy of this program. Feel free to speak to me. I leave it up to you. I've had situations where people haven't felt comfortable and that's fine. It's whatever you're comfortable with. But I will caution you that my family and my friends do know what I do for a living. They may suspect that's how I know you. But I have a very complicated life and so I might know you through some other avenue.").

MARY: How about you, Barbara, any problems with anger this week?

BARBARA: Things seem to be better.

MARY: In what way?

BARBARA: I guess because whatever we've been doing in group, I tried. I did have that talk with him about how he makes me feel.

MARY: The "I" statements . . . Aren't you glad that you did that? Cool, everyone, give her a hand. (clapping) So how did that work for you?

BARBARA: Well at first he kind of just was, well we'll talk about this later, and he tried to brush me off, and I said OK because I was trying not to be bitchy about it, you know. Then I started talking about it later, in a technical way. And he asked why did it happen? What exactly did he do to make me feel like that? He don't remember too much because of him drinking. He's not drinking now and he's bored out of his mind. 'Cause he drinks when he plays music so when his friends are in the room what they do is drink beer and jam until they pass out. He's just like, it's really hard to change your whole life like that.

MARY: It's not an easy thing to cope for someone who has a problem with alcohol. One thing you might want to do is make sure he's got something in his hand. A Coke or a 7-Up. Hopefully, when all the other guys are drinking, that will be OK, or he may need to distance himself from his friends, which is really going to be tough for him 'cause he plays music.

BARBARA: He is so bored; he just walks around the house, following me, asking what should he do?

MARY: So, one of the things you might want to do is talk to him about it.

BARBARA: Well, I told him "I really appreciate what you're going through."

MARY: So you're being supportive of him. That's great. Just realize that if you don't change the things that trigger patterns of behavior, you're going to slide right back into those same habits because habits are hard to break. Addiction is a habit. It's something your body has gotten used to. But we're real proud for you that you're trying this and we hope that it works for you, and I strongly suggest Al-Anon for you. They have a lot of suggestions about how do you handle things when your partner is not drinking for the first time and he's acting bored. They may have suggestions that I don't know because that's what they do all the time. Wanda, how's your week been?

WANDA: Last week, I was really stressed because it was the last week of classes, but I hopefully made an A in that class.

MARY: Give her a hand! (clapping)

WANDA: I don't know. No conflict with my husband. I am supposed to go and meet him and get my name off of the truck title.

MARY: All right, so then you're still looking out for yourself then.

WANDA: Oh yeah!

MARY: Jane, you get your evaluation tonight since next week is your last week here. Are you still working on your plans?

JANE: Yeah, I know what I've got to do. I know what I want to do but if it doesn't work out, I can accept that, too. I want to be happier but if it doesn't work out, then I'm outta there. If he can't accept the things that I want to do or if he can't treat me like a human being, then he can leave 'cause I'm not leaving.

MARY: And you know your options?

JANE: Yes. I'm smart enough to not get arrested again, to not let it happen like that again. I mean, I did do what I did, but I was forced to, you know. But I do know the way the law is now, and how things go. You have to be careful how you handle situations.

MARY: So if I hear you correctly, what you are telling me is that you were able to recognize what was an abusive situation and that if you find yourself in a car with him again and he starts berating and choking you . . . well, what would you do if you found yourself in the exact same situation?

JANE: I guess what I can do is, 'cause I know how he can get, I won't be running my mouth. I have a problem with my mouth. He starts it and I finish it. Because I have that much of a temper, but I've spent all these years trying to argue with someone that there's no sense arguing with. He won't change but I can change.

MARY: Fill out the evaluation form and return it next week. Be as truthful and honest as you can. Please answer all the questions. If there is something you like about the program, that's fine. If there's something you don't like, put that down too. We really want honest answers. We change things based on what people put on the evaluations. Who's next with check-in? Jen?

JEN: Friday, my son's father came to pick him up. You know he's been picking him up 'bout almost three or four months now, but I didn't want to see him. What can I do about him just popping in whenever he feels like it? He kept my son up Sunday night until 11:30 p.m. and he has to go to school on Monday. Why don't I go to family court? I don't have the money to keep going to family court and pay the $40 for the filing fee. I want him to see my son but the things he does are crazy.

MARY: How about using the visitation center? It's here, in this building, on the other end.

(Mary explains that the visitation centers allow for drop-off and pickup of children, or supervised visitation on the premises with the non-custodial parent, without the possibility of running into an ex-partner. The rules are such that if the designated pickup person is fifteen minutes late, he forfeits his time with the child. This way, any game-playing is diminished and the visit is really about the child, and not about manipulating the situation to cause hardship for the mother. Mary also encourages the women to keep a record of events like this, when a former partner fails to show up or evades other responsibilities—she calls it "journaling." Keeping track of these incidents helps in establishing a paper trail for the court. A number of the women express worries about parental kidnapping, so Mary explains the benefits of using the visitation center so that the risks are decreased. Mary also explains the difference between anger management classes, which is a six-week program, and domestic violence offender programs, which run sixteen weeks and are designed for men arrested for intimate partner abuse. She also tells the group about the state's resources available for children who need counseling.)

Fern, a new woman, begins telling a convoluted story describing why she ended up arrested.

FERN: I had to give him back money from my tax refund; he lived with me so I claimed him. I bought a new car with the money. But I sold my old car, which was in bad condition, and now he wants the money. So we argued over that. Then we got into it that I hadn't been sticking to the rules with my daughter, but he's not around. I'm like, that's not my problem. I'm at an age where, I mean, I'm not very old. I'm not even thirty yet but I want a family. I want a marriage. I want a life, something I can call my own. Someone who will be there for me and it's just not happening with him. I asked him, "Do you know where you're going to be at five years down the road?" and he said, "No, it might be just like it is now." I'm not living that way. He needs insulin shots and he has a lot of medical problems, but that's not the problem, I want something more stable. He wants me to be a home nurse and I can't do that. Enough is enough.

MARY: As long as you are OK with it; as long as you can handle it non-violently.

FERN: I am just worried about my daughter. He hasn't really been around, so maybe she'll be OK.

MARY: Domestic violence has an impact on children. How you handle it is how she is going to handle it. Lucky that she's already in counseling. You might want to give the counselor a heads-up that something's coming 'round the bend.

FERN: She's acting like a baby again.

MARY: You can't expect the perfect child. You can expect to have a regressed child. A four-year-old might go back to sucking his thumb or wanting a bottle. Go back to diapers. It depends on the children and how they deal with it. How they cope with it. It's a lot like adults: how we feel and how we cope with a situation.

(a silence while Mary looks over her clipboard)

MARY: How many of you have done your homework assignment? For the new people, the first assignment asks you to look at your relationship. Our whole program is based on the fact that domestic violence is a learned behavior and the basis for it is power and control: who is doing that in a relationship is always what's in question. We ask you to take one color highlighter and highlight any behavior you've done from the list on the page. Take another color highlighter, and highlight any behavior your partner has done. If both of you have done a behavior, it will turn into a third color since the two highlighters will overlap. Also, let me know if you need any assignments you are missing.

(Mary explains that it is not her responsibility to keep up with their homework; she merely has to check off that they completed the assignments when it is "graduation" time. The treatment agency provides a letter of completion to the court, written by Mary, and it will not be sent if the woman's file is not complete.)

> MARY: If you do not feel safe taking any of the assignments home with you, please let me know after group. I will make arrangements for you to come in early to do it here or to stay afterwards a little bit. I do not want anyone to feel like they are putting themselves in jeopardy doing their homework.

(Next, Mary introduced a video they will watch from the 20/20 TV news show on female offenders.)

> MARY: It's about women who have been arrested for domestic violence. Who does that sound like? Does it describe you? I want you all to watch it, then afterwards, we're going to critique it. So listen carefully and then let me know what you think about this video.

(The group watches the video, which runs about thirty minutes; there are audible sighs of understanding as well as expressions of outrage throughout the program from the women. When it ends, Mary asks the group what they thought of it).

> AUDREY: I know there was a lot of Hollywood role-playing going on, but I'd get knocked on my butt if I did something like what the women did in that.
> MARY: Someone said you could identify. What is it you could identify with?
> AUDREY: I see myself as being like some of those women. Like, the physical violence is just the end product of being upset that he was with another woman.
> MARY: How many of you grew up in a home with domestic violence or a very controlling situation? OK—that's half of the group. How many of you prior to this relationship or in your current relationship had a partner who was abusive to you? Have you ever had a partner physically abuse you in the past or does this partner physically abuse you prior to your being violent to him?
> AUDREY: He bats me around and I defend myself but he just laughs.

MARY: We look at domestic violence here as being about power and control. How many of your partners were afraid of you? How many of your partners changed their behavior or changed their appearance, changed their job, changed something about them because of fear of what you would say or do to them?

LEE: Well, my partner cut off his dreadlocks but not because he was scared of me. I told him he couldn't be in any pictures with my daughter anymore unless he cut his hair.

MARY: Is the partner afraid of you? Do they change their behavior because of things that you've said or done? According to the federal government right now, 95 percent of domestic violence is still done by men to women. The woman is the primary victim. Out of that 5 percent remaining, about 2 percent are going to be gay and lesbian relationships, that leaves 3 percent. Of that 3 percent, probably about 2 percent are real victims. The other 1 percent involves women who are violent on the streets, to their friends, their neighbors, their mothers, etc. There are violent women in this world. So, where do you fall in here? You're not men, so you're not in the 95 percent group.

SARA: What about me? My nephew came home drunk Saturday night.

MARY: How old is he?

SARA: Nineteen. And I kept telling him to go to bed, get out of my face, and I don't take my husband disrespecting me and he kept calling me a bitch and cunt, so then he grabbed me by the throat and set me on the sink, and I took a lid from my pot and just struck him and said, "Get out of my house! My husband threw you out Friday." We felt bad 'cause you know he don't have nowhere to go. But I am tired of taking care of this kid. He's a grown man. He's old enough to go down the street and work and pay his own bills and stuff like instead of living off us.

MARY: I guess I am concerned that the situation got as violent as it did and that it got to the point that the arguing escalated to him grabbing you by the throat and with you hitting him with a pan. Also, you realize you just violated your contract with our agency.

SARA: What? When? It wasn't my husband and me.

MARY: You contract says that you can't use violence with any person.

SARA: But what was I supposed to do? What else was I supposed to do?

MARY: Let's go back. Before it got to his hand around your throat. Walk me though it.

SARA: Well, he kept sitting there calling me names and I said, "Look Jim, you're nineteen years old. I'm not your mother; I'm not your sister. I'm your aunt. I don't allow my husband to call me them names. If anybody was going to call me names it would be him [my husband] because he earned that right." He shouldn't disrespect me, so I told him, "You can just get your stuff and get out. Your mother don't even want you." We've had him since he was born.

MARY: Now he's drunk, right?

SARA: Yes.

MARY: OK, so you're arguing with a drunk.

SARA: I wasn't really arguing. I just told him to get out; I didn't want him here.

MARY: You're arguing with a drunk. You're trying to tell him things and it's going to go in one ear and right out the other. You can't argue with a drunk.

SARA: I know that. It was more that I just wanted him to get out of my house.

MARY: But trying to tell him all the reasons, what the problems are isn't going to work when someone is drunk. (OK, can't whisper in group; that's one of the rules.) You can't argue with a drunk. What happened after you went through all these explanations telling him to get out?

SARA: I told him that I was gonna call his mom and tell his mom to send him some money so he could go down to Florida and let his stepfather and mother finally deal with him. And then when I went to pick up the phone, that's when he pushed me and I said, Jim, don't touch me."

MARY: Anyone have any suggestions for Sara?

SARA: I don't want to call the cops on him.

MARY: Why not?

SARA: 'Cause he's nineteen and I'm more like his mother.

MARY: He's an adult. He's making poor choices. He has put you at risk for violating your probation and for violating your contract with this program. So you got yourself jammed up by letting your situation escalate. OK? One of the things we talk about in this group is looking to see what happens in a situation so that you keep yourself from being put at risk. If you were further along in the program, I'd probably be excluding you from the group. My concern is that this could have gotten yourself killed. It's rough, especially when you're working with a relative, someone you care about. But when the person is an alcoholic, by allowing him to stay in your residence, he's affecting all of you and you're not helping him.

SARA: We tried to talk him into going to a program, but we can't force him.

MARY: But you can't enable him to continue. I know Kelly's been through programs—maybe you could help me out here.

KELLY: He's like, living in a fog. By letting him stay, he has a place he can come crash to after he's been drinking. He doesn't have to worry about living on the streets or being in a homeless shelter, which, if anyone has ever lived in a homeless shelter, they are not fun. You can't stay in the building during the day, after you do your chores in the morning, you have to be out looking for a job, and that includes when it's raining.

MARY: Do you see where you put yourself at risk? Because if I stuck to the letter of our contract, you'd be terminated at this point. When you abuse somebody and you're in this program, you are terminated. Since you are at the beginning and are doing fairly well in group, I'll put it aside. I figured that's what we're here for, to work on these issues. One of the things you may want to think about is boundaries. That if he shows up on your property and he's been drinking anything, he's not allowed on your property.

SARA: I told him if he can't come home by midnight, then don't come in but he said he'll break through the window.

MARY: If he does, then you call the police. You call the police. If someone is calling you names, threatening you, trying to do harm to you, you pick up the phone and you call 911. OK?

SARA: My husband could, but neither one of us wants to get violent about it 'cause we've been doing so well in our marriage that we don't want anyone else to bring us down.

MARY: In the long run, you really didn't help him by not calling the police. And you really put yourself at risk. I am concerned, but we're going to work through it. We're out of time. I will see you all next week. Have a good one. Let me know if anyone needs any homework papers.

(The group session is over.)

Analysis and Emergent Themes

Since very few studies exist that describe the inner workings of women's treatment programs, and no outcome studies have been conducted, it is difficult to know whether the format of this program is effective or even consistent with other existing programs. Overall, as the transcripts indicated, the program environment was one that helped participants to understand and manage their emotional lives and experiences. They shared conflict management strategies and problem-solving, with suggestions made by the group facilitator Mary as well as other group members. The facilitator prodded the women to take responsibility for their thoughts and behaviors, and offered positive reinforcement when presented with examples of growth.

In many ways the content of the female offender's program examined in this state resembled the curriculum discussed by Lynn Dowd (2001) as implemented in a Massachusetts anger management treatment program. The organization of the sessions' curriculum was similar—a check-in period of thirty minutes or so where the women have the opportunity to discuss the past week, followed by presentation of new material. Anger management facilitators offered resource lists of needed services for the women, and paid particular attention to the relevance of a variety of factors pertinent to the women's lives that might sabotage their success with anger management, such as depression, substance abuse, and drinking by the women or their partners.

Mary educated the women about making "I" statements, an example of an effective communication skill also endorsed in the anger management program. "The differences between passive, assertive, and aggressive behavior are demonstrated, and the women brainstorm the characteristics of each, including quality of voice, choice of words, physical posture, and overall nonverbal messages" (Dowd 2001, 95). This exercise is novel to the women, who may never have seen problems worked out through the use of words by family members in their childhood.

In addition, anger management facilitators in both programs (here and in Massachusetts) raise the fact that increasing women's assertiveness may disrupt power balances in their current relationships, so women have to be prepared for dealing with the repercussions of a partner who might be threatened by the change in her behavior. Dowd (2001) describes how stress management and relaxation techniques are used, which include progressive muscle relaxation and guided imagery exercises (p. 95). Mary also used such techniques at different points in the twelve-week program. Since most treatment programs that are being used with women who have used force in their relationships draw upon elements of the popular Duluth model (discussed in chapter 3), it is not surprising that they share similar content, structures, and techniques.

Listening to women's stories and their perceptions and descriptions of their experiences can provide the context in which later policy decisions and implementation are generated. Through an analysis of women's characterizations of their experiences, the rhetoric, or hype, about women's use of violence can be checked with reality. Although ostensibly a program designed to treat female "offenders," most of the weekly sessions in the three groups observed were disproportionately spent addressing the larger context of the arrests and how they affected women's daily lives; much less time focused on the women's specific domestic violence incidents that led to their arrests.

The female offender's program uses the weekly therapeutic environment to discuss salient issues to ensure group members' forward movement and to help them change their behaviors. Anger education—how to recognize anger, discussions of prevention and management of such emotions, and the creation of alterative strategies to anger—was the dominant theme of each session. Weaving in and out of anger-related discussions were three other prominent themes: the effects of domestic violence on children; support networks and resources; and criminal justice system experiences.

ANGER

The women discussed their lives each week, and how they faced much stress and many frustrations due to their arrests. The effects were cumulative, and included inconvenience associated with finding transportation or childcare during session times, the gloating some received from their partners, their indignation about being arrested in the first place, ongoing financial difficulties, and conflict within their social networks and with their partners or former partners. The group facilitator Mary, while not sanctioning anger that caused poor choices of behavior, placed anger in a context that made the emotion acceptable to feel under certain circumstances. Making angry feelings normative assisted in opening the women up to talk about their general experiences with anger, including events that did not lead to their arrests. The quote below illustrates a typical way that Mary discussed anger and its appropriateness:

> It's OK to be angry, but sometimes it's the way we express it and the way we handle it, when anger boils up, that's the problem. For women, it's the one emotion that we're taught growing up, that it's not appropriate for women to be angry. So lots of women tend to push it down inside and they don't know how to express is. We've learned that it's a man's world and we keep a lot of this stuff in and sometimes what happens is over the years it builds up and builds up and builds up, so you really become an angry person; inside you're angry, so the littlest things make you go off. That's what we're talking about here. When you stuff and stuff and stuff things inside, until you are a walking volcano, waiting to explode. We need to think about this, figure out how to deal with the little things before they become big explosions.

It was common for the women during check-in to describe potentially volatile incidents they had experienced in the past week, telling the group if they averted an explosion and how this was accomplished, or if they resorted to old behavioral patterns. Often, the women shared the outcome of the situation, relating it back to strategies learned in group, such as "taking a time-out" and "self-talk" (talking yourself through the dilemma, considering the options). The following illustrates a typical dialogue between a group member and Mary:

> JAYNE: I had a good week, except we're wall papering our kitchen and yesterday I had a real problem with anger because the wallpaper would not go on straight no matter what he did. I ripped it off the wall, crying . . .
>
> MARY: So after you ripped it off the wall and you were angry, how did you get calmed down?
>
> JAYNE: I just went and sat down.
>
> MARY: Like a time-out?
>
> JAYNE: Yeah, I took some time away from it.
>
> MARY: So your self-talk worked.
>
> JAYNE: Yeah.
>
> MARY: Instead of going off, you were talking to yourself coolly and logically. You took a timeout and you didn't take out your anger and frustration on your husband. You said to him, "Don't talk to me for a moment; I am taking a time out," which is OK.

Mary acknowledged that anger is a part of life, but choosing what one does with that anger is important. Her style was not pedantic; she spoke to the women without condescension, but with an eye toward empowerment:

> Frustration and anger often go hand in hand. So please don't think your coming to group means you are going to walk out at the end and never be angry again. Anybody who does think that I'd be worried about. So please know that I am not going to be concerned if you come in and tell me you got angry about something this week. That's OK, but what did you do with that anger? Did you use it or did you abuse it? This is part of being assertive; the way you raise your self-esteem by being open and direct about how you feel inside. It is taking a risk. It is also setting up boundaries. By letting someone know you are angry, you're letting them know they're pushing your buttons and you're saying this is how far you can go before I will get angry . . .

In discussing anger, one of Mary's techniques was to have the group explore the physical signs conveyed by their bodies. For instance, women talked about getting headaches, feeling nauseous, pacing the floor, shaking, stomach tightening, lack of hunger, and insomnia. Mary used these symptoms to demonstrate that there are early warning signs to pay attention to, and she encouraged women to think about their individual anger cues. Many women talked about using these early warning signs as wake-up calls to change or leave the situation.

The women had a homework assignment to write down any physical signs of anger in the subsequent week. The next week, they were amazed that they recognized their personal cues. Mary would follow up at this second discussion with a guided imagery relaxation exercise, having members close their eyes, focus on breathing, and listen to her reading relaxation messages designed to relieve stress. In the weeks following these sessions, members would voluntarily refer back to these discussions, using physical cues to recognize and sometimes avert anger.

When a member told the group about successful responses to situations that pushed her buttons and made her angry, Mary emphasized the healthy change in dealing with such difficult emotions. She encouraged the group to give the member a round of applause, reinforcing her progression. When a member was stuck in responding with old behavior patterns, Mary choreographed role-playing in addition to eliciting suggestions from other group members. Rather than castigating or judging women when they talked about anger, Mary gave constructive ideas and encouragement. New members heard about courage and behavioral changes from old members, as well as a spirit of optimism concerning gaining control over one's powerfully felt emotions.

CHILDREN

As evidenced by how often (every session) clients raised the issue of children, the women were or became increasingly aware of the impact of domestic violence on children. Discussions focused on how to address children's fears and "acting out" behavior, and how to empower themselves to be better parents. Part of the program included using handouts that provided exercises to uncover the connections between individuals' feelings and how these affect children. Mary explained:

> These handouts are the same tools a lot of therapists use in client therapy. This helps you to get more insight into yourself and to hopefully grow as a person. Then, you can pass on something different to your kids. And that's the real important thing . . . that we are trying to pass on something different.

Mary provided a lot of information (through group discussion, videos, and handouts) about the effects on children when they hear or see battering in their homes:

> When you see children acting out, a lot of times it is because that is how they can express their anger. They don't know how to say "I am

really mad that my dad is not here, and I am really mad at you because I think it is your fault." They just don't know how to say those things. They have it all bottled up inside and all they know to do is to kick and scream and carry on and have a temper tantrum and not go to bed, and fight you all the way.

Unrelated to domestic violence, additional problems with children were raised constantly by group members, who solicited assistance from other group members who may have encountered similar problems. For instance, one group member told the group that her eighteen-month-old son was waking up crying every night at 3 a.m. Other members asked questions about sleeping habits, offered information about what they did when faced with the same problem, and discussed whether he was at the age when children begin to experience nightmares. Having children acted as a bonding element between the women: announcements of pregnancies were celebrated with cheers and clapping, photographs of children were passed around, and so forth.

Another common issue involved children whose fathers were incarcerated. Mary and group members provided helpful information about prison video hookups as a way to visit, transportation, how to talk about other issues with the children, and how to negotiate relationships between children and the women's new partners or husbands.

The common ground—motherhood—offered a safe avenue to solidify group dynamics. When these discussions about children occurred, and seemed sometimes unrelated to domestic violence, Mary often made comparisons between the larger issues and how abusive homes or parents affect children.

SOCIAL SUPPORT NETWORKS AND RESOURCES

Another theme that emerged was the resource referrals made by the group facilitator. Whenever a member raised an issue where she faced strain or trouble, Mary provided multiple suggestions, including names, phone numbers, and addresses if needed, for members to pursue. She was a wealth of information, and it was extremely clear that most of the women were hearing about some of these resources for the first time. They asked for paper or pulled out a scrap of paper from their purses to write down contact information. They called Mary during the week with follow-up questions and for advice. Routinely, group members chimed in with their experiences and information about agencies or advocates who had provided help. Since most of these women had never been residents at battered women's shelters and, in fact, had never shared some of their frustrations about their children or other family members or their poverty circumstances before, this information was invaluable.

Although this list is not exhaustive, some of the resource material include children's psychiatrists; family social workers; an agency that handles mental health issues for elderly parents; help with getting an insurance card to pay for a child's medicine; consumer affairs; child support enforcement; getting Protection From Abuse orders (PFAs); shelters; GED; colleges; Alcoholics Anonymous, Narcotics Anonymous, and Al-Anon (the support group for friends and family of alcoholics); and all kinds of criminal justice system help (e.g., questions about police, probation, public defenders).

The advantage of a group setting meant that women were able to share resource information as well as their frustrations and triumphs. The women openly appreciated Mary's willingness to spend group time giving practical information about social service agencies and criminal justice issues, and seemed more relaxed about participating in the group as a whole. Information exchanged allowed better rapport to be established, and Mary was not just dismissed as the authority figure but instead recognized as someone who cared about their situation and played an active role in helping the women negotiate through the mazes of their lives.

CRIMINAL JUSTICE SYSTEM

As discussed in chapter 5, the interviews with social service providers and criminal justice professionals revealed many concerns about police behavior and legal decision making and case processing that were echoed by the women's conversations in treatment groups. The most common issue raised by women was their lack of familiarity with the criminal justice process, leaving them vulnerable to manipulations by their abusive partners' threats or outright lies and to the consequences of accepting a guilty plea. Wanda's and Deidre's cases illustrate this commonality. Although Wanda said she was told at arraignment that she didn't have to plead guilty, she "didn't know what would happen to my kids. He wouldn't watch them. I just wanted to get home and the first offender's program sounded like a good deal so I wouldn't go to jail." Deidre had a similar situation. Her public defender told her the charges she faced, and "I stood in front of the judge and they read off what was on the police report and then asked me was it true. And I said yes. They charged me." Deidre had never been arrested before and had a long history of victimization; in contrast, her husband had a criminal record with several domestic violence charges.

The first offender's program provided an option for women who had no prior domestic violence convictions. (Women were often still eligible for treatment even if they were not first offenders, and they received the same deal.) Under this program, they received probation for a year that mandated specific conditions, such as attending the female offender's program or the substance abuse program. Faced with the option of the first offender's program and, upon successful completion (with no new charges incurred), expungement of the arrest from their records,[1] many women grabbed it, regardless of the consequences or whether they would have been successful with a self-defense defense.

Very few women pled not guilty. Tammy initially pled not guilty for the charge of possession of a deadly weapon and assault in the second degree. She had been assigned a public defender. However, her attorney changed several times, without her prior knowledge, and she had to keep going to court to deal with the case. When her employer threatened that she would lose her job if she kept taking time off, the public defender suggested, "Why don't you just plead guilty to third degree assault for a misdemeanor?" Tammy said, "And I decided I just wanted whatever it takes to get this thing over with so I don't lose my job. So, I took that and I started coming to these classes." Keesha pled not guilty because she did not like the plea bargain offered. She was one of the only two women (in six months of groups observed) who hired a private attorney.

On the whole, the women were unaware of potential negative consequences of pleading guilty. Mary explained to them that employment could be jeopardized because some jobs are based on whether the employee has a criminal record. For the majority of the women, this was the first time the aspects and consequences of the criminal justice system and case decisions were explained to them; they also had the opportunity to ask questions for the first time. For instance, Mary told them that they should have multiple copies of PFAs for their purse, their car, the house, and the kids' schools, and that they must make sure the seal is intact or police officers will not honor it. She explained the role of mediators in family court and what happens if PFAs are violated as well as a myriad of other case-related topics such as: the role of probation officers; advice and warnings about how not to violate PFA provisions by contacting their abusers; the use of visitation centers for ex-partners to see children; where to wait at the courthouse so they didn't have to face their abusers; how to keep a journal to establish a paper trail for a PFA if he had not been arrested before.

The women raised many legal questions. The majority of them were not represented by attorneys. They fell between the cracks, making too much money to qualify for a public defender, yet too little to afford a private attorney to represent them. For those women who were assigned a public defender, most said they felt shut down by the public defenders: the women had never met them before and the attorneys did not have much time for them and thus did not explain options and meanings behind choices the women needed to make about their case. From the women's comments, it was clear that they were intimidated by the process and by the attorneys.

The most common charge used to arrest women was "offensive touching." Most of the women did not understand the meaning of that charge, despite the fact that their case had already been processed, their plea entered, and punishment imposed (typically, probation with required attendance in the female offender's program and maybe the substance abuse program).

Rhonda described an incident where her husband tried to strangle her and she kicked him in his crotch so he would let go of her. He did let go, but then punched her in the face and locked her out of the house. When he finally let her back inside, she broke a lot of his CDs. He called the police as she destroyed the CDs and she was arrested. As Rhonda said, ". . . my understanding was that if we went to court and I told them I was protecting myself when I kicked him in his privates, I still would get in trouble for breaking the CDs . . . I didn't want a charge on my record so I took the program option so I could keep myself clean." In other words, a guilty plea for offensive touching allowed her to enter into the female offender's program with a possible dismissal of her conviction upon successful completion of the program; a criminal damage to property charge did not carry the possibility of a later conviction dismissal.

Amy felt that her attorney was mad at her for insisting she was guilty; he told her she could have gotten off on self-defense. This scenario was very rare, however, as self-defense was never mentioned by attorneys to most of the women.

A handful of women mentioned that a few police officers apologized to them during the arrests. Although not persuaded that their arrest was just, the women did feel better that the police treated them as potential victims who got somewhat unfairly ensnarled in a new policy. Many women discussed the embarrassment they felt when arrested in front of their children. Typically, in abusive situations the male partner or ex-partner was the one to leave with police, so this alternative scenario was foreign to the children and caused the children more anxiety in addition to the stigma the women experienced.

Prior emotional support or criminal justice system assistance from victim services personnel was lacking. Very few of the women had ever talked to victim services providers. For the counties addressed in the present research, part of the reason is that victim services providers are not routinely notified when women are arrested on domestic violence charges; hence, there is little or no involvement at the earliest stages of the criminal justice system, precisely when victim assistance may be most needed. Although women participated in the female offender's program and even noted some benefits they received from the program, most women were angry about being mandated to attend treatment programs when they felt that they were not the abusers. Their anger increased when they learned that program participation meant shelling out several hundred dollars in fees as well as the hassle of orchestrating transportation and childcare.

A final observation from the treatment groups seems relevant: after reaching their final session in week twelve, participants were invited to share with the group any comments about how the program had affected them. All but one of the women in the six months of observation chose to speak up. Overwhelmingly, the women spoke of several ways they felt changed by the program. First, the women said they realized that they made conscious choices about how to act or react in a given situation: "No one made me do it; I choose to do it." Second, they learned to recognize warning signs of simmering anger in themselves and in their partners, and how to handle these signs. Third, the women learned how to make "I" statements so their feelings weren't so "stuffed" inside them (e.g., "I feel unattractive when you make fun of my body."). The women also talked about their new understandings of their right to say "no" (e.g., to undesired sexual practices, to his rules) and the self-respect and validation that goes along with the ability to say "no." And finally, the women discussed strategies they learned to help deal with situations before they escalate into conflict (e.g., use of time-outs and walk-outs).

Discussion

The various themes that emerged from the weekly group sessions suggest that regardless of the punitive or coercive nature of court-ordered treatment, some good came out of the sessions. First, the supportive structure of the group and the facilitator's participation coalesced to create an environment conducive to women's growth and empowerment. Women not only received practical information about resources stretching far beyond domestic violence concerns, but also they learned to discuss "messy" issues such as anger or violence or jealousy in a manner that did not further demonize the women as "offenders," or not "good women." Second, the holistic approach was very beneficial. By placing violence and anger within a larger framework, women were able to discuss and figure out how anger and frustration triggered inappropriate emotional responses. Women openly discussed the vicissitudes of their daily lives and how violence affected their children, employment, and social and family connections. Finally, the sessions provided information about the criminal justice system to the women, which de-mystified a process over which the women felt ignorant and powerless.

I turn now to the next chapter, which explores the circumstances surrounding the use of force by women in the treatment groups and the categories derived from their stories.

Chapter 7	The Contexts of "Violent" Behavior

THIS CHAPTER EXPLORES the different types of behavior exhibited by women that led them to be arrested on domestic violence charges.[1] To reiterate some information about the research design from chapter 3, weekly participant observation of the three treatment groups was conducted over six months; ninety-five women attended the programs. Group sessions were tape-recorded and later transcribed. Following grounded-theory methods, themes were utilized only if they were discussed at length by at least three of the women in the groups.

Three uses of violence were identified in the data from the participant observation conducted with the treatment groups: generalized violent behavior, frustration response behavior, and defensive behavior. A coding validation method was used in the categorization whereby a colleague and I independently coded the incidents; there was virtually no disagreement over the three categories that emerged.

Generalized Violent Behavior

The first category, *generalized violent behavior*, included women who used violence in many circumstances, not just in intimate relationships, such as against neighbors, other family members, strangers, or acquaintances. This also accounted for the smallest number of women, five, comprising about 5 percent of the program's clients. Rather than selecting a representative slice of the stories from this category as I do in the discussion of the other two categories, I relate all five stories. What was consistent with this group of female "abusers" or "perpetrators" was that the nature of their violence differed from what is typically associated with "batterers." A batterer uses violence as a vehicle for getting his or her partner to do something. Often, the batterer operates with a sense of entitlement, and uses violence as a way to punish or control a partner. However, from what was observed, the women who used violence against intimate partners did not have control or power over the men, but used violence as an expression of anger. The women were not able to control or change men's behavior; in fact, the male targets did not fear them, nor change their behavior out of a sense of intimidation, responses that would be typical for female victims abused by men.

Linda's case typified this category. Linda was mandated to treatment based on three violent episodes; her current offense involved threatening a female neighbor for parking too close to her truck. Prior to this, Linda had attacked her wheelchair-bound uncle during a family quarrel as well as attacked her live-in boyfriend due to jealousy over another woman. She did not believe that her violence changed anyone's behavior. In the group sessions, Linda was argumentative and non-apologetic.

Another example is Tyra's story. Tyra and her husband were separated at the time of the incident and Tyra had a drug addiction. Although she never physically hit him, she was arrested for terroristic threats. Tyra does not have a history of victimization and she freely admitted that her husband, although emotionally distant and a workaholic, was not physically abusive. Here is how Tyra described the incident that brought her to the treatment group:

> TYRA: I went out partying and never came home and my husband was a little upset, and I threatened him.
> MARY: You threatened him? What did you threaten him with?
> TYRA: That I was gonna get somebody to come there and kill him. I didn't strike him or nothin'. But he called the cops. The next day, they came to my work. I ended up with a year probation, this program, and drug counseling.

Tyra saw this as a wake-up call and now attends both Alcoholics Anonymous and Narcotics Anonymous (and is on probation for a year); she and her husband are attempting reconciliation.

An example of violent behavior that follows a long history of victimization is present in Dawn's story. Dawn and her husband have two children together; his abuse began when she was five months pregnant with their first child. He choked her, beat her, held a gun to her head threatening to kill her, and drove the car at dangerously high speeds without letting her out. She had a civil protection order against him from one state, but he followed her to a contiguous state. Her mother and other family members encouraged her to try to make the marriage work, and they did reconcile; months later, she was pregnant with their second child. She left her son in his care one day, but when she came home, her husband was snoring on the couch while their son was screaming and crying. He mocked her and refused to answer any questions about the child. In the past, after he was violent and she called the police, each time he ran to the woods and hid, so he never had actually gotten arrested. Suspecting the worse, afraid for her own safety, and mad as hell, she ordered him out of the house.

> I went to the kitchen; I got a knife and threatened to kill him from the other side of the door. I didn't know what I was doing with the knife 'cause I really didn't want to hurt him but he went to grab for my hand and when I switched the knife over, it cut his thumb. He got that cleaned up and he went down to the gas station and called the police on me. They came and asked me if I had cut him. Actually, they said "stabbed" him. He also had lacerations on this chest and his back. I have no idea how they got there. I know that I didn't do it with the knife. But they charged me with possession of a deadly weapon and assault in the second degree. They put me in handcuffs in front of my son.

Another woman, Carole, argued frequently with her husband about his lack of help with her ten-year-old stepson. Most of the violence that occurred in the household stemmed from both people's frustration with parenting issues. She does not describe herself as a battered woman, nor does she describe her husband as an abuser. Here is her description of her arrest:

> I picked up a globe and I threw it at my husband, and he didn't think to just throw something but instead he put his hands on my throat. When he let me up, I went to the bedroom and I was trying to get to my suitcase 'cause I was going to pack and leave. I was throwing things across the room and the mirror fell off the door. I don't know how it come off and I threw it against the wall. My husband heard glass breaking and he called the police. He said it wasn't his intention to have me arrested. He just wanted them to come in and talk to me. But we were both arrested for domestic violence.

The final example from the generalized violence category involved Sandra Lee and her second husband of many years. She described herself as a battered wife in her first marriage and a target of her current husband's abuse for over ten years. She said that both of them had serious drug addictions to cocaine and Valium. She was arrested for endangering the welfare of a child because her daughter was present during following incident:

I was using cocaine, Valium, and blacking out periodically. I went to get some more while he was out of it [from the drugs]; we had been fighting all weekend and I am not a violent person. But he started on me and I guess something just snapped because he wouldn't give me the car keys. I don't really remember all of what happened; I had had a lot of Valium, and I took a knife out of the kitchen drawer and my intent was to slit the tires on the car. When he seen me in that state, he took the knife out of my hands and he flipped out. My daughter was in the house. She flipped out. He called 911 and I was arrested and charged and the judge sent me to [a residential drug treatment center] for seventeen days.

When Sandra Lee came home, she was clean and sober, and found another woman with her husband in her house. She responded calmly, telling the woman to leave and telling her husband to pack his bags and get out. Then she took her daughter and went to stay with her mother. She remains in recovery, attending substance abuse sessions four times a week, and she and her husband are separated; he has remained a drug user.

These examples suggest that far from being a batterer (in the conventional sense of the word), these women used violence in a response to a volatile situation, and the consequences were negligible. They were not successful in establishing or reestablishing control or power over their partner or former partner as a result of their actions. Only one woman had a long history of victimization. In three of the five cases, physical violence was not directed solely towards a partner (one case involved threats; another woman was violent toward three people; another woman threw an object). These three women were not victims of battering nor enmeshed in violent relationships. They were angry and could not control their actions. In later group sessions, they described additional incidents when they used violence outside the intimate context. While the remaining two women, Dawn and Sandra Lee, were battered women, their use of violence in the specific incidents were not preceded by violence by their partners. Again, it is important to note the rarity of this behavior: five women from the six months of observation of three treatment programs.

Frustration Response Behavior

Approximately 30 percent (twenty-eight women) of the sample comprise the second category, *frustration response ("end of her rope") behavior*. These women often had histories of domestic abuse (with their current partners or in earlier relationships) and reacted violently when nothing else seemed to stop the partners' behavior. Typically, the women responded to stressful situations or encounters with partners that might lead to violence. These women were different from the first category of offenders (generalized violence) because they overwhelmingly exhibited violent behavior with a partner who was abusive (emotionally, sexually, and physically) toward them. In some cases, the man was the primary aggressor, but the woman responded with violence.[2] The case of Kelly exemplifies the frustration response category. Kelly left an abusive sixteen-year marriage with Tim. When her new boyfriend Danny started becoming emotionally abusive, she flashed backed to what emotional abuse in her marriage had led to. (Tim's emotional abuse had typically led to both sexual abuse and physical battering.) Kelly was hitting her boyfriend with both hands, causing no injury, when a neighbor called the police to report the noise.

An example of a case involving a stressful situation in which there was no known history of abuse is Sheila and Bobby. Sheila and her husband Bobby were drinking at a local bar. He was flirting and dancing with another woman that Sheila hardly knew. Sheila got on the dance floor and punched Bobby on his shoulder and threw her drink at him. Although her actions caused no injury, Bobby was humiliated in front of his friends; his brother called the police.

Eunice's situation epitomizes the frustration response category. In her words:

> I was charged with offensive touching. My husband and I got into an argument one night because the baby had a diaper rash and it was really, really late and he didn't feel like it was important to get the diaper rash medicine and I did and we got into an argument and it escalated. There was a lot of yelling involved and then I said that I was going to leave with the baby and he didn't want me to so he was standing there in front of the door, and I tried to move him out of the way. I scratched him. [Mary: "How did you scratch him?"] With my nails. And someone heard the yelling and called the police. The police showed up and then I was charged.

Eunice's story reflects a physical response to a frustrating situation that involved potential harm to her child.

Shauna's incident involved jealousy. Her ex-boyfriend, with whom she had a child, was "messing around with another girl and got her pregnant." While all three were at family court (Shauna and her ex-boyfriend were working out child support), "we got fighting over the top of the stairwell and she came up behind me and grabbed me and I grabbed her by her hair and started dragging her. And he started dragging me down the stairs. She had a bruise on the side of her head, but I didn't hit her with anything though. I got worse than her from him dragging me." Throughout their relationship, Shauna's boyfriend cheated on her. It was "the final insult," she said, when he showed up with his new (pregnant) girlfriend at court.

June described a situation in which she and her estranged husband were constantly fighting about custody over their children. They did not have any formal court agreement, but tended to let the children decide when they wanted to stay with each parent. Initially, because June kept the couple's trailer and her estranged husband had several girlfriends, the children were content to stay with her. But their four-year-old son started crying for his father, so she sent him over to stay with him. The next day the little boy called her, wanting to come home. She talked to her husband to determine whether she should come to get her son, and he said he did not care because he didn't want to keep him. When June arrived with the children to pick him up, he started to berate her in front of the children and several other adults in the house. He shoved her and June shoved him back, saying, "I am not having you put your hands on me; we are not together." She took the children and left.

Four days later, he went to the police station and filed criminal trespassing, offensive touching, and terroristic threatening charges. "I ended up taking the plea bargain because, see, we got back together in that time after that. I also had gotten a PFA against him, and he keeps begging me to drop it, but I won't because I dropped it once time before, he tricked me, and then slammed into me, wham, in front of all his friends, so I am not doing it this time with me and him back together not even two days."

Natalie and her ex-husband were arguing about child support for their two-year-old. This was in a public parking lot—they had met there because she did not want him near the house and she wanted to be in a public setting. He told the police that Natalie was yelling at him and slapped him, demanding a watch that she had given him. Then she punched him in the face and hit the back of his car with her hand. Natalie's version was that the husband began screaming at her first, and then started hitting her and taunting her that he would never give her a dime, and so forth. Natalie was afraid, based on his past violence, so she flagged down a police officer and followed him to the station to file a report.

Lily is a mother of three children; one of them is profoundly handicapped and can only get around in a wheelchair. After a fight, her husband moved in across the street with a female "friend," denying she was a girlfriend, and he also stopped seeing the children. Lily was overwhelmed and depressed, and verbally abusive with her husband whenever she saw him, mostly about how he shirked his parenting responsibilities and lied about the female "friend." On the day of her arrest, Lily paraded her kids in front of his house, and he still refused to talk to the kids. She then barged into his house, and they screamed at each other, and he told her that he was sick of the kids and the "cripple." Lily hit him. Meanwhile, a neighbor called the police because the yelling was so loud.

Another woman, Laurie, described her arrest:

> I acted out of the depression and pain that was inflicted on me from years of his abuse. That day, he had been baiting me and he was trying to lure me back into the van since I had jumped out at a stoplight because I was sick of hearing his mouth. It was a nice warm day and the agreement was that if I got back in the van, I could drive since it was my vehicle. So, we changed seats. We kept arguing and he kept verbally abusing me so I got kind of heavy with the foot on the gas so he wanted to get out. When he got out, I thought, "I'm going to give this prick a feeling of what he gave me," so I chased him in the van. The field the car was on was really dry. The van overheated and the field caught on fire and the next thing I knew the firemen was out and the police came and I was arrested and charged with reckless driving and endangerment of a child since my son was in the car.

Sunny's experience is the final example for this category. From the time that she was fourteen years old until she turned twenty-four, she was a victim of many beatings (father, stepfather, boyfriends). Her current husband physically assaulted her for the past two years, and she said, "I got to the point that . . . if you are gonna put your hands around me, choking me, or throwing me out of the car, I am not taking it no more." They reconciled after he beat her up (because her mother would no longer let Sunny and the three children stay with her).

The incident that led to her arrest involved Sunny pushing her husband out of the doorway when she was trying to leave because he was smoking pot in front of her kids. Her house had become a drug hangout for her husband's friends, and she did not want her kids to be raised the way that she felt she was raised. Despite his past beatings, she attempted to leave while he was stoned and verbally abusive, especially toward their handicapped child. Sunny decided that her children's safety was more important than obeying her tyrannical husband, so she risked further abuse by deciding to leave.

For these women, their use of violence did nothing to change the abuse and power dynamics of their current or former relationships. Without analyzing options or planning ahead, the women in this category responded to a situation with force, with much of the present situation being reminiscent of past abuse in their lives. The women's use of force suggests a playing out of older patterns in which they learned to use force as a reaction to conflict. In a number of situations, women used violence when verbal arguments about child visitation or custody escalated. In general, these women expressed that they had no other options—they either had not received or not asked for help from the criminal justice system or the social support networks during earlier abusive incidents. They used violence as an expressive tool to demonstrate their outrage or frustration over a situation in which they felt powerless.

Defensive Behavior

The final category, *defensive behavior*, comprised the majority (sixty-two women), or about 65 percent, of the women. Women who exhibited defensive behavior were trying to get away during a violent incident or were trying to leave in order to avoid violence. In many cases, particularly when children were at home, the women were not able to get away. Typically, a woman's violence occurred after her male partner was the first to use violence. When women perceived their children were in danger because of men's violence, they acted violently toward the man in an attempt to make him quit what he was doing. The violence used by women, then, was in response to either an initial harm or a threat to them or their children.

Examples of women in the defensive category include Tonja and Gail. Tonja's boyfriend had her in a choke hold as he attempted to strangle her. She bit his arm in order to get him to loosen his grip so she could get away from him. Gail's husband Randy was drinking too much at home and Gail wanted to leave before it got violent, as it had in the past. Randy blocked the doorway so she could not leave, so Gail scratched him and pushed him away.

Becky endured severe beatings from her boyfriend for approximately a year, including broken ribs that caused so much pain she was unable to walk. She said, "I got to the point where I fought back at times, blocking parts of my body so that he wouldn't hurt me so bad." For Jennifer, her abusive, drunken husband came at her when she had her child in her arms, so she "poked him in the forehead" and then found herself arrested for offensive touching. Patty returned to her abusive husband after a two-month separation. He begged her to come back after he was shot by a drunken friend, so she decided to try to make things work. They went out partying on his boat. When they got back home, her mother-in-law was there. Because they didn't get along, Patty tried to leave. Here is her description:

I tried to leave but he doesn't want me to leave, but I walked out the door and he jumps on me. I hopped in my car, and he moves behind my car and in front of my car and tries to break into the windows with a stick. So I tried to put my car in drive and pinned him up against the garage wall. I didn't realize what I was doing until he looked at me and said "Patty, please go." I felt like total shit, I put my car in reverse and just left.

Patty was arrested the next day for assault with a deadly weapon and assault with intent to harm. Facing a possible jail term of twenty-five years, she hired an attorney and pled guilty to a lesser charge, received probation, substance abuse treatment, and the female offender's program.

Wendy's experience mirrored many of the women in the group. Her ex-husband was abusive, striking both her and her son (by another man) for the several years they were together. As Wendy describes it: "He was pushing and beating on me and he would beat up my son all the time just because he [the son] was at home. He did drugs in front of him. I got sent to jail for not doing anything, for child endangerment." When she got out of jail, she found him at home with another woman. She was mad that she had been jailed for three days. "He started pushing and hitting me again in front of my kids, so I just hauled off and I struck him. And then I heard the cops come. My daughter had called the cops and she said he is beating me mom. When the cops came, she told them to help me, but they let him tell the story instead. They saw that I had just come from jail." Although her ex-husband had been physically abusive to her and the children, Wendy had never called the police or filed a protection order, so there was no paper trail that designated him as the batterer. The police did not investigate the circumstances of the prior arrest, the shared history, or the current incident.

Terry was with her boyfriend as he drove his car. They were engaged in an argument where he accused her of flirting with, and maybe sleeping with, another guy. He began punching her as he drove. He accelerated, so she could not jump out. He stopped the car, grabbed her, and put his arms around her neck in a choke hold, pulling her hair and almost strangling her so that she could scarcely breathe. Terry bit his arm to force him to stop choking her. Despite the marks around her neck and her hair being disheveled, she was arrested. Terry acknowledged that the police told her that she did not have to plead guilty. However, Terry assumed that it was her fault ("I deserved it"), and that pleading guilty and getting the first offender's program would avoid jail time. Terry described herself as someone with a temper who has a lot of pent-up anger. She had a long history of being a victim of abuse. She minimized his actions to the group, saying, "Since I know how he can get, I shouldn't be running my mouth. I have a problem with my mouth. He starts it; I finish it, because I have that much of a temper. I spent all these years trying to argue with someone that there's no sense in arguing with. I should know better." Quickly, Mary interjected, trying to put the violence into perspective for Terry: "When someone puts their hands around your neck, they are strangling you. It only takes seven pounds of pressure on the windpipe to kill you. And it only takes cutting off the oxygen to the brain for death; I think it's six minutes for a brain injury and anything under that you can be resuscitated, hopefully."

Nicole's situation involved her ex-husband and child. Tom had asked Nicole for a Christmas suggestion for their daughter, and she said that sneakers were what the daughter wanted. Christmas came and went, and their daughter never received the present. Nicole spotted Tom at the shopping mall a few days after New Year's Day and asked him about it, insinuating that he spent the money to support his drug and alcohol addiction.

> NICOLE: I said, "I am quite sure you wasted the money on your beer." He shoved me, hard, and knocked me down, so when he shoved me again, I just hit him. I didn't hit him hard, but he had said to me, "She [their daughter] deserves to suffer sometimes. Don't no kid deserve to have everything she want in life." Maybe that's true, but the point is that if he had told me that, I could've gotten her the sneaks.
>
> MARY: What did you hit him with?
>
> NICOLE: A closed fist. I punched him. I don't know actually where I hit him. I didn't hurt my hand, so it wasn't like I hit him real hard.
>
> MARY: What were things like when you were together?
>
> NICOLE: We did drugs together. I stopped, and that busted him up. He hit me a lot. I hit him back, but actually I can't hurt him. He's bigger than me. I can only sting him, just like a little bit or nothing, get him away from me so I could leave.

Gina's situation was different from the others because of the prominent position her family occupied. Her husband was a former high official in the town, and he personally knew all of the police and prosecutors. According to Gina, she and her husband had never experienced physical abuse prior to the incident that led to a dual arrest. Here are her words:

> What had happened was me and my husband got into an argument at our family business. When I got home, I was upset. When he came home, he got mad at our oldest daughter and threw a phone at her. My other daughter asked, "When are you gonna fix my car, Daddy?" He was still mad at the younger daughter, so he went to push her and she used profanity with him, which she never had done ever, and he

got upset with her and he started punching her. And I went to break them up, stop him from hitting her, and he hit me and I hit him back, and then he punched me and I punched him. I'm not bragging about it but I'm just saying I saw him hitting my child. So the police were called in and the court's solution was very political because of who our family is.

The police and prosecutors wanted them to work it out, but Gina remained upset because her husband had hit their daughter in her face and he was refusing to take responsibility for it, saying "you know who I am, I can't be arrested." According to Gina, this is what happened next: "That ticked me off, him saying 'you know who I am.' So I told the police, if you don't arrest him, I'm calling [the chief prosecutor]. They still didn't want to arrest him because he was their prior boss but they were in between a rock and a hard place. So they arrested me and him and my two daughters and they drummed up some charges on all of us." Because Gina worked with teenagers at her job and one of the charges against her was reckless endangerment because children were present, she felt pressured to plead guilty and accept the female offender's program and probation, rather than follow her attorney's advice to hold out on self-defensive defense. "All I could think about was my job. My boss said get rid of the charges or you will have no job. So, I plea-bargained and they dropped the reckless endangerment charges and I took assault in the third degree and disorderly conduct and here I am in group."

Emily's situation involved a former boyfriend who raped her and burned her arms with cigarettes. Although he was arrested and faces over twenty years in jail, she remained torn about her feelings for him and wondered if he really deserved all that prison time. She said, "I still have some kind of feeling for the guy. He's not supposed to contact me but he writes me letters. And it was not really rape because we were in a relationship. After he burnt me, he made me have sex with him. I don't really feel like I was raped even though I didn't want to have sex. But I have burns on my body now." Emily was arrested for terroristic threats because she told people that she was going to ambush him and kill him because of the burns (but not because of the rape).

Bettina and her husband had been drinking for a couple of hours and they got into a verbal argument that led to a fight. He started hitting her and knocked her down on the floor in front of the kids. The name-calling was getting ugly, so Bettina made the kids get in the car so they could leave. He came after her again, and "I bit him. On his butt, on his ankle. We were really messed up but I couldn't breathe, my ribs hurt so bad." Bettina and the kids left in the car but the husband called the police to report her drunk driving. The police pulled her over and gave her a Breathalyzer test, arrested her for

DUI, endangering the welfare of a child, and offensive touching. He also was arrested.

Erin had recently reunited with her husband of seven months. They were renting a house, and had many arguments about whose turn it was to mow the yard and take out the garbage and so forth. He also blamed her for damaging his '57 Camaro. Verbal fights eventually escalated into more violent ones where he did the hitting. Erin said, "Instead of being violent, I became the person with the hugs and the loving touch." It never worked, so she defended herself when she could. When he was kicking her, as she lay on the floor, she reached up and grabbed his neck and he yanked away from her, twisting it. Erin was arrested for offensive touching; the police arrested both of them, never giving her a chance to tell her story.

Many of these women expressed feelings of injustice that they were mandated to the group, such as Jayne: "I don't want to come back here; I don't want to spend money out of my pocket . . . I feel like a man brought me to this class and it's just not fair." Most of the women mentioned that following their arrest, their partners or former partners taunted them and said belittling comments, such as they were "crazy" or "stupid." They also described how the men placed the blame on the women for their own arrests or for the arrests of both of them. In the defensive behavior category, a number of the violent situations resulted in dual arrests.

As women committed more time to the treatment program and examined their own behavior as well as their relationships, they felt that the men were angry and uncomfortable with any changes or challenges to the power dynamics or "understandings" about the roles they each played in their relationships. Most of the women thought that the empowerment they felt was a new, exciting feeling, but the repercussions of this personal transformation were uncomfortable.

What the incidents described in the defensive behavior category demonstrate is that most women used violence to defend themselves or their children or to escape an impending violent attack—a threat they knew was realistic, given their past experiences with the batterer. The women had long histories of victimization, and most expressed feeling as though they had no choice but to fight back. A number of the women expressed sentiments that reflect descriptions of the classic cycle of violence in which the women hate the violence, but for a variety of reasons, still love the abuser and feel trapped or powerless in their situations. Often, the women's social support networks or the criminal justice system had failed to support or protect them. Many lived isolated lives, either geographically exiled in the countryside or by design of the batterer, who cut off the women's contact with friends and family. Similar to the other categories, children and drugs and alcohol were common factors. Often, the women were arrested because the male batterer called the police, but it was equally likely another family member at the scene or a neighbor called. In all cases, the women were surprised and outraged at the arrest. The outrage was present because their perceptions of the situations were that they were defending themselves or their children, and often the man had not been arrested for beating her at the time of the incident or earlier in their violent relationship.

Discussion

What the three paths to arrest indicate is that the truly violent woman is an anomaly. The analysis reveals that most women used violence in order to thwart their husbands' or boyfriends' egregious actions, to defend themselves or their children, out of frustration based on past abuse or current custody disagreements, or because their current situation mirrored earlier circumstances in their lives where they perceived or experienced danger and violence.

The women described in this project are the very people that the criminal justice system is supposed to help, not hurt by first arresting them, then treating them as perpetrators, and finally mandating them to batterer intervention programs. This is one unintended side effect of relying too heavily on the criminal justice system to be the primary answer to domestic violence (Mills 1999; Osthoff 2002; S. Miller 2001). The purported gender neutrality of domestic violence policies may in actuality constitute gendered injustice (Renzetti 1999) as women who are not batterers get arrested under laws designed for men who are. Consistent with the majority of research findings, the female offenders observed in the three treatment groups demonstrate that most women who use violence do so to escape or stop abuse.

There is support for two of the four violence categories introduced by Johnson (1995, 2000) as well as for the three categories distinguished by the Duluth manual (Hamlett 1998). Only five of the ninety-five women in six months of (often tri-weekly) treatment group meetings exhibited preemptive, aggressive violence, the category of violence most similar to Johnson's *mutual violent control* type. The remaining ninety women's use of violence cannot be characterized as battering; nor could any women's violence in this sample be characterized as *intimate terrorism* (Johnson 1995, 2000). According to their stories, the women never achieved power or control over their partner or former partner; nor did the men fear for their safety at the time of the incident or afterward, or change their behavior as a result of women's use of intimidation. Women's use of violence was either an instrumental act that was primarily used to defend themselves or their children (Johnson's *violent resistance*) or an expressive act that conveyed frustration with an abusive situation that seemed beyond their control. There were no examples of Johnson's final violence category, *common couple*, exhibited in this data; perhaps minor violence unconnected to control did not reach the new arrest threshold under pro-arrest policies.

Despite the frustrating circumstances that underlie women's use of violence, the need to take responsibility for their choices to use violence was an important message conveyed by Mary and the overall treatment group philosophy. Most readers would no doubt agree that the arrests of the women from the first group, the generalized violence category, were justified. In those five cases, the women either responded violently to a situation that was not threatening their safety, or their use of violence was unprovoked. Moreover, the arrests of the women from the second category, frustration response behavior, might also be viewed as warranted; if one reverses the genders, surely a male who used violence against a female partner in the same context would be arrested. But a woman's use of violence does not accomplish the same outcomes as a man's use, such as creating greater fear, causing injury, and reinforcing his control over her. This gendered difference in the motivations behind and the result of violence are important to consider when assessing blame. Moreover, that these women's arrests are understandable does not make the women "batterers," and the question about whether the female offender's program is appropriate remains. The arrests of the women from the largest category, defensive behavior, seems the most clearly unjust, for the women suffered in long violent relationships and typically used violence to fend off an attack on themselves or their children.

Women's articulation of their behavior provides insight into gender differences regarding the use of violence. The women readily took responsibility for their behavior, but their acknowledgment differed considerably from that of men in that, according to research on male batterer's treatment groups, men typically minimize and deny their violent behavior (Dobash et al. 1998). Women, on the other hand, freely admitted their role and actions—admissions that may have initiated police proceedings against them. When group members were asked if they considered themselves "victims, offenders, or survivors," the majority put themselves in the survivor category, after explaining that they knew they broke the law. Many had endured long histories of victimization. Again, this self-labeling differs from men who batter. Women couched their experiences in terms of morality: they knew the act was wrong, but they did not think it was illegal. Once they learned that there were laws against the actions they took, the women uniformly acknowledged that they broke the laws, but believed their actions to be morally justifiable, given the circumstances. In contrast, men often simply deny the illegality of their actions and project responsibility onto the women, or deny the abuse all together (Kimmel 2002).

The analysis of the group sessions revealed that the meanings and roles that anger (and sometimes violence) played in women's lives were explored to a much greater extent than the specific acts that got them arrested. A large part of the program was devoted to guiding the women to recognize what triggers their anger and how to appropriately redirect such feelings so that they are constructive and not destructive. Through resource information exchange and active participation in discussions, women received invaluable information about how domestic violence affects family life, how to get help so that they do not feel so isolated or without options, and how to understand and negotiate the criminal justice system. It was clear from the participants' evaluations at the end of their program that they achieved insight and that they felt more empowered and better able to deal with the frustrations and issues in their lives. For this sample of arrested women and in the studies conducted by Hamberger and his colleagues (see chapter 2), women responded positively to the programs and wanted to learn techniques for taking responsibility (not blame) for their own behavior and changing that behavior by seeking nonviolent ways to ensure the safety of themselves and their children. The treatment programs examined in this book and the Wisconsin programs examined by Hamberger offered information to women that was similar to that provided in battered women's shelters. Most of the court-mandated women had not been exposed previously to these resources through residential or community outreach programs.

Given some of the positive feelings and experiences the women attributed to the group sessions, it would be accurate to say that they benefited from attending the female offender's program. However, this assertion introduces a dangerous, slippery slope. Although ostensibly an "offenders" program, this particular agency's philosophy, Mary's orientation and her background in victim services, and the program's curriculum coalesced to produce a nascent victim-centered program. This makes sense, given that most (95 percent) of the participants were not batterers, and a victim-centered emphasis is consistent with the programs described earlier in Minnesota and Wisconsin. However, the format of the female offender's program may not address what the courts intended, despite the appropriateness of the curriculum. This particular treatment program emphasized context—what were the meanings, motivations, and consequences of the acts and how did these shape and constrain women's choices. Not all female offender's programs would validate women's experiences and have the foresight to explore the use of violence within the full context of women's lives. For instance, other programs within the same state, or across the country, might follow a very different philosophy that is incident-driven and thus more in line with typical criminal justice system practices.

The issues that came to light in the treatment groups speak to a range of concerns. An incident-driven treatment group that fails to contextualize women's use of force would define, treat, and address women as perpetrators or batterers. Endorsing this kind of program is risky in that it is never appropriate to send a victim to a treatment program designed for batterers. Contextualizing women's use of violence is of paramount importance, given prior research findings and what this present analysis reveals. Ironically, this examination of context occurs at the wrong end of the criminal justice process; it should begin when police are initially called to a domestic violence incident rather than at the culmination of case processing.

It is easy to prosecute women in these cases. As demonstrated in this data and elsewhere, women tend to tell their stories with much detail (i.e., exactly where they hit, how hard they hit. See McMahon and Pence 2003). Compared to men arrested on domestic violence charges, arrested women are less demanding that attorneys argue their innocence to get them acquitted (George and Wilson 2002). This characteristic, albeit unknown to the women, feeds right into an incident-driven criminal justice system that focuses on the act and not on relationships or the contexts in which violence occurred. It was almost solely in the treatment groups that the context of the incident and its consequences were addressed, such as how the arrest would affect the women's lives.

For most of the women, the criminal justice process was alienating and foreign to them. Since the women feared jail time or loss of custody, it was often easier to accept a guilty plea than to contest the arrest. It is a sad commentary that the bulk of the women's legal knowledge was gleaned after the fact, in the treatment groups, rather than at earlier decision-making points where the knowledge mattered more. Desperate to prevent the familial, employment, or financial crises posed by a conviction, women were eager to accept the first offender's program if it was offered, or plead guilty and enroll in the female offender's program. Moreover, because women court-mandated to treatment are placed under the probation department's auspices, women are at risk for violations. Thus, probation violations could result in harsher penalties when it comes to custody issues or jail time, and threats of jeopardizing probation status are used by abusers to intimidate their victims (S. Miller 2001, 1366). In addition, there remains a coercive element to female offender's programs: the women must attend and participate in the group discussions and homework assignments[3] or their probationary status could be rescinded, with jail time a potential outcome.

When victims who are arrested for fighting back plead guilty, the context of the relationship in which the use of force occurred fails to get addressed by the criminal justice system, leaving treatment groups as the forum to examine issues of self-defense, fear of retaliatory violence, and so forth. The expansion of the numbers of women under control by the criminal justice system has far-reaching implications. Since many organizations that control treatment groups will not be as forward-minded in their approach as the one analyzed in this book, there is an enormous danger of continued reliance on incident-driven solutions that disingenuously designate all women arrested on domestic violence charges as batterers.

I turn now to the final chapter for a larger discussion of the major findings of the research project and their policy implications.

Chapter 8   Implications

R<small>EGARDLESS OF THEIR ROLE</small> in the system or the nature of their experiences with violent women, respondents in this study unanimously agree that women's violence differs significantly from men's violence. While not all violence stems from women's responses to victimization, a clear pattern emerged. Typically, women's use of force is in response to their current or former partner's violence or can be characterized as a reaction that results from past abuses and their relative powerlessness in the relationship.

Although the police and the rest of the criminal justice system—at least from a policy standpoint—have answered the call to take battering more seriously by arresting and punishing perceived offenders, the "tough on crime" stance is not effective if it penalizes women when issues of self-defense or gendered power dynamics are not taken into account. As described powerfully by the women mandated to treatment programs, the consequences can be costly: women will have arrest and conviction records, which may affect employment prospects, possibly resulting in even less power in their relationships. Additionally, due to distrust of the criminal justice system and its failure to protect them by virtue of arresting and prosecuting them, women might be less likely to rely on the police for further help and more likely to resort to violence in the future. Continuing to use arrest policies that do not ascertain the primary aggressor or the contextual dimensions of the domestic violence essentially increases a woman's victimization: the original abuse she endured coupled with the victimization by a system that does not understand her circumstances.

While the evidence gathered from in-depth interviews with system professionals, police ride-along observations, and descriptions from the arrested women themselves demonstrates that women do use violence, it is also exceedingly clear that actual or threatened abuse by their current or former partners plays a role in women's behavior, and the choices they make in responding have been constrained by social and economic factors. Abusive relationships are characterized by asymmetric power, and women typically have fewer options and resources than do men. Failure to fully consider the circumstances under which violence is used inhibits our understanding of the motivations for violent actions and facilitates one-size-fits-all policies that are wholly inappropriate for victims who use violence for defensive reasons.

The criminal justice system is by its very nature incident-driven. It is difficult to imagine the possibility for such an entrenched manner of operation to really change and look beyond dichotomous thinking (did the person break the law or not) to a more contextualized approach. Yet police exercise discretion at every citizen-police encounter and use selective enforcement strategies in deciding whom to arrest. Surely it is not too much to desire a more considered and informed approach to making arrest decisions in domestic violence situations. Pro-arrest and mandatory arrest policies curtail discretion, and can result in the kinds of over-enforcement discussed by so many of the people interviewed and observed in this study. The officers with the least experience on the police force seem to exercise less flexibility in their enforcement decisions; perhaps as they learn more and practice more, greater understanding of the complexity inherent in domestic violence will be reached. Moreover, the more-experienced officers may be able to impart their wisdom to the newer officers.

Police officers and the criminal justice professionals and social service providers did not believe that women's violence was increasing, and universally acknowledged that women resorted to violence for reasons that markedly differed from those of men. Two factors seemed to be related to increased arrests of women: one, changes in police policies to favor arrest; and two, officers' fear of being named in a civil lawsuit. In fact, the economic risk of nonintervention could devastate a small police department. Early cases such as the Tracy Thurman civil suit in Torrington, Connecticut, outraged activists in the battered women's movement because they highlighted police reluctance to intervene in domestic violence cases. The cases strengthened the call for enacting pro-arrest policies.

This reaction raises a larger issue related to the advantages and disadvantages of the criminalization of domestic violence. Feminist activists initially fought for greater use of legal remedies such as pro-arrest and pro-prosecution (no dropping of charges) policies because the state was deficient in protecting battered women. They are imperfect solutions at best due to their infringement on a woman's autonomy over making her own choices about whether to pursue prosecution in the face of economic dependency, guilt, feelings of love, or concern about children. Pro-arrest and pro-prosecution policies can be helpful in that they send a deterrent message to batterers and others that domestic violence is a crime that will be treated punitively; relieve the victim of the burden of deciding to pursue the case herself since the responsibility is transferred to the state; disempower batterers and prevent their further manipulation of the victim; and transform the private nature of domestic violence into a public matter, one that encourages victim cooperation and support (Schneider 2000). On the other side, however, critics of pro-arrest and pro-prosecution policies contend that:

> . . . they are paternalistic and essentialize women's experiences by
> presuming that society knows what is right for all women; they re-
> victimize women by subjecting them to further coercion at the hands
> of the state; they increase the risk of retaliation against the victim by
> the batterer; and, finally, they disempower women by taking their au-
> tonomy away from them. (Schneider 2000, 186)

In addition, as demonstrated clearly by the current study, an increased reliance on pro-arrest policies for domestic violence results in criminalizing victims' use of self-defensive action in abusive situations because the victims are falsely identified as offenders.

In contrast, respondents in this study did not view women's violence as occurring within the power-control dynamic that is typical of male domestic violence. The context and nature of women's violence was qualitatively different from men's violence, given that the majority of women's violence bears little resemblance to male batterers' use of violence. Instead, the respondents in the police ride-along and in-depth interviews with criminal justice professionals and social service providers state that women's violence is due to frustration over an enduring abusive relationship, entanglements with drugs and alcohol, or self-defensive action against violent current or former male partners.

Relevant here is Michael Johnson's (1995, 2000) development of intimate violence categories, particularly the one called "violent resistance," which covers situations in which violence is used but does not emanate from a controlling or intimidating pattern. Rather, the violence is used to express frustration or to defend one's self. Similarly, Beth Richie's (1996) study of black battered women arrested for committing other crimes reveals the process of gender entrapment, in which women "who are vulnerable to men's violence in their intimate relationship are penalized for behaviors they engage in even when the behaviors are logical extensions of their racialized gender identities, their culturally expected gender roles, and the violence in their intimate relationships." This explains how some women commit illegal acts "in response to violence, the threat of violence, or coercion by their male partners" (Richie 1996, 4). Both Johnson's and Richie's distinctions among violence categories and the findings of their research demonstrate the importance of a contextualized approach to evaluating women's use of violence, one that allows for the consideration of complexity of relationships and the social and economic realities of their lives.[1]

Another unintended consequence of curtailing much of police discretion through pro-arrest and mandatory arrest laws is that the number of dual arrests may increase because police feel they need to arrest anyone involved due to fear of lawsuits (Martin 1997); and in turn, dual arrests could deter women from calling the police again (Buzawa and Buzawa 1990, 94; Martin 1997, 145). For example, after mandatory arrest was implemented in Duluth, Minnesota, calls to the police were reduced by 47 percent, with similar reductions reported in Detroit (Martin 1997, 145).

When women have fewer options (because they become reluctant to call police for help following enactment of these new policies), the emotional ramifications are costly: isolation is reinforced, as are their beliefs that there are no resources or that they are to blame. When women are themselves arrested, they do not call police during future abusive episodes, putting them at greater risk (Abel and Suh 1987; Stafne 1989). In Lyon's (1999) analysis of two jurisdictions in Michigan, it was found that officers who learned that women had suffered prior abuse were less likely to arrest them. However, it was also found that if a woman had called the police before, she was more likely to be arrested, suggesting "either conscious or unconscious retaliation by the police against women for staying in an abusive situation." Lyon contends that this retaliation may occur due to police officers' feelings of not being trusted when policies take away their discretion.

In the present study, the relationship between pro-arrest policies and an increase in dual arrests is murky: the perception of police in the ride-along component was that dual arrests were rare. They attribute the rarity to their own competence in investigative policing, and with that, their ability to distinguish between primary aggressor and victim. Moreover, many officers also stated that they would be in "hot water" with their supervisors or the district attorneys if they made too many dual arrests. In fact, in the three months of participant observations, only one dual arrest was made.

On the other hand, in-depth interviews with criminal justice professionals and social service providers told a different tale: these professionals strongly criticized police for their over-zealous law enforcement efforts that resulted in many dual arrests. When one considers the analysis of the treatment group sessions, the women's stories reinforce the professionals' admonishment to police, since quite a number of the women arrested for frustration-related violence or defensive violence indicated that their situation resulted in arrests of both parties. The fact that respondents unanimously deplored the use of dual arrests offers hope that changes in policy and practice may be possible.

The propensity to arrest is exacerbated if police have little sympathy for female victims to begin with (Lyon and Mace 1991; Stafne 1989). In particular, Saunders (1995) found that when police had negative attitudes about victims, especially women, and they believed domestic violence was justified in some cases and that some stereotypes about why battered women stay were true, they were more likely to make arrests (see also Ford 1987). In the present study, only the police from the ride-along component but not the police in the interviews of criminal justice professionals expressed prejudicial beliefs about battered women. They made these comments in the context of class, not race. Comments were targeted against poor people who have "pitiful lifestyles" and "don't take responsibility for their lives" and live in "dirty houses and scummy neighborhoods." Although there was some superficial acknowledgment that battering occurs in "nicer" neighborhoods and with "richer" people, for the most part, the police said that most battering occurred in the trailer parks (in the middle and southern parts of the state) or subsidized public housing (in the most urban area of the state), which are more indicative of lower socioeconomic classes. The officers' emphatic explanations that reveal race and class prejudices belie the many hours of domestic violence training police receive in the state, which always includes a training session on the diversity of battering across income and racial groups. Despite the difficulties encountered when trying to "bend granite" (Guyot, 1979)—change police cultural values—it might prove beneficial to identify effective police training efforts nationwide and adopt some of their practices.

Nationally, some research indicates that women who use violence are punished more severely than male batterers, particularly women of color and poor women, due to fewer resources, language barriers, and racism. Women who are deemed the primary aggressor, particularly women of color, receive harsher sentences than violent men. (Browne 1987; Burrell 1995, cited in Hooper 1996, 178). But women's violence cannot always be characterized as purely dichotomous (self-defensive or primary aggressor); it is far more complicated. Women of color may not fit into generic female offender models since men's violence models were modified to accommodate white women (Allard 1991). "Poor women are also more likely to live in dangerous areas where gangs are active, where gun and knife violence is not uncommon, and where the risk of violence outside the home is great" (Hooper 1996, 179). Racism by the criminal justice system compounds the issue for battered women of color. Fighting back may be viewed by some women as an available and desirable alternative to being trapped in a battering relationship, especially when calling the police means an encounter with a system perceived as racist that is likely to blame them for the violence. Both police and prosecutors need to be more cognizant of cultural nuances that shape women's responses to battering.

Not only do police and prosecutors need to be cognizant of gender, class, and racial differences in how they respond to intimate violent situations, but the process of offering court diversion programs, such as a treatment program for female "offenders," needs to be examined for any implicit bias. Although it was not the case in the treatment groups observed here, other jurisdictions may find that women of color are underrepresented in treatment groups. An underrepresentation could reflect differences in how cases were handled at the post-arrest stage, with women of color less likely to be offered the treatment group option. It would be useful to explore the determinants of jail versus probation or treatment options to see if race or ethnicity or poverty play a role, given the extant research that suggests that women of color or impoverished women receive harsher sentences due to fewer resources, language barriers, cultural nuances, and racism (Hooper 1996; Browne 1987; Allard 1991; Osthoff 2002; Richie 1996).

Moreover, police who possess rigid sex-role beliefs and find justifications for domestic violence in marriages appear to have an increased tendency to arrest women (Stith 1990). For instance, while police in the ride-along component were somewhat sympathetic when explaining why women would resort to violence, they framed their comments around negative assessments of women's behavior. They were tired of responding to the same address and wondered why she did not just leave or why she was "stupid" enough to stay in a bad relationship. It was rare for officers to focus their blame on the male offenders or do more than mention the desperate conditions and economic limitations faced by battered women.

In general, arrest propensity is compounded when women are viewed as stepping out of traditional feminine roles. Rasche (1986) contends that some people view violent women as the "epitome of unrestrained female aggression" because they discard socially prescribed roles of submissiveness and subservience. The police officers in the present study offered a new twist: they admired battered women's greater willingness to fight back, and they attributed women's feistiness to features of the modern women's liberation movement. At the same time, however, the police would arrest women without thoroughly exploring the circumstances that led them to use force. This ambivalence by the police shows how imperative it is to examine the situational origins and context of domestic violence. These findings are consistent with other research conducted with arrested battered women that shows women may not view themselves as helpless, so they may not perceive their own violence as self-defensive (Hooper 1996). As the stories told by women in the treatment groups in this study demonstrate, battered women who fight back are stuck in a survival mode, and do not have the luxury to reflect on their circumstances when they are trying to save themselves or their children from harm.

Inability or unwillingness by police to distinguish between being the primary aggressor and taking self-defensive action is an enormous problem, one that highlights the importance of police training that teaches officers how to distinguish between aggressive and defensive action and how to ask a range of questions to help in this determination. For instance, self-defensive actions, such as blocking blows, may be missed by the police since bruising occurs underneath the victim's arms. If officers stayed longer at the crime scene, bruises would show up after approximately forty-five minutes on a light-skinned individual; however, this would not be the case for darker-skinned individuals. In addition, due to men's larger size and greater strength, women often grab an object that is handy in order to effectively fight back. This gender difference was frequently illustrated in the observational data gathered from the ride-along component as well as reported in the women's descriptions of their use of violence in the treatment groups; it also is confirmed in Dasgupta's (1999) study of battered women who use violence against their abusive partners. Thus, women often get charged with a felony because of their use of a deadly weapon—typically, a kitchen knife is used because it is most handy—while men are charged with a misdemeanor. The result is that a man may have a more visible and serious wound, though the woman's intent may be defensive, not malicious.

Further, if men are indeed using the criminal justice system as another tool to manipulate women, as many of the criminal justice professionals and social service providers expressed, police must be cognizant of this and strive to look beyond who called 911 or who appears calmer in order to address victim-offender ambiguity. Lyon (1999) suggests that prosecutors may want to form review teams that would evaluate whether the "right" person was arrested and that would look at the history of domestic violence in the relationship. While prosecutorial review is helpful, police as the first responders should be urged to investigate domestic violence calls more thoroughly and focus on context, not just on whether or not a law has been broken.

The court process is more foreign to many women than it is to their male partners. Interviews with criminal justice professionals and social service providers indicated that there were many times that women made important case decisions, such as accepting a plea bargain versus pleading not guilty, without regard for their guilt or innocence but in relation to their fears of jail or losing custody of their children. The lack of legal advice available to women was astonishing. Further training of the defense bar is needed to raise awareness of this dilemma. Moreover, cronyism between the defense attorneys and the prosecutors may reinforce women's feelings of powerlessness and women's beliefs that case efficiency is valued more highly than truth.

Female Offender's Programs: Pro and Con

The "gender neutral" enforcement of domestic violence laws that has resulted in the increase of women arrested introduces implications for court-mandated treatment. Given that acceptance into the female offender's program in the research state includes probation status, women are at risk for violations, which are often orchestrated by vindictive batterers. Probation violations could result in harsher penalties when it comes to custody issues and jail time, and threats of jeopardizing probation status are used by abusers to intimidate their victims. Ostensibly, the female offender's program offers a win-win situation for the court and for the women, but the downside is that the context of women's violence is often left unexamined.

Moreover, once state control of batterers through criminal justice intervention and mental health programs is achieved, it becomes institutionalized. Once a program becomes institutionalized and bureaucratized, the people who run it often become invested in its continued operation, for it brings in funding to their organization, legitimacy, and a recognition of the practitioners as "experts." This cooptation is a common occurrence in social movements (Ferraro 1996; Piven and Cloward 1979). The consequences of becoming institutionalized include prioritizing fund-raising and satisfying funding agencies' requirements, rather than challenging the underlying causes of battering or the appropriateness of the criminal justice system's response.

The trend in this particular state and elsewhere across the country appears to support treatment programs for women arrested on domestic violence charges. One advantage of these programs is that they connect with a population that has had very little access to battered women's shelters or advocates (see Hamberger and Potente 1994). The information the women receive about the cycle of violence, dynamics of power and control, emotional, sexual, and physical abuse, and the criminal justice system is information that they may not otherwise encounter.

For many women, being in a group setting with other women sharing their experiences shows them that they are not alone, that they did not deserve the abuse, and that they can make changes in their lives. Women typically receive advice and information from the treatment group facilitators regarding social service referrals and helpful techniques (i.e., medical care for children, how to handle ongoing disputes with partners, Protection From Abuse orders information, networking, "time-out" strategies and anger management techniques). This distribution of helpful information may not be the norm for all facilitators or all female offender's groups, but it was well received by the women in the treatment groups we observed in this state. In fact, there may be enormous variation among treatment programs' philosophies across the country; for instance, not all facilitators will view arrested women as primarily "victims" who made "bad choices" as Mary did. This distinction highlights how a particular philosophical orientation of the group facilitator can make a tremendous difference, and these variations could greatly affect program structure and emphases. By their explicit acknowledgment of "offenders" who are "victims," and their treatment of women in that light, Mary and the female offender's program are covertly subversive in carrying out the court's mandate. Admittedly, there still remains a coercive element to these programs: the women must attend and participate in the group discussions and homework assignments or their probationary status would be rescinded and jail time could be a realistic outcome.

Perhaps for some women the trade-off is worth it. Positive assessments of programs by women, however, should not obscure the issues of early identification of the primary aggressor, establishment of context, and better police and prosecutorial training. When so few women in the studies nationwide are found to actively engage in the kind of violent behavior that typifies battering, the increase in female offender treatment programs continues to raise questions of legitimacy and appropriateness.

The accounts of the women in the three treatment groups observed for this study revealed three types of violence that led to their arrests. Women who lash out at anyone in any context clearly fall within the appropriateness of an arrest. However, this group reflected just a tiny percentage (5 percent) of the women mandated to treatment.

The second group of women, those who acted out of frustration in situations where their partners (or ex-partners) were abusive in some manner or the current incidents were eerily reminiscent of past abusive situations, raises the most perplexing questions about what is the appropriate response to women's use of violence. Clearly, these women possess some level of responsibility; retaliatory violence is not equivalent to self-defense. However, upon examination of the context in which violence occurred, the women's choices were constrained. Their use of violence does not make them "batterers," for the women's actions did not engender fear in the men, result in serious injury to the men, or cause the men to change their behavior through women's attempts to intimidate or hurt them. On the other hand, if the gender of the combatants were reversed, we would find it difficult to excuse the men's use of violence under the same circumstances. I believe this "switching" exercise illustrates the immense gender difference present in violent relationships and how contextual understanding is shaped by gendered dynamics and power. For example, if the genders were reversed and a man used violence in the same way described in the women's stories, she would be afraid, injured, and intimated by him enough to acquiesce to his controlling demands.

Finally, the third and largest group described their use of violence as defensive, in protection of themselves or their children. Arrest is never warranted under those circumstances, nor is the designation of these women as "batterers."

Advocacy programs designed to help domestic violence victims should endeavor to reach all battered women, even those charged with or convicted of crimes. Accomplishing this is tricky, as some programs that choose to help victims who are defendants face withdrawal of funding support and legal assistance from prosecutors (Osthoff 2002). Bloom and Covington (1998), in their work on women's prison programs, contend that women-centered environments are crucial for providing support, empowering women, and creating a trusting, culturally sensitive environment. These feminist ideals resonate with innovative reentry programs for female inmates that connect them through a "continuum of care" to the community, including "wrap-around" services that address goals of reintegration into society (Jacobs 2001; Acoca 1998, 1999). A program that addresses women who use violence in relationships as a means of self-defense could address women's issues in a similar kind of women-centered program, incorporating community resources and key support people. As Busch and Rosenberg (2004) argue, "Women may need intervention, but not as batterers. Treatment should focus on their victimization and provide them with the psychological tools and material resources to leave their abusive relationships and to avoid subsequence ones" (p. 56).

Inviting women who have been both victims and users of violence in relationships to tell their stories adds a crucial dimension to exploring this issue. Their elucidations emerged in the present study as well as in an analysis by Perilla and colleagues (2003) of an ongoing group where women who were not in crisis situations could go to openly discuss the ways in which they used vio-lence. These contextually-based discussions, occurring between women of dif-ferent ethnicities, backgrounds, and sexual orientations, reveal the dynamics that led to their actions, similar to those discussed by the women in the female offender's program in the present state: (a) the ways in which they learned the effectiveness of violence as a control mechanism as they saw violence being enacted in their lives, (b) opportunities that presented themselves as a result of the imbalance of power in relationships, and (c) their choices to use or not use violence, along with the consequences (Perilla et al. 2003, 40).

A contextual understanding of an abusive situation would hopefully re-sult in more just law enforcement and court action. The interview data ana-lyzed in this book suggest that the vast majority of the criminal justice professionals and social service providers believe that women who are charged with domestic violence offenses cannot be treated with the same paradigm used for male batterers. Women's actions are typically self-defensive or protec-tive, and the social and economic factors that influence women's violence op-erate in ways that vary greatly from the ways they operate in men's lives. As the treatment group analysis revealed, women do not typically use violence to exert power or control over partners. Instead, women are often responding to a loss of power resulting from abuse inflicted on them, and their violent re-sponse may not have been immediately precipitated by an attack. Women are further disadvantaged by their savvy batterers whose greater familiarity with the criminal justice system facilitates manipulation of their victims and oper-ates to their advantage against their female partners as yet another tactic of domination. Since female victims are officially labeled as offenders, they do not have the benefit of receiving emotional support and legal advice from victim services workers. It would be helpful for victim advocates to become involved with cases at an earlier stage in the process so that the ambiguities can be ad-dressed before the system is in high gear.

Criminalization of Domestic Violence

By aligning themselves with the state, feminist activists in the battered women's movement have had to compromise their political analyses of batter-ing and transform their grassroots activism into a more state-controlled enter-prise in which shelters have become social service agencies that serve clients instead of empower women (Schechter 1982; Schneider 2000). Rather than challenging male privilege and prioritizing broad social transformations that would increase women's well-being and make available the resources needed for them to survive away from a violent relationship, the conservative crime-control model sacrifices goals such as affordable housing, child care, low-interest educational loans, and child support in order to shore up law enforcement powers (Ferraro 1996; see also Rothenberg 2003). Thus, the feminists' compromise comes at a price: feminist philosophy that once challenged patriarchy and women's dependency on men is replaced by crime-control efforts that criminalize all intimate violence without regard to context. Despite the legitimacy achieved by state recognition, many advocates within the battered women's movement deplore the state's appropriation of the issue, seeing it as malevolent and paternalistic.

Gender neutrality and equal treatment, though laudable in the abstract, further confuse an already complex issue when we explore victim resistance to abuse. In light of the scholarship explored in this book and elsewhere, the criminal justice system must recognize that the same standards of assessing legal blame cannot be applied to evaluate battered victims' use of violence in relationships vis-à-vis abusers' use of violence. When advocates for battered women demanded an end to discrimination in law enforcement between intimate and stranger victims of violence, the intention was that female victims of violence (more often assaulted by intimate partners in the home) would be accorded the same protections as male victims (more often assaulted by strangers or acquaintances rather than intimate partners). Instead, rather than victims of violence being treated the same regardless of gender, female victims are again subject to discrimination. An arrest policy intended to protect battered women as victims is being misapplied and used against them. Battered women have become female offenders.

While the symmetrical application of arrest pays lip service to the equality tenet inherent in liberal feminism, the differences between violence committed by women and men are being masked. Though changes in police arrest practices may be commendable and seemingly gender-neutral, unreflective enforcement of pro-arrest and mandatory arrest statutes results in inappropriate arrests of women. The incorporation of primary aggressor laws that distinguish between preemptive and defensive violence as well as a contextual understanding of the violent relationship would greatly assist in clarifying the proper role of arrest. Only when the entire continuum of women's experiences is considered will the ambiguous dichotomy of "victim" and "offender" be better understood.

Serendipitously and informally, the female offender's program described in this book explores many levels of an ecologically nested model[2] (see Bronfenbrenner 1977, 1979, 1986; Dasgupta 2002) that include examining women's childhood and socialization experiences, present employment, family, relationship situations, larger social structural issues and patterns, as well as the uniqueness of one's culture and ethnicity or race. The female offender's program curriculum uses group discussions, worksheets, videos, and homework assignments to address these influences. By addressing the antecedents of violence, gender roles, and power dynamics in relationships, the female offender's program is able to richly contextualize the meanings, motivations, and consequences of women's use of violence. It would be interesting to see how other programs would more consciously incorporate the levels of an ecologically nested model into their curriculum. Providing these resources and services at the post-arrest stage in the process is laudable, but it disguises the dire need to offer access and support prior to the arrest incident. As Osthoff (2002, 1537) contends: "Perhaps with more options, women would be less likely to use violence (particularly when they are forced to do so in order to defend themselves) and, therefore, would be less likely to get arrested."

Unmistakably, given the women's experience with the criminal justice system, certain key issues must be reexamined and addressed. This study reveals that women's lack of familiarity with the system as well as the ease with which their emotions can be manipulated (by abusers or practitioners) and (poor) decisions made based on these emotions create barriers to achieving justice. Victim advocates need to enter at earlier stages in the case process, regardless whether the women are designated as "offenders." Most of the women in the treatment groups expressed anger at police officers' reluctance to "figure out" what transpired that led to the women's use of force. Police can be better trained to discern acts of self-defense from acts of aggressive violence, and in fact, evaluations of such trainings have begun to demonstrate declines in dual arrests in jurisdictions that provide such training to their officers (Hirschel and Buzawa 2002).

Prosecutors can play a more direct role in uncovering the context in which the use of force occurred, using their discretion to distinguish "true" offenders from victims who fought back. Previous research has recognized that prosecution may not always be the safest and most appropriate response (Mills 1999), so it is incumbent upon prosecutors to assess fully the situation before pursuing cases. As Epstein (1999) cautions, "We have become increasingly content—even complacent—to serve as technicians and tinkerers in the law rather than aspiring to the role of transformers, system shakers who risk alienation but seek real substantive change" (p. 3).

While civil lawsuits and changes in arrest policies have ensured that police take domestic violence more seriously, we now see potential dangers present in police and prosecutorial over-enforcement. This book highlights the need for further thinking and improvements within the criminal justice system, including an increased role for victim advocates for all women arrested on domestic violence charges.

Discussion

An over-reliance on the criminal justice system to protect women from domestic abuse has helped to create the issues examined in this book. It is a specious argument to insist that gender neutrality in law enforcement practices succeeds in identifying batterers; this utopian vision conflicts with women's realities within intimate relationships as well as fails to address the gendered nature of violence itself. As McMahon and Pence (2003, 57) contend, part of this failure can be attributed to the movement away from a critique of the underlying social, legal, and political structures that underpin male privilege and use of violence, and toward a more individual focus on the pathologies of offenders and victims, as well as the intricacies related to service providers' styles, practices, and specific procedures.

While some battered women may be helped by court-mandated treatment programs, failing to listen to women's stories about the context of their relationship violence and coercing women to attend batterer groups (presented as gifts in exchange for guilty pleas) replicate the very system of power and control that antiviolence advocates and scholars seek to eradicate. As indicated by the data presented in this book and discussions elsewhere, most women who are arrested for and charged with domestic violence offenses are not batterers. It is time for some difficult and serious reflection about this "vengeful equity," namely, on the appropriateness and misapplication of some domestic violence policies. Devising ways to evaluate individuals' actions within the context of their situations is paramount in order for the criminal justice system to respond in a more just and humane manner. Instituting policies that ignore or fly in the face of women's realities will only serve to increase the alienation and isolation experienced by victims of battering. Adopting a contextually based framework within which to evaluate domestic violence arrests of women will serve to monitor police power while simultaneously contributing to a more enlightened and efficacious response to women's use of force in intimate relationships.

Appendix

Domestic Violence Calls for Police Service: Summaries by Researchers

COUNTY POLICE (COUNTY A, SEVENTEEN INTIMATE VIOLENCE CALLS)

(June 19) Officer called to assist on a domestic call since the policy is to send out two officers. The police were dispatched to a white man's house in a lower-SES neighborhood in New Castle. The man's son and his son's girlfriend were engaged in a loud verbal fight. A different officer had been sent to the same home earlier that night when she punched him in the face with a kid's toy truck, but no arrest was made at that point. The other responding officer was annoyed because if she had been arrested earlier, there would have been no need for a second dispatch to this address. It was unclear what happened next as we were diverted to respond to a 911 hang up call somewhere else in the city. UNCLEAR IF ARRESTED. (white)

(June 24) A girlfriend and her ex-boyfriend got into a fight over shared custody with their son. He threw her against the wall and grabbed the child and stormed off. He was no longer on the premises when we arrived. The other officer on the scene took the call and sent us on our way. NO ARREST. (unknown race)

(June 26) We stopped a white guy, trashy looking with lots of tattoos, for a traffic violation and ran his name through the computer, finding that he had an outstanding PFA; the guy bragged about it: "I beat the shit out of her." Brought into station to book. ARRESTED ON PFA VIOLATION. (white)

(July 1) While student was waiting to be taken on the evening ride-along, another officer brought in a domestic where the woman had just bitten the man in the chest (both white). They were boyfriend/girlfriend. This ended up as a dual arrest. Both were junkies and she said he pushed her while he said she pushed him. Both parties had marks on them. DUAL ARREST. (white)

(July 4) 72-year-old white married couple. The wife told officer that her husband was drunk and pushed her. Initially the husband was arrested and handcuffed. But then the officer realized that he had pushed her last week, not that day, so the officer decided not to arrest but had their daughter pick her up and remove her from the home. The husband said that he was aggravated with his wife and the officer was too young to understand. NO ARREST. (white)

(July 4) White mother concerned about an argument between her white daughter and her daughter's black boyfriend. Two officers arrived and separated them to get full stories. An eight-year-old child was brought in to tell about the injuries that the daughter incurred. The daughter was screaming the whole time that her mother hates black people. No arrest was made, despite what the boy said, because officers compared stories and determined that the mother's story did not add up. Both the boyfriend and the girlfriend said the mother had been drinking and placed her somewhere where she would not have been able to witness their argument. The daughter did not have any visible injuries. NO ARREST. (white and black)

(July 8) Call from a nice trailer park where wife and husband had been drinking at the beach all day. She did most of the driving home and was tired. The car ran out of gas on the way home and she could not get her husband up to help get the gas. So, she had had it with him by the time they got home. She started an argument and started beating on him. He had a bloody contusion on his face and other bruises on his arms and back. She admitted to everything that she did. ARREST. (white)

(July 10) Officer called as backup to case involving custody dispute between divorced white couple, but officers told the couple that they had to go to family court to resolve. NO ARREST. (white)

(July 10) Second officer on scene. Took the husband outside and he explained that he was trying to leave the house and his wife was mad because she wanted to go out that night and wanted him to watch the kids. So, she was physically holding him back. When he went to get into the car, she had jumped onto the back of the car. When he realized she was there, he stopped and she called the cops. The first responding officer made no arrest, which the second officer disagreed with, saying that if it was the other way around, the guy would have been locked up in a second. But the officer in charge decided not to make any arrest because the husband said that she was not actually hitting him, but trying to restrain him. NO ARREST. (white)

(July 17) A man, no longer at the scene, slapped his girlfriend after giving her a hard time about drinking. Since it was in the city's jurisdiction, the county officer did nothing. NO ARREST. (black)

(July 17) Answered a call that involved a nonviolent argument between white husband and wife. Both wanted to use the only car with air conditioning. He claimed that both cars were really his since he was the only one who worked. One of the officers said, "Hey, your wife takes care of your three babies; that's work. Do you want your kids to ride around in a car without a/c?" So, the husband gave in. Later, the officer said that if they had arrested anyone, it would have been the wife since she had pushed him during the dispute. NO ARREST. (white)

(July 24) Officer working on a PFA case involving a mentally retarded divorced couple. The ex-wife had assaulted him. They still share their only car; she wanted it today and he got in the car with her and she told him to leave. But, he offensively touched her and would not leave. He pulled the keys out while she was driving and she crashed. Officer was filing out a warrant to arrest him for Offensive Touching and destruction of property. WARRANT TO ARREST.

(August 6) When officer arrived on the scene, she was gone but had ripped up his clothes. NO ARREST. (white)

(August 7) White girlfriend arguing with black boyfriend over their baby. The guy said that he was going to kill her and take his son. Another officer was already there and had already separated the two. Found out later from the first officer that she would not fill out a restraining order; she just wants to get him in trouble, but he's never hurt the baby and he pays support. If she was bruised or if he had admitted to threatening her, they could have arrested him for terroristic threatening. NO ARREST. (white and black)

(August 7) Another officer met them at scene. It was in a nice house in a nice neighborhood, with a white married couple in their 40s. The wife answers the door crying. The husband is in the other room, pissed off. She said they were fighting about getting her car fixed and they are having financial difficulties and he was mad at her because she doesn't work for his company anymore. When she questioned him about getting the car fixed, he yelled at her and went upstairs to sleep. She followed him and kept bothering him; he told her to leave but they kept arguing. He got up and pushed her out of the way. She followed him back downstairs arguing, and she went to the phone. He hit it out of her hand and broke it, and she bit his wrist. The husband basically said the same story, but said that he never pushed her and that she has been depressed and was on medication because of their financial difficulties. She had no visible injuries. The husband did not want her arrested, but they did arrest her because the officer felt she was the aggressor because she had many chances to get away from him yet she kept following him around the house. ARREST. (white)

(August 8) Picked up middle-class white guy wanted for PFA violation. ARREST. (white)

(August 19) Call involved mother and son and a verbally harassing ex-girlfriend. NO ARREST. (white)

(There were also seven non-intimate domestic calls, not included here.)

STATE POLICE (THREE TROOPS IN COUNTIES B AND C, ELEVEN INTIMATE VIOLENCE CALLS)

(June 19) Answered call that someone saw a man beating his wife in a car with kids. They tried to find the car with no luck. NO ARREST. (unknown race)

(July 10) Answered call to boyfriend's house where girlfriend had done some vandalism. She wasn't home—had left threatening suicide. NO ARREST. (white)

(July 17) Dispatched to restaurant to fight between white girlfriend and boyfriend. She said he grabbed her in an attempt to detain her during an argument. Officer drove to her residence with the victim (nice neighborhood, middle class) and found offender. ARREST. (white)

(July 29) Answered call at convenience store; a terroristic threat incident between a white female, about 25, threatened by her ex-boyfriend who she had cheated on her fiancé with. He was on heroin and had several warrants on him. ARREST. (white)

(August 1) Responded to verbal domestic at gas station. Black girlfriend accused black boyfriend of cheating on her. She had just left and threatened to go tear up their apartment. State made courtesy call to local police department to advise that State would go there. She wasn't there. NO ARREST. (Black)

(August 1) Domestic call reported by neighbor. Officer flew there, lights and sirens, but no one was at location. (unknown race)

(August 6) Officer called to station to handle walk-in domestic involving white husband and wife. The husband had been drinking and punched her in the back as she left. She said that they've been married 14 years, and this is the third time he'd done this when drinking. ARREST WARRANT FILLED OUT. (white)

(August 11) Domestic in courthouse; a 22-year-old white female complained that her ex-fiancé had broken her $180 stroller. Officer negotiated with the ex-bf that if he paid $100, the officer wouldn't arrest him. NO ARREST. (white)

(August 11) Picked up guy wanted from breach of PFA from night before. ARREST. (unknown race)

(August 13) Ex-girlfriend said that he cut her, but he wasn't there. Outstanding warrant for PFA violation for him. ARREST WARRANT. (white)

(August 20) Answered call to poor development, with junk lying around the yard. White woman was sobbing, surrounded by friends and kids. One woman was saying to her: "You don't have to take this anymore. You have to make it stop." No visible injuries. The white male was drunk and high and fled to woods. When officers found him, he swung keys on long cord and they tackled him. He shouted: "I fuck her in the cunt. I pay the bills. It is my goddamn money. Fuck her. I am done with her." He had a marijuana pipe with him. ARREST. (white)

(There were also two non-intimate domestic calls, not included here.)

CITY POLICE (COUNTY A, TWENTY-TWO
INTIMATE VIOLENCE CALLS)

(June 14) Call involving gun. Car was third or fourth on scene and boyfriend had already fled with gun. NO ARREST. (Unknown race).

(June 14) Oral argument boyfriend with girlfriend; neighbor called. No injuries. NO ARREST. (unknown race)

(June 14) Obese black naked lady crying. Black husband very pissed off. Neighbor said this is the first time it happened. First officer came out with husband in handcuffs. She was injured and blamed him. ARREST. (black).

(June 18) Verbal between white husband and wife. Other officer was already on scene and had husband leave. NO ARREST. (white)

(June 18) Domestic in progress in parking lot. White male and female, both teenagers, and female was in a stage of undress. "I guess they made up pretty quickly, huh," says officer laughing. NO ARREST. (unknown race)

(June 25) DV in progress: boyfriend beating on girlfriend in public. Not found. NO ARREST. (unknown race)

(June 26) DV: saw 3 black people on street gesticulating wildly—2 women and one guy. Woman with bandage on face arguing with guy. Guy had restraining order against her. Police escorted her away and told guy to go into house and not to argue, just call police if she came back. Wrote it down as disturbing the peace. Officer told student he would not write it up as a domestic because of paperwork. Too much time to spend on something so little when there is "real" stuff to do. NO ARREST. (black)

(June 29) DV call: middle class neighborhood. Black man finally came to door and said "my bitch been on me all week. She cut my wires in my truck and I kicked her out of the house. I ain't gonna let her back in." She wasn't there. Officer said he would write up report. They went back to car and ran her name through computer and she had an outstanding warrant. Officer was sure more was going on—she probably called police (guy was sweating and too worked up—officer believed that he definitely did more than he said he did) and she had fled, probably because she didn't want cops picking her up on the outstanding warrant. Officer thinks she'd get shit kicked out of her tonight, but nothing they can do since she wasn't there. (NO ARREST). (black)

(July 3) DV call: black female hit with chair over her head by boyfriend and he also attacked girlfriend's daughter by kicking her in back and punching her. Met by another officer. Small row house. Advised her to obtain PFA. Subject gone when arrived at scene. Officer explained that other officer went to station to sign warrants on the subject. Felt that if they left it up to the victim and the subject returned that night and seriously injured or killed her, then he would get his face plastered all over the local newspaper and get fired for not having taken proper action. (Victim was sister of recently retired city police officer). WARRANTS. (black)

(July 3) DV: flagged down by black female about domestic in progress. Black female and black male were fighting. Woman did not stop so handcuffed each and put in separate police car. Woman had bite marks from him and he had scrapes and cuts inflicted by her. Offered both subjects the option of signing warrants against the other and both refused. Officer said that he had dealt with the male subject before that and "he's an asshole." Shared a child but separate residences. (NO ARRESTS). Officer felt that since both committed act of violence but did not share residence, it made him comfortable that they would be safe from each other for the night. Officer said that he would not have arrested both of them unless the abuse was more severe in both subjects. Explained that he had covered his liability because they had both refused warrants.

(July 9) 78-year-old black man stabbed in his apartment by black girlfriend. Transported to hospital. She wasn't on scene and victim covered for her and minimized incident. NO ARREST. (black)

(July 9) Black boyfriend pushed black girlfriend and she broke bottle over his head. We left and first officer kept call. We took guy to hospital. UNCLEAR IF ARRESTED LATER. (black)

(July 10) Neighbors heard screams, drinking, but nothing visible with girlfriend or missing boyfriend. NO ARREST. (unknown race)

(July 13) Homeless woman needed to get to a battered women's shelter. Huge bruises on arm. Said husband beat her after she found out he was cheating on her. OF-FICER DID NOT GIVE HER WARRANT INFO. NO ARREST. (white)

(July 14) Possible dv call. Black woman jumped off bridge; possible her boyfriend pushed her. We did not answer call since paramedics were on the way there. NO ARREST. (black)

(July 20) Domestic in progress. White woman in early 40s met them and said white boyfriend had not taken medication and they got into a verbal fight and he punched the wall. No signs of injury on her. Boyfriend had no injuries either. NO ARREST. (white)

(July 27) Hispanic woman had taken her 3 kids to police station to get away from drunken ex-husband. Needed interpreter. We were back-up, and escorted her back to house after getting call that ex-husband had left. NO ARREST. (Hispanic)

(July 30) 17-year-old white girl (with 2 kids) said that she was thrown through a screen door by black boyfriend of 3 weeks. Told she could file warrant. NO ARREST. (white/black)

(August 12) Black female, working class, said that ex-boyfriend (they share son) has new girlfriend who threatened to kill her at the mall. Officer wrote up dv report for terroristic threatening and gave it to woman and told her to go to court to file warrants against girlfriend and girlfriend's mother who was also involved. NO ARREST. (black)

(August 17) We were back-up for other officer. Verbal between husband and wife. Nothing happened. NO ARREST. (unknown race).

(August 19) DV call—black woman flagged them down; lived in projects and screamed she wanted her black fiancé arrested. Called for back up since guy was getting upset she wanted him arrested. She was jealous—saw him drinking out of another women's cup on porch. He had hit her three times in the face. She kept threatening him that she was going to get him later. Officer tried to get version from man but he was very drunk and wouldn't tell it. He just kept screaming that it didn't matter what he said since he was going to be the one getting arrested anyway. Finally he started talking and he said that she was swinging also. Two women backed up her story. Officer filled out dv incident report for offensive touching and gave woman a copy, saying she could take it to court the next day if she wanted to press charges. She had no visible bruises and offi-cer told the student he filled out the report so he would not be called to court to testify. Then he took her to her mother's house and told her not to go back to their house that night. When in the car, officer told student that he did not arrest the guy because he saw no bruises on the woman, which would be unusual for someone who got hit in the face three times. Also, since the lady told him that nothing like this ever happened before, and he didn't really believe her story anyway, he didn't want to make an arrest. Didn't arrest the man because didn't believe the woman. NO ARREST. (black)

(August 27) DV complaint: black female was hit by ex-boyfriend. Minor swelling on either side of face but also could have been from crying. Black boyfriend; not on scene. Officer told her he would write up a crime report for her and she would have to go to the station to file a complaint against him and she said she would. PAPERWORK, NO ARREST. (black)

(There were also four non-intimate domestic calls, not included here.)

Notes

Chapter 1   Defining the Dilemma

1. Some of this chapter draws upon S. Miller (2001) and Iovanni and Miller (2001).
2. See Dobash and Dobash 1992; Matthews 1994. For example, in the pro-choice movement, as funding became available for activists to "make careers out of being movement leaders," the movement itself became more professionalized and formal (Staggenborg 1988).
3. Many of these laws were constructed in order to avoid civil liability suits charging that police did not respond appropriately to domestic violence calls for police service when crimes involve intimate partners rather than strangers (Lyon 1999), and ignored or delayed response, which violates the equal protection clause of the Fourteenth Amendment (see *Thurman v. City of Torrington*, 1994).

Chapter 2   The Controversy about Women's Use of Force

1. However, other researchers believe that hitting even once conveys the possibility to everyone that hitting could happen again, and that violence does not have to happen again to remind who has the power (Belknap and Potter 2005).
2. The use of "same-gender" was coined by Perilla et al. (2003).
3. Perilla et al. (2003) offer a caution about the risks of using a feminist analysis to explain same-gender intimate violence, maintaining that it could fuel myths such as: "(a) gay male violence is logical because men are violent and violence is uncommon in lesbian relationships because women are nonviolent; (b) same-gender partner violence is not as severe as that which men perpetrate against their female partners; (c) because both partners are of the same gender, it is mutual abuse; and (d) as a reflection of heterosexual domestic violence, the perpetrator in homosexual couples must be the 'man' or 'butch' and the victim must be the 'woman' or 'femme'" (p. 21; see also Merrill 1996).

Chapter 3   The Research Project

1. Reliability concerns the extent to which findings can be replicated. Validity concerns the extent to which data actually reflect what investigators set out to measure.
2. Although battering occurs within same-sex relationships, the focus for this analysis is on heterosexual domestic violence because at the time of the data collection, there were no lesbian clients arrested and mandated for treatment who participated in the groups. Lesbian clients have the option to participate in group or individual

counseling. Material was presented in group sessions using references to both heterosexual and lesbian relationships.

3. This twelve-week commitment differs from the men's program commitment of sixteen weeks. Both programs operate with sliding scales, based on an individual's income. Since women typically earn less than men, their program costs were often less expensive.

4. The facilitator's name, Mary, is a pseudonym. All names of group participants are also pseudonyms.

Chapter 4 **On the Beat**

1. Before beginning, the researchers were trained to follow Lofland and Lofland's fieldwork steps (1995, 89–98): During the period of observation, take notes to aid memory and to let respondents know that they are being taken seriously; convert these to full field notes at the end of each shift to minimize the time between observation and writing so that crucial material is not lost; write up observations fully before the next trip to the field; and, when additional information is recalled, add it to the written notes. For the research team, field notes were a "running description of events, people, things heard and overheard, conversations among people, conversations with people. Each new physical setting and person encountered merit[ed] a description" (Lofland and Lofland 1995, 93). Investigators distinguished between the respondents' verbatim accounts and their own paraphrasing and general recall.

2. For instance, one white male officer, who commented on the appearance of all women they passed during the shift and talked a lot about sex with his girlfriend, said to a male student ride-along, "I am so glad I got you to ride-along with. We could talk about pussy all night. You never know who you are gonna get when you get a ride-along, and it would have sucked to get a girl or some loser guy. This is really cool."

3. The two most common misdemeanor charges for domestic violence offenses in this state are offensive touching (OT) and terroristic threatening. "A person is guilty of offensive touching when the person intentionally touches another person either with a member of his or her body or with any instrument, knowing that the person is thereby likely to cause offense or alarm to such other person; a person is guilty of terroristic threatening when he or she commits any of the following: (1) the person threatens to commit any crime likely to result in death or in serious injury to person or property; (2) the person makes a false statement or statements: a. knowing that the statement or statements are likely to cause evacuation of a building, place of assembly, or facility of public transportation; b. knowing that the statement or statements are likely to cause serious inconvenience; or c. in reckless disregard of the risk of causing terror or serious inconvenience" (see state criminal code).

Chapter 5 **After Arrest**

1. This chapter draws on S. Miller (2001).

2. The police officers interviewed for this component of the study held supervisory and leadership positions, such as the head or director of their department's domestic violence task force.

3. Social workers in the prosecutor's office exercised enormous power. Typically, they were responsible for the background work, which essentially became the charging decision. Prosecutors rarely got involved until later in court. There had been a

high turnover of prosecutors in County A, yet the unit's two social workers had been there for four and nine years. As one social worker related (and she acknowledged that they are the key people making the decisions):

> We have a lot of input because we are the ones who talk to the victims . . . and we can say when we see "Jane Smith"—well, "Joe Smith"—has been here twenty times before, but that particular prosecutor won't know it because he's only been in family court maybe six months to a year.

4. Victim services personnel believed that the prosecutor's office was very reluctant to pursue dual arrests. Throughout the state, respondents mentioned that the turnover was high and retention was low in the prosecutor's offices, leaving little continuity in policy and procedure—and little institutional memory. There was a sense that the court personnel sought to dispose of most of the cases at arraignment. There was also the sense that only the most junior prosecutors had this job, and they were just biding their time until they could be promoted or transferred elsewhere, and nobody was watching them because it was "only" family court.

Chapter 6 A Day in the Life

1. In reality, however, the charges remain on the women's records, with "dismissed" noted next to them.

Chapter 7 The Contexts of "Violent" Behavior

1. Some of this chapter draws on S. Miller and Meloy (2005).
2. The Domestic Abuse Project in Minnesota designates a category similar to the frustration response category, one they call "Never Again." This motivation is often characteristic of women who have had long or repeated relationships in which they were battered. They adopted a survival mode of thinking: "No one is ever going to hurt me that way again," and used violence to decrease their chances for further victimization (Domestic Abuse Project 1998). The research team did not observe this kind of motivation very often. However, prior abuse often manifests in a mindset of defiance and a refusal to accept further abuse.
3. The facilitator makes allowances for those women who can not complete homework assignments at home because of ongoing conflict with their partners.

Chapter 8 Implications

1. In their work with delinquent girls who commit crimes serious enough to be sentenced as adults, Gaardner and Belknap (2004) explore also the fluidity involving victim and offender classifications, seeing these girls as both victims and actors in lives that are constrained by social structural limitations.
2. Ecologically nested models can be useful in understanding violence because they explore macro-level interactions of social, historical, and institutional variables as well as individual level (micro) factors. (See Edleson and Tolman (1992), and Heise (1998) for general discussions of how this model is used in a domestic violence context.)

References

Abel, E. M., and E. K. Suh. 1987. Use of police services by battered women. *Social Work* 32:526–628.

Acoca, L. 1998. Diffusing the time bomb: Understanding and meeting the growing health care needs of incarcerated women in America. *Crime and Delinquency* 44 (1):49–70.

Acoca, L. 1999. Getting healthy and staying healthy: Physical and mental health/ substance abuse. In *National Symposium on Women Offenders*, 33–36. Washington, DC: U.S. Department of Justice.

Allard, C. A. 1991. Rethinking battered woman's syndrome: A black feminist perspective. *UCLA Women's Law Journal* 1:191–207.

Ammons, L. L. 1995. Mules, madonnas, babies, bathwater, racial imagery and stereotypes: The African American woman and the battered women's syndrome. *Wisconsin Law Review* 5:1003–1080.

Anderson, K. L., and D. Umberson. 2001. Gendering violence: Masculinity and power in men's accounts of domestic violence. *Gender & Society* 15 (3):358– 380.

Anderson, T. Forthcoming (2006). Women in prison. In *Rethinking gender, crime, and justice: Feminist perspectives*, ed. C. M. Renzetti, L. Goodstein, and S. L. Miller. Los Angeles: Roxbury.

Archer, J. 2000. Assessment of the reliability of the Conflict Tactics Scales: A meta-analytical review. *Journal of Interpersonal Violence* 14:1263–1289.

Bachman, R. 2000. A comparison of annual incidence rates and contextual characteristics of intimate partner violence against women from the National Crime Victimization Survey (NCVS) and the National Violence Against Women Survey (NVAWS). *Violence Against Women* 6:839–867.

Bachman, R., and D. C. Carmody. 1994. Fighting fire with fire: The effects of victim resistance in intimate versus stranger perpetrated assaults against females. *Journal of Family Violence* 9:317–331.

Bachman, R., and L. Saltzman. 1995. *Violence against women: Estimates from the redesigned survey*. Washington, DC: U.S. Department of Justice.

Bachman, R., and B. Taylor. 1994. The measurement of rape and family violence by the redesigned National Crime Victimization Survey. *Justice Quarterly* 11:702– 704.

Bandura, A. 1973. *Aggression: A social learning analysis*. Englewood Cliffs, NJ: Prentice Hall.

Barnett, O. W., and A. LaViolette. 1993. *It could happen to anyone: Why battered women stay*. Newbury Park, CA: Sage.

Barnett, O. W., C. Y. Lee, and R. E. Thelan. 1997. Gender differences in attribution of self-defense and control in interpartner aggression. *Violence Against Women* 3:462–481.

Barnett, O. W., and R. E. Thelan. 1992. Gender differences in forms, outcomes and motivations for marital violence. Unpublished manuscript.

Belknap, J., and K. Holsinger. 2000. Gender discrimination and status offenders. In *Encyclopedia of women and crime*, ed. N. H. Rafter, 98–99. Phoenix, AZ: Oryx Press.

Belknap, J., and H. Potter. Forthcoming (2005). Intimate partner abuse. In *Women, crime, and criminal justice* (2nd ed.), ed. C. M. Renzetti, L. Goodstein, and S. L. Miller. Los Angeles: Roxbury.

Bell, D. J. 1986. Domestic violence in small cities and towns: A pilot study. *Journal of Criminal Justice* 9:163–181.

Berk, R. A., A. Campbell, R. Klap, and V. Western. 1992. The deterrent effect of arrest in incidents of domestic violence: A Bayesian analysis of four field experiments. *American Sociological Review* 57:698–708.

Berns, N. 2001. Degendering the problem and gendering the blame: Political discourse on women and violence. *Gender & Society* 15 (2):262–281.

Black, D. J. 1980. *The manners and customs of the police*. San Diego, CA: Academic Press.

Bloom, B., and S. Covington. 1998. Gender-specific programming for female offenders: What is it and why is it important? Paper presented at the 50th annual meeting of the American Society of Criminology, Washington, DC, 1998.

Blumner, R. December 12, 1999. Men get slapped around: Who cares? *Sunday Star Ledger*, 1, 6.

Bowker, L. H. 1983. Beating wife beating. *Response* 4–5 (January–February), Washington, DC: Center for Women's Policy Studies.

Bowman, C. G. 1992. The arrest experiments: A feminist critique. *Journal of Criminal Law and Criminology* 83:201–208.

Boyd, S. C. 2004. *From witches to crack moms: Women, drug law, and policy*. Durham, NC: Carolina Academic Press.

Bronfenbrenner, U. 1977. Toward an experimental ecology of human development. *American Psychologist* 32:523–621.

Bronfenbrenner, U. 1979. *The ecology of human development: Experiments by nature and design*. Cambridge, MA: Harvard University Press.

Bronfenbrenner, U. 1986. Development as action in context: Problem solving behavior and normal youth development. In *Recent advances in research on the ecology of human development*, ed. R. Silbereisen, K. Eyferth, and G. Rudinger, 287–308. New York: Springer.

Brown, S. E. 1984. Police responses to wife beating: Neglect of a crime of violence. *Journal of Criminal Justice* 12:277–288.

Browne, A. 1987. *When battered women kill*. New York: Free Press.

Buel, S. M. 1988. Recent developments: Mandatory arrest for domestic violence. *Harvard Women's Law Journal* 11:213–226.

Burke, L. K., and D. R. Follingstad. 1999. Violence in lesbian and gay relationships: Theory, prevalence, and correlational factors. *Clinical Psychology Review* 19:487–512.

Burrell, B. C. 1995. Women's movements in America: Their successes, disappointments and aspirations. *Women & Politics* 15 (1):69–90.

Burroughs, D. R. March 4, 1999. Who has heard of a battered men's shelter? *Delaware State News*, 5.

Busch, A. L., and M. S. Rosenberg. 2004. Comparing women and men arrested for domestic violence: A preliminary report. *Journal of Family Violence* 19 (1):49–57.

Buzawa, E. S., and C. G. Buzawa. 1990. *Domestic violence: The criminal justice response.* Beverly Hills, CA: Sage.

Buzawa, E. S., and C. G. Buzawa. 1993. The scientific evidence is not conclusive: Arrest is no panacea. In *Current controversies on family violence*, ed. R. J. Gelles and D. R. Loseke, 337–356. Newbury Park, CA: Sage.

Buzawa, E. S., and C. G. Buzawa. 2003. *Domestic violence: The criminal justice response.* Thousand Oaks, CA: Sage.

Buzawa, E. S., and G. Hotaling. 2000. *The police response to domestic violence: Calls for assistance in three Massachusetts towns, Final Report.* Washington, DC: National Institute of Justice.

Cain, M. 1990. Realist philosophy and standpoint epistemologies, or feminist criminology as a successor science. In *Feminist Perspectives in Criminology*, ed. L. Gelsthorpe and A. Morris, 124–140. Philadelphia: Open University Press.

Campbell, J. C. 1995. *Assessing dangerousness: Violence by sexual offenders, batterers and child abusers.* Thousand Oaks, CA: Sage.

Campbell, J. C., L. Rose, J. Kub, and D. Nedd. 1998. Voices of strength and resistance: A contextual and longitudinal analysis of women's responses to battering. *Journal of Interpersonal Violence* 13:743–762.

Cantos, A. L., P. H. Neidig, and K. D. O'Leary. 1994. Injuries of women and men in a treatment program for domestic violence. *Journal of Family Violence* 9:113–124.

Cascardi, M. D., and D. Vivian. 1995. Context for specific episodes of marital violence: Gender and severity of violent differences. *Journal of Family Violence* 10: 265–293.

Cascardi, M. D., D. Vivian, and S. L. Meyer. 1991. Context and attributions for marital violence in discordant couples. Paper presented at the meeting of the Association for the Advancement of Behavior Therapy, New York.

Chaudhuri, M., and K. Daly. 1992. Do restraining orders help? Batterered women's experiences with male violence and the legal process. In *Domestic violence: The changing criminal justice response*, ed. E. S. Buzawa and C. G. Buzawa, 227–252. Westwood, CT: Auburn House.

Chesney-Lind, M. 1998. Women in prison: The forgotten offender. *Corrections Today* 60 (7):66–73.

Chu, J. L., and D. L. Dill. 1990. Dissociative symptoms in relation to childhood physical and sexual abuse. *American Journal of Psychiatry* 147:887–892.

Clark, M. L., J. Beckett, M. Wells, and D. Dungee-Anderson. 1994. Courtship violence among African American college students. *Journal of Black Psychology* 20:264–281.

Cook, P. W. 1997. *Abused men: The hidden side of domestic violence.* New York: Praeger.

Danner, M. J. E. 1998. Three strikes and it's women who are out: The hidden consequences for women of criminal justice policy reforms. In *Crime control and women: Feminist implications of criminal justice policy*, ed. S. L. Miller, 1–14. Thousand Oaks, CA: Sage.

Dasgupta, S. D. 1999. Just like men? A critical review of violence by women. In *Coordinating community response to domestic violence: Lessons from Duluth and beyond*, ed. M. F. Shepard and E. L. Pence, 195–222. Thousand Oaks, CA: Sage.

———. 2002. A framework for understanding women's use of nonlethal violence in intimate heterosexual relationships. *Violence Against Women* 8 (11):1364–1389.

DeKeseredy, W. S. 2000. Current controversies on defining nonlethal violence against women in intimate heterosexual relationships: Empirical implications. *Violence Against Women* 6:728–746.

DeKeseredy, W. S., D. G. Saunders, M. D. Schwartz, and S. Alvi. 1997. The meanings and motives for women's use of violence in Canadian college dating relationships: Results from a national survey. *Sociological Spectrum* 17:199–222.

DeKeseredy, W. S., and M. D. Schwartz. 1998. Measuring the extent of woman abuse in intimate heterosexual relationships: A critique of the CTS. Violence against women online resources: http://www.vaw.umn.edu/documents/vawnet/ctscritique/ctscritique.html

Denzin, N. K. 1997. *Interpretive ethnography: Ethnographic practices for the 21st century.* Thousand Oaks, CA: Sage.

Denzin, N. K., and Y. S. Lincoln. 1994. *Handbook of qualitative research.* Thousand Oaks, CA: Sage.

Dobash, R. E., and R. P. Dobash. 1979. *Violence against wives.* New York: Free Press.

———. 1992. *Women, violence and social change.* New York: Routledge.

———. 1998. Violent men and violent contexts. In *Rethinking violence against women,* ed. R. E. Dobash and R. P. Dobash. Thousand Oaks, CA: Sage.

Dobash, R. E., R. P. Dobash, and K. Cavanagh. 2000. *Changing violent men.* Thousand Oaks, CA: Sage.

Dobash, R. P., R. E. Dobash, K. Cavanagh, and R. Lewis. 1998. Separate and intersecting realities: A comparison of men's and women's accounts of violence against women. *Violence Against Women* 4:382–414.

Dobash, R. P., R. E. Dobash, M. Wilson, and M. Daly. 1992. The myth of sexual symmetry in marital violence. *Social Problems* 39:71–91.

Domestic Violence Abuse Project. 1998. *Women who abuse in intimate relationships.* Minneapolis, MN: Domestic Violence Abuse Project.

Double-Time. 1998. (Newsletter of the National Clearinghouse for the Defense of Battered Women) 6:1–2.

Dowd, L. 2001. Female perpetrators of partner aggression: Relevant issues and treatment. *Journal of Aggression, Maltreatment & Trauma* 5 (2):73–101.

Dubois, B. 1983. Passionate scholarship: Notes on values, knowing, and method in feminist social science. In *Theories for women's studies,* ed. G. Bowlers and D. R. Klein, 105–116. London: Routledge and Kegan Paul.

Dunford, F. W. 1992. The measurement of recidivism in cases of spouse assaults. *Journal of Criminal Law and Criminology* 83 (1):120–136.

Dutton, M. A. 1992. *Empowering and healing the battered woman: A model of assessment and intervention.* New York: Springer.

Eaton, M. 2004. Abuse by any other name: Feminism, difference, and intra-lesbian violence. In *The public nature of private violence: The discovery of domestic abuse,* ed. M. A. Fineman and R. Mykitiuk, 195–223. New York: Routledge.

Edleson, J. L., and R. L. Tolman. 1992. *Interventions for men who batter: An ecological approach.* Newbury Park, CA: Sage.

Elliott, P. 1996. Shattering illusions: Same-sex domestic violence. In *Violence in gay and lesbian domestic partnerships,* ed. C. M. Renzetti and C. H. Miley, 1–8. Binghamton, NY: Harrington Park Press.

Epstein, D. 1999. Effective intervention in domestic violence cases: Rethinking the roles of prosecutors, judges and the court system. *Yale Journal of Law & Feminism* 11:3–50.

Fagan, J. 1989. Cessation of family violence: Deterrence and dissuasion. In *Family violence,* ed. L. Ohlin and M. Tonry, 427–480. Chicago: University of Chicago Press.

Faith, K. 1993. *Unruly women: The politics of confinement and resistance.* Vancouver, Canada: Press Gang.

Farrell, W. 1999. *Women can't hear what men don't say.* New York: Tarcher/Putnam.

Feld, S. L., and M. A. Straus. 1989. Escalation and desistance of wife assault in marriage. *Criminology* 17:141–161.

Ferrante, A., Morgan, F., Indermaur, D., and Harding, R. 1996. *Measuring the extent of domestic violence*. Perth, Australia: Hawkins Press.

Ferraro, K. J. 1989. Policing woman battering. *Social Problems* 36:61–74.

———. 1996. The dance of dependency: A genealogy of domestic violence discourse. *Hypatia* 11 (4):77–91.

———. 2003. The words change, but the melody lingers: The persistence of the battered women's syndrome in criminal cases involving battered women. *Violence Against Women* 9:110–129.

Fiebert, M. S. 1997. References examining assaults by women on their spouses or male partners: An annotated bibliography. *Sexuality & Culture* 1:273–286.

———. 1998. References examining assaults by women on their spouses or male partners: An annotated bibliography. http://www.vix.com/menmag/fiebert.htm.

Field, M. H., and H. F. Field. 1973. Marital violence and the criminal process: Neither justice nor peace. *Social Science Review* 47:221–240.

Finn, P., and S. Colson. 1990. *Civil protection orders: Legislation, current court practice, and enforcement (issues and practice report)*. Washington, DC: National Institute of Justice.

Fisher-Giorlando, M. 2000. Gender disparity in prisons. In *The encyclopedia of women and crime*, ed. N. H. Raftner, 99–102. Phoenix, AZ: Oryx.

Flavin, J. 2001. Feminism for the mainstream criminologist. *Journal of Criminal Justice* 27:271–285.

Follingstad, D. R., S. Wright, S. Lloyd, and J. A. Sebastian. 1991. Sex differences in motivations and effects of dating violence. *Family Relations* 40:51–57.

Ford, D. A. 1987. The impact of police officers' attitudes toward victims on the disinclination to arrest wife batterers. Paper presented at the Third National Conference for Family Violence Researchers, University of New Hampshire, Durham, NH.

Fox, J. A., and M. W. Zawitz. 2000. *Homicide Trends in the United States: Intimate homicide*. Washington, DC: U.S. Department of Justice, Bureau of Justice Statistics.

Gaardner, E., and J. Belknap. 2004. Tenuous borders: Girls transferred to adult court. In *The criminal justice system and women: Offenders, prisoners, victims, and workers*, ed. B. R. Price and N. J. Sokoloff, 95–112. New York: McGraw-Hill.

Gelb, A. 1994. *Quincy court model domestic abuse program manual*. Swampscott, MA: Productions Specialties.

Gelles, R. J. October 12, 2000. Domestic violence: Not an even playing field. *The safety zone*: http://thesafetyzone.org/everyone/gelles.html

Gelles, R. J., and M. A. Straus. 1988. *Intimate violence: The causes and consequences of abuse in the American family*. New York: Touchstone.

George, L., and A. Wilson. 2002. *Community-based analysis of the U.S. legal system's interventions in domestic abuse cases involving indigenous women*. Unpublished report, National Institute of Justice. (Available from MPDI Inc., 202 East Superior Street, Duluth, MN 55806).

Gelsthorpe, L. 1990. Feminist methodologies in criminology. In *Feminist Perspectives in Criminology*, ed. L. Gelsthorpe and A. Morris, 89–106. Philadelphia: Open University Press.

Gil, D. G. 1986. Sociocultural aspects of domestic violence. In *Violence in the home: Interdisciplinary perspectives*, ed. M. Lystad, 128–149. New York: Brunner/Mazel.

Gilbert, P. R. 2002. Discourses of female violence and societal gender stereotypes. *Violence Against Women* 8:1275–1304.

Gilfus, M. E. 1992. From victims to survivors to offenders: Women's routes of entry and immersion into street crime. *Women & Criminal Justice* 4 (1):63–88.

Giorgio, G. 2002. Speaking silence: Definitional dialogues in abusive lesbian relationships. *Violence Against Women* 8 (10):1233–1259.

Gondolf, E. W., and E. R. Fisher. 1988. *Battered women as survivors: An alternative to treating learned helplessness.* Lexington, MA: Lexington Books.

Gonzalez, D. M. 1997. *Why females initiate violence: A study examining the reasons behind assaults on men.* Master's thesis, California State University, Long Beach.

Gordon, L. 1988. *Heroes of their own lives.* New York: Penguin Books.

Gottfredson, M., and D. Gottfredson. 1988. *Decision-making in criminal justice.* 2nd ed. Cambridge, MA: Ballinger.

Greenfeld, L. A., and T. L. Snell. 1999. *Women offenders.* Bureau of Justice Statistics, special report. Washington, DC: U.S. Department of Justice.

Greenfeld, L. A., M. R. Rand, D. Craven, P. A. Klaus, C. A. Perkins, and C. Ringel. 1998. *Violence by intimates: Analysis of data on crimes by current or former spouses, boyfriends, and girlfriends.* Washington, DC: U.S. Department of Justice.

Guyot, D. 1979. Bending granite: Attempts to change the rank structure of American police departments. *Journal of Police Science and Administration* 7 (3):253–284.

Hamberger, L. K. 1991a. Characteristics and context of women arrested for domestic violence: Context and implications. Give in section titled Marital violence: Theoretical and empirical perspectives, Indiana University Conference on Research and Clinical Problems, Bloomington, IN.

Hamberger, L. K. 1991b. Research concerning wife abuse: Implications for training police and physicians. In State-of-the-art research in family violence: Practical applications, R. Geffner (Chair), symposium presented at the meeting of the American Psychological Association, San Francisco, CA.

Hamberger, L. K. 1997. Female offenders in domestic violence: A look at actions in context. *Journal of Aggression, Maltreatment & Trauma* 1 (1):117–129.

Hamberger, L. K., and C. E. Guse. 2002. Men's and women's use of intimate partner violence in clinical samples. *Violence Against Women* 9:1305–1335.

Hamberger, L. K., and J. M. Lohr. 1989. Proximal causes of spouse abuse: Theoretical analysis for cognitive-behavioral interventions. In *Treating men who batter: Theory, practice, and programs,* ed. P. L. Caesar and L. K. Hamberger, 53–76. New York: Springer.

Hamberger, L. K., J. M. Lohr, and D. Bonge. 1994. The intended function of domestic violence is different for arrested male and female perpetrators. *Family Violence and Sexual Assault Bulletin* 10 (34):40–44.

Hamberger, L. K., J. Lohr, D. Bonge, and D. F. Tolin. 1997. An empirical classification of motivations for domestic violence. *Violence Against Women* 3:401–423.

Hamberger, L. K., and T. Potente. 1994. Counseling heterosexual women arrested for domestic violence: Implications for theory and practice. *Violence and Victims* 9 (2):125–137.

Hamlett, N. 1998. *Women who abuse in intimate relationships.* Minneapolis, MN: Domestic Abuse Project.

Hamner, J., and S. Saunders. 1984. *Well-founded fear: A community study of violence to women.* London: Hutchinson.

Harding, S. 1991. *Whose science? Whose knowledge?* Ithaca, NY: Cornell University Press.

Harrison, L. A., and C. W. Esqueda. 1999. Myths and stereotypes of actors involved in domestic violence: Implications for domestic violence culpability attributions. *Aggression and Violent Behavior* 4 (2):129–138.

Hart, J. Fathers' rights activists plan suit. *The Boston Globe*, August 18, 1999, B1, 5.

Haviland, M. Frye, B. Rajah, V. J. Thukral, and M. Trinity. 2001. *The Family Protection and Domestic Violence Act of 1995: Examining the effects of mandatory arrest in New York City.* New York: Urban Justice Center.

Hearn, J. 1998. *The violence of men: How men talk about and how agencies respond to men's violence against women.* Thousand Oaks, CA: Sage.

Heise, L. 1998. Violence against women: An integrated, ecological framework. *Violence Against Women* 4:262–290.

Hirschel, J. D., and E. Buzawa. 2002. Understanding the context of dual arrests with directions for future research. *Violence Against Women* 8:1449–1473.

Hirschel, J. D., and I. W. Hutchinson. 1992. Female spouse abuse and the police response: The Charlotte, North Carolina experiment. *Journal of Criminal Law and Criminology* 83 (1):73–119.

Holtzworth-Munroe, A., N. Smutzler, and L. Bates. 1997. A brief review of the research on husband violence: Part 3. Sociodemographic factors, relationship factors, and differing consequences of husband and wife violence. *Aggression and Violent Behavior* 2:285–307.

Hooper, M. 1996. When domestic violence diversion is no longer an option: What to do with the female offender. *Berkeley Women's Law Journal* 6:168–181.

Hunt, J. 1984. The development of rapport through the negotiation of gender in field work among police. *Human Organization*, 43:283–296.

Hutchinson, I. W., J. D. Hirschel, and C. E. Pesackis. 1994. Family violence and police utilization. *Violence and Victims* 9:299–313.

IACP (International Association of Chiefs of Police), 1967. *Training Key 16: Handling Disturbance Calls.* Gaithersburg, MD: IACP.

Iovanni, L. Forthcoming (2006). The violent victimization of women: An overview of legal, empirical and theoretical issues. In *Exploring policies and politics of violence against women*, ed. S. L. Miller and M. L. Meloy, 69–122. New York: Oxford University Press.

Iovanni, L., and S. L. Miller. 2001. Criminal justice responses to domestic violence: Law enforcement and the courts. In *Sourcebook on violence against women*, ed. C. M. Renzetti, J. Edleson, and R. Bergen, 303–327. Thousand Oaks, CA: Sage.

Jacobs, A. 2001. Give 'em a fighting chance: Women offenders re-enter society. *Criminal Justice Magazine* 16 (Spring):1.

Jacobson, N. S., J. M. Gottman, J. Waltz, R. Rushe, J. Babcock, and A. Holtzworth-Munroe. 1994. Affect, verbal content and psycho-physiology in the arguments of couples with a violent husband. *Journal of Consulting and Clinical Psychology* 62:982–988.

Johnson, M. P. 1995. Patriarchal terrorism and common couple violence: Two forms of violence against women. *Journal of Marriage and the Family* 57:283–294.

———. 2000. Conflict and control: Images of symmetry and asymmetry in domestic violence. In *Couples in conflict*, ed. A. Booth, A. C. Crouter, and M. Clements, 178–204. Hillsdale, NJ: Erlbaum.

Johnson, M. P., and K. J. Ferraro. 2000. Research on domestic violence in the 1990s: Making distinctions. *Journal of Marriage and the Family* 62:948–963.

Jones, D. A., and J. Belknap. 1999. Police responses to battering in a progressive pro-arrest jurisdiction. *Justice Quarterly* 16:249–273.

Joseph, J. 1997. Woman battering: A comparative analysis of black and white women. In *Out of the darkness: Contemporary perspectives on family violence*, ed. G. Kaufman Kantor and J. Jasinski, 161–169. Thousand Oaks, CA: Sage.

Kaufman Kantor, G., and M. Straus. 1987. The "drunken bum" theory of wife beating. *Social Problems* 34:213–230.

Karmen, A. 1982. Women as crime victims: Problems and solutions. In *The criminal justice system and women*, ed. B. R. Price and N. J. Sokoloff, 181–196. New York: Clark Boardman.

Kimmel, M. S. 2002. "Gender symmetry" in domestic violence: A substantive and methodological research review. *Violence Against Women* 8:1336–1367.

Klein, A. R. 1996. Re-abuse in a population of court-restrained male batterers: Why restraining orders don't work. In *Do arrests and restraining orders work?* ed. E. S. Buzawa and C. G. Buzawa, 192–213. Thousand Oaks, CA: Sage.

Krueger, R. 1994. *Focus groups: A practical guide for applied research.* 2nd ed. Newbury Park, CA: Sage.

Langhinrichsen-Rohling, J., P. Neidig, and G. Thorn. 1995. Violent marriages: Gender differences in levels of current violence and past abuse. *Journal of Family Violence* 19 (2):159–176.

Lerch, I. 1999. Letter from Chair, AAAS Committee on Scientific Freedom and Responsibility, to Ray Fowler, Executive Director of the American Psychological Association. *Science Directorate Newsletter* November-December 12 (6):2–3.

Lerman, L. 1986. Prosecution of wife beaters: Institutional obstacles and innovations. In *Violence in the home: Interdisciplinary perspectives*, ed. M. Lystad, 251–295. New York: Brunner/Mazel.

Lillja, C. M. 1995. Why women abuse: A study examining the function of abused men. Master's thesis, California State University, Long Beach.

Lischick, C. W. 1999. Coping and related characteristics delineating battered women's experiences in self-defined, difficult/hurtful dating relationships: A multicultural study. Doctoral dissertation, Rutgers, The State University of New Jersey, Newark.

Litz, B. T., and T. M. Keane. 1989. Information processing in anxiety disorders: Applications to the understanding of posttraumatic stress disorder. *Clinical Psychology Review* 9:243–257.

Lofland, J., and L. J. Lofland. 1995. *Analyzing social settings: A guide to qualitative observation and analysis.* 3rd ed. Belmont, CA: Wadsworth.

Lyon, A. D. 1999. Be careful what you wish for: An examination of arrest and prosecution patterns of domestic violence cases in two cities in Michigan. *Michigan Journal of Gender & Law* 5:253–267.

Lyon, E., and P. G. Mace 1991. Family violence and the courts: Implementing a comprehensive new law. In *Abused and battered: Social and legal responses to family violence*, ed. D. D. Knudson and J. L. Miller, 167–180. Hawthorn, NY: Aldine de Gruyter.

Margolies, L., and E. Leeder. 1995. Violence at the door: Treatment of lesbian batterers. *Violence Against Women* 1 (2):139–157.

Marshall, L. L., and P. Rose. 1990. Premarital violence: The impact of family of origin violence, stress, and reciprocity. *Journal of Family Violence* 5:51–64.

Martin, M. E. 1997. Double your trouble: Dual arrest in family violence. *Journal of Family Violence* 12:139–157.

Matthews, N. A. 1994. *Confronting rape: The feminist anti-rape movement and the state.* London: Routledge.

Mauer, M., C. Potler, and R. Wolf. 1999. *Gender and justice: Women, drugs and sentencing policy.* Washington, DC: The Sentencing Project.

McLeod, M. 1984. Women against men: An examination of domestic violence based on an analysis of official data and national victimization data. *Justice Quarterly* 1:171–193.

McMahon, M., and E. Pence. 2003. Making social change: Reflections on individual and institutional advocacy with women arrested for domestic violence. *Violence Against Women* 9:47–74.

Meloy, M. L., and S. L. Miller. 2002. Focus group findings of women mandated to domestic violence treatment groups. Unpublished manuscript.

Melton, H. C., and J. Belknap. 2003. He hits, she hits: Assessing gender differences and similarities in officially reported intimate partner violence. *Criminal Justice and Behavior* 30 (3):328–348.

Merrill, G. S. 1996. Ruling the exception: Same-sex battering and domestic violence theory. In *Violence in gay and lesbian domestic partnerships*, ed. C. M. Renzetti and C. H. Miley, 9–21. Binghamton, NY: Harrington Park Press.

Messner, M. A. 1998. The limits of the "male sex role": An analysis of the men's liberation and men's rights movements' discourse. *Gender & Society* 12 (3):255–276.

Miller, B. A., W. R. Downs, and M. Testa. 1993. Interrelationships between victimization experiences and women's alcohol use. *Journal of Alcohol Studies* 11:109–117.

Miller, N. 1997. *Domestic violence legislation affecting police and prosecutor responsibilities in the United States: Inferences from a 50-state review of state statutory codes*. Alexandria, VA: Institute for Law and Justice.

Miller, S. L. 1989. Unintended side effects of pro-arrest policies and their race and class implications for battered women: A cautionary note. *Criminal Justice Policy Review* 3 (3):299–316.

———. 1998. *Crime control and women: Feminist implications of criminal justice policy*. Thousand Oaks, CA: Sage.

———. 1999. *Gender and community policing: Walking the talk*. Boston, MA: Northeastern University Press.

———. 2000. Mandatory arrest and domestic violence: Continuing questions. In *It's a crime: Women and justice*, ed. R. Muraskin and T. Alleman, 283–310. New York: McGraw-Hill.

———. 2001. The paradox of women arrested for domestic violence. *Violence Against Women* 7:1339–1376.

Miller, S. L., and R. Barberet. 1994. A cross-cultural comparison of social reform: The growing pains of the battered women's movements in Washington, DC, and Madrid, Spain. *Law & Social Inquiry* 19 (4):923–966.

Miller, S. L., and M. L. Meloy. Forthcoming (2006). *Exploring policies and politics of violence against women*. New York: Oxford University Press.

———. Forthcoming (2005). Women's use of force: Voices of women arrested for domestic violence. *Violence Against Women*.

Mills, L. G. 1999. Killing her softly: Intimate abuse and the violence of state intervention. *Harvard Law Review* 2:550–613.

Moffit, T., and A. Caspi. 1999. *Findings about partner violence from the Dunedine Multidisciplinary Health and Development Study*. Washington, DC: National Institute of Justice.

Morse, B. J. 1995. Beyond the Conflict Tactics Scale: Assessing gender differences in partner violence. *Violence and Victims* 10:251–272.

Moss, V. A., C. R. Pitula, J. C. Campbell, and L. Halstead. 1997. The experience of terminating an abusive relationship from an Anglo and African American perspective: A qualitative descriptive study. *Issues in Mental Health Nursing* 18: 433–454.

Mullender, A. 1996. *Rethinking domestic violence: The social work and probation response*. New York: Routledge.

Najavits, L. M., R. D. Weiss, and B. S. Liese. 1996. Group cognitive-behavioral therapy with women with PTSD and Substance Use Disorder. *Journal of Substance Abuse Treatment* 13 (1):13–22.

National Clearinghouse for the Defense of Battered Women. February 2001. *The impact of arrests and convictions on battered women*. Unpublished manuscript.

Osthoff, S. 2002. But, Gertrude, I beg to differ, a hit is not a hit is not a hit. *Violence Against Women* 8:1521–1544.

Pagelow, M. 1981. *Women-battering: Victims and their experiences.* Beverly Hills, CA: Sage.

Pagelow, M. 1992. Adult victims of domestic violence: Battered women. *Journal of Interpersonal Violence* 7:87–120.

Parnas, R. E. 1967. The police response to the domestic disturbance. *Wisconsin Law Review* 31:914–960.

Pate, A. M., and E. E. Hamilton. 1992. Formal and informal deterrents to domestic violence: The Dade County spouse assault experiment. *American Sociological Review* 57:691–697.

Pearson, P. 1997. *When she was bad: Violent women and the myth of innocence.* New York: Viking.

Pence, E., and M. Paymar. 1993. *Education groups for men who batter: The Duluth model.* New York: Springer.

Perilla, J. L., R. Bakeman, and F. H. Norris. 1994. Culture and domestic violence: The ecology of abused Latinas. *Violence and Victims* 9:325–339.

Perilla, J., K. Frndak, D. Lillard, and C. East. 2003. A working analysis of women's use of violence in the context of learning, opportunity, and choice. *Violence Against Women* 9 (1):10–46.

Piven, F. F., and R. A. Cloward. 1979. *Poor people's movements: Why they succeed, how they fail.* New York: Vintage.

Pleck, E. 1987. *Domestic tyranny: The making of social policy against family violence from colonial times to present.* Oxford: Oxford University Press.

Ptacek, J. 1990. Why do men batter their wives? In *Feminist perspectives on wife abuse,* ed. K. Yllo and M. Bograd, 133–157. Newbury Park, CA: Sage.

Rasche, C. E. 1986. Women who kill their men: Are they violent women or women against violence? Paper presented at the American Society of Criminology Conference, Atlanta, GA.

———. 1995. Minority women and domestic violence: The unique dilemmas of battered women of color. In *The criminal justice system and women: Offenders, victims, and workers* (2nd ed.), ed. B. R. Price and N. J. Sokoloff, 246–261. New York: McGraw Hill.

Rennison, C. M., and S. Welchans. 2000. *Intimate partner violence.* Washington, DC: U.S. Department of Justice Statistics.

Renzetti, C. M. 1992. *Violent betrayal: Partner abuse in lesbian relationships.* Newbury Park, CA: Sage.

———. 1999. The challenges to feminism posed by women's use of violence in intimate relationships. In *New versions of victims,* ed. S. Lamb, 42–56. New York: New York University Press.

Richie, B. E. 1996. *Compelled to crime: The gender entrapment of battered black women.* New York: Routledge.

———. 2000. Exploring the link between violence against women and women's involvement in illegal activity. In *Research on women and girls in the criminal justice system.* Vol. 3, 1–14. Washington, DC: National Institute of Justice.

Rothenberg, B. 2003. "We don't have time for social change": Cultural compromise and the battered women's syndrome. *Gender & Society* 17 (5):771–787.

Russell, D. 1986. *The secret trauma: Incest in the lives of girls and women.* New York: Basic Books.

Russell, M. N., E. Lipov, N. Phillips, and B. White. 1989. Psychological profiles of violent and nonviolent martially distressed couples. *Psychotherapy* 26:81–87.

Ryan, G. W. and H. R. Bernard. 2003. Techniques to identify themes. *Field Methods* 15 (1):85–109.

Saunders, D. G. 1986. When battered women use violence: Husband abuse or self defense? *Violence and Victims* 1:47–60.

———. 1988. Wife abuse, husband abuse, or mutual combat? In *Feminist perspectives on wife abuse*, ed. K. Yllo and M. Bograd, 90–113. Beverly Hills, CA: Sage.

———. 1995. The tendency to arrest victims of domestic violence: A preliminary analysis of officer characteristics. *Journal of Interpersonal Violence* 19 (2):147–158.

———. 2002. Are physical assaults by wives and girlfriends a major social problem? A review of the literature. *Violence Against Women* 8:1424–1448.

Savran, D. 1998. *Taking it like a man: White masculinity, masochism, and contemporary American culture.* Princeton, NJ: Princeton University Press.

Schechter, S. 1982. *Women and male violence: The visions and struggles of the battered women's movement.* Boston: South End Press.

Schneider, E. M. 2000. *Battered women and feminist law-making.* New Haven, CT: Yale University Press.

Schur, E. M. 1984. *Labeling women deviant: Gender, stigma, and social control.* New York: McGraw-Hill.

Schwartz, M. D. 1987. Gender and injury in spousal assaults. *Sociological Focus* 20: 61–75.

Sens, R. 1999. Between a rock and a hard place: Domestic violence in communities of color. *Colorlines* 2(1). Retrieved from http://www.arc.org/C_Lines/CLArchive/story2_1_07.html.

Shelden, R. G. 1981. Sex discrimination in the juvenile justice system: Memphis, TN, 1900–1917. In *Comparing male and female offenders*, ed. M. Q. Warren, 55–72. Newbury Park, CA: Sage.

Sherman, L. W., and R. A. Berk. 1984a. The Minneapolis domestic violence experiment. *Police Foundation Reports* 1:1–8.

Sherman, L. W., and R. A. Berk. 1984b. The specific deterrent effects of arrest for domestic violence. *American Sociological Review* 49:261–272.

Sherman, L. W., J. D. Schmidt, D. P. Rogan, P. R. Gartin, E. G. Cohn, D. J. Collins, and A. R. Bacich. 1991. From initial deterrence to long-term escalation: Short custody arrest for poverty ghetto domestic violence. *Criminology* 29 (4):821–850.

Sherman, L. W., and D. A. Smith. 1992. Crime, punishment and stake in conformity: Legal and informal control of domestic violence. *American Sociological Review* 57:680–690.

Smith, D. A. 1987. Police response to interpersonal violence: Defining the parameters of legal control. *Social Forces* 65(3):762–782.

Smith, M. D. 1994. Enhancing the quality of survey data on violence against women. *Gender & Society* 8:109–127.

Sommer, R. 1994. *Male and female partner abuse: Testing a diathesis-stress model.* Unpublished doctoral dissertation, University of Manitoba, Winnipeg, Canada.

Stafne, G. 1989. *The Wisconsin Mandatory Arrest Monitoring Project: Final report.* Madison, WI: Wisconsin Coalition Against Domestic Violence.

Staggenborg, S. 1988. The consequences of professionalization and the formalization in the pro-choice movement. *American Sociological Review* 53:585.

Stanko, E. 1985. *Intimate intrusions: Women's experiences of male violence.* London: Unwin Hyman.

Stanley, L., and S. Wise. 1983. *Breaking out: Feminist consciousness and feminist research.* London: Routledge and Kegan Paul.

Stark, E. 1996. Mandatory arrest: A reply to its critics. In *Do arrests and restraining orders work?* ed. E. S. Buzawa and C. G. Buzawa, 115–149. Thousand Oaks, CA: Sage.

Stark, E., and A. Flitcraft. 1988. Violence among intimates: An epidemiological review. In *Handbook of family violence*, ed. V. V. Van Hassett, R. L. Morrison, A. S. Bellack, and M. Hersen, 293–317. New York: Plenum.

Steffensmeir, D., and J. Schwartz. 2004. Contemporary explanations of women's crime. In *The criminal justice system and women: Offenders, prisoners, victims, and workers*, ed. B. R. Price and N. J. Sokoloff, 113–126. New York: McGraw-Hill.

Stets, J. E., and M. A. Straus. 1990. Gender differences in reporting marital violence and its medical and psychological consequences. In *Physical violence in American families: Risk factors and adaptations to violence in 8,145 families*, ed. M. A. Straus and R. J. Gelles, 151–165. New Brunswick, NJ: Transaction Publishers.

Stith, S. M. 1990. *The Wisconsin Mandatory Arrest Monitoring Project: Final report*. Madison, WI: Wisconsin Coalition Against Domestic Violence.

Straton, J. C. 1994. The myth of the "battered husband syndrome." *Masculinities* 2 (4):79–82.

Straus, M. A. 1990. The Conflict Tactics Scale and its critics: An evaluation and new data on validity and reliability. In *Physical violence in American families: Risk factors and adaptations to violence in 8,145 families*, ed. M. A. Straus and R. J. Gelles, 3–16. New Brunswick, NJ: Transaction Publishers.

———. 1993. Physical assaults by wives: A major social problem. In *Current controversies on family violence*, ed. R. J. Gelles and D. R. Loseke, 67–80. New Brunswick, NJ: Transaction Publishers.

———. 1999. The controversy over domestic violence by women: A methodological, theoretical, and sociology of science analysis. In *Violence in intimate relationships*, ed. X. B. Arriaga and S. Oskamp, 17–44. Thousand Oaks, CA: Sage.

Straus, M. A., and R. J. Gelles. 1990. *Physical violence in American families: Risk factors and adaptations to violence in 8,145 families*. New Brunswick, NJ: Transaction Publishers.

Straus, M. A., R. J. Gelles, and S. Steinmetz. 1980. *Behind closed doors: Violence in the American family*. Newbury Park, CA: Sage.

Straus, M. A., S. L. Hamby, S. Boney-McCoy, and D. B. Sugarman. 1996. The revised Conflict Tactics Scale (CTS2): Development and psychometric data. *Journal of Family Issues* 17:283–316.

Strauss, A. L. 1987. *Qualitative analysis for social scientists*. New York: Cambridge University Press.

Strauss, A. L., and J. Corbin. 1990. *Basics of qualitative research: Grounded theory procedures and techniques*. Thousand Oaks, CA: Sage.

Swan, S. C., and D. L. Snow. 2002. A typology of women's use of violence in intimate relationships. *Violence Against Women* 8:286–319.

Taslitz, A. E. 1999. *Rape and the culture of the courtroom*. New York: University Press.

Thurman v. City of Torrington, CT. 595 F Supp. 1521 (D. Conn. 1984).

Tjaden, P., and N. Thoennes. 1998. *Prevalence, incidence, and consequences of violence against women: Findings from the National Violence Against Women Survey*. Washington, DC: Department of Justice, National Institute of Justice, and the Centers for Disease Control and Prevention.

———. 2000a. *Extent, nature and consequences of intimate partner violence: Findings from the National Violence Against Women Survey*. Washington, DC: Department of Justice, National Institute of Justice, and the Centers for Disease Control and Prevention.

———. 2000b. Prevalence and consequences of male-to-female and female-to-male intimate partner violence as measured by the National Violence Against Women Survey. *Violence Against Women* 6:142–161.

———. 2000c. *Full report of the prevalence, incidence, and consequences of violence against women: Findings from the National Violence Against Women Survey.* Washington, DC: Department of Justice, National Institute of Justice, and Centers for Disease Control and Prevention.

Turrell, S. C. 2000. A descriptive analysis of same-sex relationship violence for a diverse sample. *Journal of Family Violence* 15:281–293.

Van der Kolk, B. A. 1996. The body keeps the score: Approaches to the psychobiology of posttraumatic stress disorder. In *Traumatic stress: The effects of overwhelming experience on mind, body and society*, ed. B. A. Van der Kolk, A. C. McFarlane, and L. Weisaeth, 914–941. New York: The Guilford Press.

Visher, C. A. 1983. Gender, police arrest decisions, and notions of chivalry. *Criminology* 21:5–28.

Vivian, D., and Langhinrichsen-Rohling, J. 1996. Are bi-directionally violent couples mutually victimized? A gender-sensitive comparison. *Violence and Victims* 9:107–124.

Waldner-Haugrud, L. K., L. V. Gratch, and B. Magruder. 1997. Victimization and perpetration rates of violence in gay and lesbian relationships: Gender issues explored. *Violence and Victims* 12 (2):173–184.

Walker, L. E. 1984. *The battered woman syndrome.* New York: Springer.

Wanless, M. 1996. Note, mandatory arrest: A step toward eradicating domestic violence, but is it enough? *University of Illinois Law Review* 9:533–547.

Websdale, N. 2001. *Policing the poor: From slave plantation to public housing.* Boston: Northeastern University Press.

West, C. M., and S. Rose. 2000. Dating aggressing among low income African American youth: An examination of gender differences and antagonistic beliefs. *Violence Against Women* 6 (5):470–494.

White, J. W., and R. Kowalski. 1994. Deconstructing the myth of the nonaggressive female: A feminist analysis. *Psychology of Women Quarterly* 18:477–498.

White, J. W., P. H. Smith, M. P. Koss, and A. J. Figueredo. 2000. Intimate partner aggression—What have we learned?: Comment on Archer (2000). *Psychological Bulletin* 126 (5):690–696.

Wilson, K., R. Vercella, C. Brems, D. Benning, and D. Refro. 1992. Levels of learned helplessness in abused women. *Women & Therapy* 13:53–67.

Women's Prison Association. December 2003. Focus on women and justice. www.wpaonline.org.

Worcester, N. 2002. Women's use of force: Complexities and challenges of taking the issue seriously. *Violence Against Women* 8:1390–1415.

Worden, R., and A. Pollitz. 1984. Police arrests in domestic disturbances: A further look. *Law & Society Review* 18 (1):103–119.

Wright, E. A. 2000. Not a black and white issue: For battered and abused Latinas and Black women, dialing 911 may be risky business. In *Women's health: Readings on social, economic, and political issues*, ed. N. Worcester and M. H. Whatley, 549–552. Dubuque, IA: Kendall/Hunt.

Zorza, J. 1992. The criminal law of misdemeanor domestic violence 1970–1990. *Journal of Criminal Law and Criminology* 83 (1):46–72.

———. 1994. *Must we stop arresting batterers? Analysis and implications of new police domestic violence studies.* New York: National Center on Women and Family Law.

Zorza, J., and L. Woods. 1994. *Mandatory arrest: Problems and possibilities.* New York: National Center on Women and Family Law.

Index

About the Author

Susan L. Miller is a full professor in the department of sociology and criminal Justice at the University of Delaware. Her research interests include gender and criminal justice policy issues, victimology, violence against women, and social justice. Dr. Miller has published numerous articles in the areas of domestic violence, community policing and gender, and criminal justice policy. Her books include *Crime Control and Women: Feminist Implications of Criminal Justice Policy* (Sage, 1998), *Gender and Community Policing: Walking the Talk* (Northeastern University Press, 1999), and two forthcoming books, *Exploring Policies and Politics of Violence Against Women* (with Michelle L. Meloy, Oxford University Press) and *Rethinking Gender, Crime, and Justice: Feminist Perspectives* (with Claire M. Renzetti and Lynne Goodstein, Roxbury).

CPSIA information can be obtained
at www.ICGtesting.com
Printed in the USA
LVHW041837120619
621039LV00001B/3